This second, revised edition is dedicated to the movers, shakers, and dogsbodies of the American Conference on Oriental Rugs:

Servants of rugs, well done! Well hast thou fought the better fight!

(after John Milton)

THE OFFICIAL® PRICE GUIDE

ORIENTAL RUGS

Map of principal oriental rug-producing region.

THE OFFICIAL®PRICE GUIDE

ORIENTAL RUGS

JOYCE C. WARE

Line drawings by Wilson P. Ware

SECOND EDITION

House of Collectibles • New York

Important Notice. All of the information, including valuations, in this book has been compiled from the most reliable sources, and every effort has been made to eliminate errors and questionable data. Nevertheless, the possibility of error, in a work of such immense scope, always exists. The publisher will not be held respon-sible for losses which may occur in the purchase, sale, or other transaction of items because of information contained herein. Readers who feel they have discovered errors are invited to *write* and inform us, so they may be corrected in subsequent editions. Those seeking further information on the topics covered in this book are advised to refer to the complete line of *Official Price Guides* published by the House of Collectibles.

Published by: House of Collectibles
201 East 50th Street
New York, New York 10022

Distributed by Ballantine Books, a division of Random House, Inc., New York, and simultaneously in Canada by Random House of Canada Limited, Toronto.

http://www.randomhouse.com

Manufactured in the United States of America

ISSN: 1089-1366

ISBN: 0-676-60023-9

Text design by Holly Johnson
Cover design by Ruth Ross
Cover photograph courtesy of FPG International

Second Edition: September 1996

10 9 8 7 6 5 4 3 2 1

CONTENTS

ACKNOWLEDGMENTS

In addition to the persons acknowledged in the first edition of this guide, I wish to thank the following for their invaluable contributions to this revised version. First and foremost, the directors of the American Conference on Oriental Rugs: Connie Henderson, Mark Hopkins, Rosalie Rudnick, Paul Ramsey, and Mike Tschebull, whose kind provision of ACOR's updated list of American oriental rug societies saved me considerable time and effort.

Market information was generously shared with me by Paul Ramsey and Carolyn Shaver of Denver's Shaver-Ramsey, Cornelia Montgomery of Peter Pap Oriental Rugs, Inc., and three New York City dealers recommended to me by satisfied customers: Krikor Markarian, George Anavian, and David Zadeh. I am also indebted to Emily Sanford, David Walker, and Richard Newman for the invaluable information they provided about rug cleaning and restoration, and to Marla Mallett's lucid explications of rug structure and design.

The sales at the major auction houses continue to offer oriental rug enthusiasts an unparalleled range of weavings to admire, compare, and buy, and most of the photographs used to illustrate this guide were provided by Skinner, Inc., of Bolton and Boston, Massachusetts—thank you, Jo Kris and Cindy Tashjian!—and Christie's New York Images Department, managed by Sarah Mitchell. Several of the transparencies in the color section were loaned by Peter Pap, whose galleries in Dublin, New Hampshire, and San Francisco offer superior examples of collectible and decorative rugs; others were supplied by InnerAsia Trading Company and George Jevremovic of Tribal Visions.

Among the knowledgeable collectors willing to share their experiences and hard-earned wisdom with me were Rod Griffith, Charles Lave, Bethany Mendenhall, DeWitt Mallary, Robert Pittenger, John Sommer, and Mike and Inge Tschebull. My good friend Gayle Garrett of the Rug Project in Washington, D.C., was again always ready to listen and advise, and the unflagging enthusiasm of Afghan war rug maven Tatiana Divens saw me through the rough passages.

Special thanks are due agent Adele Leone and Stephen Sterns, my former House of Collectibles editor, who together obtained the green light for this revised edition; Tim Kochuba, for his unflappable handling of the transition, and my new editor, Randy Ladenheim-Gil, who cheerfully undertook the complex, occasionally baffling, task of interweaving new material with old.

FOREWORD TO THE SECOND EDITION

Compared to the arts commonly classified as "fine"—paintings, sculpture, ceramics—textile art remains an undervalued medium. The prices for collectible oriental rugs never approached the dizzy heights seen in other areas of the arts during the prosperous late eighties, and the economic insecurity of the nineties has set in motion a downward trend in the bids received at auction for the general run of old and antique rugs. The supply of examples fresh to the current market has slowed, and a significant number of dealers specializing in collectible rugs are, for the first time, publicly advertising reductions in prices.

On the other hand, the prices of truly superior examples are higher than ever. The best are already either in museums or private collections—even very wealthy new collectors would be hard put to assemble a major collection of early classical carpets—and the few exceptional pieces offered from time to time on the international market are in great demand. The same holds true for the finest examples of tribal rugs and trappings. In fact the only category of rugs currently experiencing a depression in price are Caucasians: the best and oldest of these will always be deservedly pricey, but mint condition turn-of-the-century Kazaks no longer command the five-figure prices often seen six years ago when the price information for the first edition of this guide was gathered.

As mentioned previously, one of the characteristics of an uncertain market is the lack of fresh material available to dealers and auction goers. Prospective sellers of fine old pieces are, understandably, biding their time until the market settles. In the meantime, rug dealers who heretofore handled only old and antique collectibles are stocking the best of a growing number of vegetal-dyed quality reproductions to satisfy the furnishing needs of clients unwilling to settle for a worn, tired-looking, run-of-the-mill Heriz.

But while dealers fret about the paucity of good examples of traditionally collected weavings available to them, collectors are themselves exploring new and unfamiliar territory: tribal flatweaves from Afghanistan and Baluchistan, and rugs from lesser known weaving areas in Central Asia, Chinese Turkestan, and Tibet. The excitement of exploring new collecting areas should, however, be tempered with caution. Expertly counterfeited antique tribal bags made with old, natural-dyed materials have appeared at auction, first in Europe, then in the United States, and a group of Baluch flatweaves imported in good faith by an American dealer were found to have cotton warps rather than the wool characteristic of genuinely old tribal pieces.

Similarly, contemporary Turkish knockoffs of antique Anatolian and Caucasian rugs have been touted to this writer as the real thing by a few unscrupulous dealers. The best of these copies, knotted with hand-spun lustrous wool and dyed with rich vegetal colors, are well worth buying, but no one wants to pay antique-rug prices for a reproduction. Your best bet? Arm yourself by heeding the precepts and suggestions given throughout this guide; buy from a reputable dealer—you will find a list in the resource section in the back of this book—and steer clear of those weekend distress sales held at motels and hotels where rug market dregs unsaleable in reputable retail outlets are flogged by fly-by-night scam artists.

To sum up, there are still exciting, reasonably priced areas of collecting for those ready to learn from their mistakes and able to adjust to the shifting values inherent in a quixotic market. Connoisseurship is a relatively new phenomenon in the field of oriental rugs, fostered in large measure by collectors and dealers who were themselves novices a decade or so ago. Given sufficient clarity of vision and the commitment to pursue it, there is no reason why today's neophyte cannot become tomorrow's expert.

ORIENTAL RUGS

INTRODUCTION

The term "oriental rug" is an arbitrary catchall for a wide variety of knotted-pile and flat-woven textiles produced in a vast area stretching from North Africa to China. Included in this territory are Turkey (Anatolia), Iran (Persia), Afghanistan, Pakistan, India, and three historically significant weaving areas that were a part of the Soviet Union: the Caucasus, Turkestan, and East Central Asia. Beautiful carpets were also made in Spain and Egypt, and an important modern industry has developed in Romania in addition to the distinctive floral-patterned kilims for which it has long been known.

A genuine oriental rug is made by hand. Some machine-made rugs, such as the popular American-made Karastan, are of good quality and certainly far superior to plain-colored carpets printed with oriental-type patterns, but both are required by law to be designated and advertised as oriental *design*.

The vast majority of rugs offered for sale by dealers or at auction are late-19th- or 20th-century examples. Only a small minority of these can be considered either collectible or antique, and although the terms are often thought to be synonymous, they are not. In fact, some rugs being made today with hand-spun wool and vegetable colors are more collectible than century-old rugs defaced by unstable synthetic dyes.

If you are less interested in rugs for their own sake than as an element of a decorative ensemble, the faded look characteristic of old unstable dyes or the untraditional palette of a computer-designed new rug may very well suit you. The true collector, however, views rugs primarily as works of woven art. Collectors may use commercially designed decorative carpets in high-traffic household areas, but they are no more likely to confuse that practical choice with collectible rugs than they would a paperback thriller with Tolstoy's *War and Peace*.

The dating of oriental rugs is often a matter for lively debate, and since some collectors value age above all other factors, the outcome can be of considerable monetary importance to buyer and seller alike. The classification of age, however, depends in large measure upon who does the determination. The international auction houses, like Sotheby's and Christie's, consider as antiques rugs woven 100 or more years ago. More conservative authorities apply that desirable label only to rugs predating the introduction of synthetic dyes in the area in which they were woven, in some cases as early as 1870. In the trade, a rug becomes an antique in about 80 years; semiantique if it predates World War II, and "old" if made at least 25 years ago.

Perhaps at this point you should ask yourself why you picked up this book in the first place. If your interest in rugs begins and ends with the wish to furnish your home with a few attractive pieces, or if you just want to know more about the rugs you already have and how to care for them, this book will help you accomplish that worthwhile goal.

Dyed-in-the-wool rug collectors, on the other hand, acquire over the years more pieces than can conceivably be used or displayed at any one time, the overflow crowding the foot lockers and closet shelves that in other households are used for out-of-season garments and sporting gear. Since I fall into that category myself, I hope what follows will help others steer clear of some of the pitfalls awaiting the unwary rug collector in the course of enjoying collecting's many delights.

The first hard lesson most collectors learn is that the coveted object bought expensively today, perhaps even excitingly dueled over at auction, is worth in dollars only what the next buyer will pay for it. With that in mind, here are a few basic truths:

1. Collectors who, for whatever worthy reason, haven't time to spare for visiting museum collections, attending exhibitions, or prowling auction previews, should put themselves in the hands of a reputable dealer. When it comes to rugs, beautiful pictures and scholarly articles just aren't enough. You have to see the colors, feel the wool, and examine the structure, preferably in the company of collectors more knowledgeable than yourself. In short, you have to develop an eye.

2. Connoisseur collecting is expensive. World-class antique rugs of exceptional color, design quality, and condition are not picked up for pocket change at a tag sale, local antique show, or rural auction. The rare exceptions are just that, very rare. Adjust your collecting sights to your pocketbook. It can be just as rewarding, and you'll sleep better. Besides, as Joseph Alsop shrewdly observed in *The Rare Art Traditions*, "the line between 'worth having' and 'not worth having' is always shifting, since collectors with limited means are constantly exploring all the things 'not worth having' for possible prizes when a new collectors' category finds favor."

3. Only buy rugs that please you. News of a high price paid for a so-called rare rug, which may have little otherwise to recommend it, invariably brings hitherto unknown but similar pieces out of attics and into the auction rooms where the rarity bought for a quick killing quickly becomes a drug on the market.

4. Finally, be prepared to make mistakes. Everyone does. Experts loftily advise beginners to collect only what they like and to buy only the best examples. Obviously, we all hope to scorn the mediocre, but the catch is that if it takes a trained eye to distinguish the best from the good, the novice is often hard put to choose between the run-of-the-mill and the embarrassingly awful. It's not easy to admit to our mistakes, but admit

them we must: do not blame the dealer who "talked you into it," or the catalog description that misled you, or the poor light, or auction fever. The decision was yours.

Since we learn much more from our mistakes than we do from inspired choices, consider the cost of yours as tuition. Let us hope the school you are about to enter offers more pleasure than hard knocks, but be ever mindful of the motto emblazoned above its gates: *Caveat Emptor*.

A LITTLE BIT OF HISTORY

According to a report given in 1995 at a meeting of the Society for American Archaeology, a clay fragment bearing impressions of woven textiles or basketry was found in a 27,000-year-old site near a river in what is now the southeastern Czech republic. This validates the long-held assumption that, since the materials used in rug making are rather perishable, the art of weaving undoubtedly antedates the existence of known specimens like the very well-preserved, finely knotted carpet found in 1949 by a Russian archaeologist in the Altai mountains of eastern Siberia and dated to between the fifth and third centuries B.C. Although newer information argues for a later dating, the skillfully balanced design, well-drawn pictorial motifs, and fine craftsmanship of this astonishing rug is *prima facie* evidence that the art of knotted textiles was well developed much earlier than the evidence available before the Pazyryk excavations had led scholars to assume.

The oldest known Islamic rug, known as the Fustat (Old Cairo) Carpet, alleged to have been excavated in Egypt, has been carbon-dated to the seventh to ninth centuries A.D. Acquired in 1986 by the Fine Arts Museums of San Francisco, its sadly faded colors and fragmentary design will no doubt fuel scholarly surmise and discussion for years to come.

The Pazyryk carpet, oldest-known knotted pile rug.

After the invasion of Egypt by Islamic armies in A.D. 640 and the domination of varying areas of Spain by the Moors from North Africa from the 8th century through the 15th century, the arts in both areas became influenced by the Islamic tradition. The best-known Egyptian weavings produced during this period are the Mamluk carpets of the 15th and 16th centuries, which, unsurprisingly, have stylistic links to both Anatolian and northwest Persian weaving of the same period. Their distinctive iridescent coloration and geometric patterning were succeeded by curvilinear designs after the occupation of Cairo by the Ottoman Turks in 1517.

Early Spanish rug design was also derived largely from eastern Islamic patterns except for the custom of knotting into the field of carpets the crests of the noble Spanish families who commissioned them. The earliest surviving examples, dating from the 15th century, are reminiscent of Egyptian work. Later, Anatolian influences prevailed, and still later, in the 16th and 17th centuries, European baroque patterns were commonly employed.

The production of pile carpets diminished in both Egypt and Spain in the 18th century, and although superb early examples may be seen in museum collections—especially noteworthy is the glowing silk Mamluk in the Osterreichisches Museum für Angewandte Kunst in Vienna—they are rarely available in the market except as fragments. There is no significant modern production in Spain, but Persian-design rugs of superb quality are being made today in Egypt, thanks to a recent revival of workshop weaving there.

The peak of the rug weaving art was reached under the patronage of the Safavid dynasty in Persia, 1499–1722. Carpets and other textiles—as well as paintings, ceramics, ironwork, and calligraphy—attained a level of extraordinary virtuosity during this period, but not as a result of the expression of individual creativity within the weaver's cultural tradition, which is prized by many collectors today. On the contrary, the highly sophisticated designs of these carpets woven in court-sponsored manufactories were created by master artists. It was a combined achievement of artistry and craft possible only in a society in which, since time itself was of little value, weavers were expected to take as much time as was necessary to produce the desired result. In terms of delicacy of ornament, subtle coloration, and mastery of technique, these glorious carpets have never been equaled.

Wonderful carpets were also made in India in the Mughal dynasty's workshops during roughly the same period, 1500–1738. "The art was borrowed," says Islamic art scholar Walter Denny, "but as with the Japanese and baseball, it was taken up with enthusiasm: Indian rugs of the classical period are the largest, most finely knotted, and most brilliantly colored carpets ever made." These classical Indian carpets employ exquisite floral motifs—more realistically drawn than those on Persian models—arrayed together with bizarre animals on distinctive claret red grounds. Except for the flat-woven dhurries, Indian weaving later became entirely dominated by Persian designs, and although these rugs may be attractive as furnishing pieces, they lack the cultural expression that make a rug collectible. The same holds true for India's sizable contemporary production, which consists largely of Persian-design knockoffs offering good value but unlikely ever to interest collectors.

Rug making in the area now known as Turkey is particularly well documented thanks to the long-established custom there of giving carpets to mosques as tokens of piety and thanksgiving. In urban centers and remote villages alike, they accumulated over the centuries, layer upon layer, awaiting discovery by scholars and removal to Turkish museum collections for documentation and conservation. The earliest carpets, whose fragments have been dated to the 13th- and 14th-century Seljuk dynasty, were large coarse weavings with textilelike repeat patterns bordered by barbarically bold motifs. Ottoman court carpets, like their Persian and Indian counterparts, used silk and fine wools for their elaborate, floral-based patterns. The arched prayer rug design has been an enduringly popular format throughout Turkey, from the finely knotted silks produced in Hereke workshops to refined village products like the tulip-decorated Ladiks and the brightly colored geometricized versions produced on cottage looms. The use of cheap European synthetic dyes wreaked havoc in the Turkish cottage weaving industry from about 1880 through most of the 20th century, but the reintroduction of vegetable dyes and hand-spun wool in the early 1980s (see chapter on contemporary collectibles) has spurred a lively revival of dealer and collector interest in these handsome traditional rugs.

By the 14th and 15th centuries, rugs began being imported by Venetian merchants, first from Anatolia—now Turkey—and later from the Caucasus, where a thriving cottage industry produced carpets with distinctive large-scale floral and stylized dragon designs. European fascination with the brilliant color and bold geometric designs of the early Anatolian rugs is confirmed by their frequent depiction in the contemporary paintings of Previtali, Bassano, Lotto, and Holbein. In fact, the names of the two latter artists have been applied to the designs of the Anatolian carpets they favored as accessories. It is interesting to note that these paintings show rugs being used as table covers at least as often as floor decoration.

The turmoil resulting from frequent hostile invasions in both Persia and Anatolia during the 18th century contributed to a decline in court carpet production in these important weaving areas. Rulers seeking to preserve their thrones have more on their minds than aesthetics. As a result, the weavings of this period of most interest to collectors originated in the rugged hills and windswept plains of the Middle East and Central Asia, where village and nomadic tribal life was affected more by local harvests and treks to pasturage than the troubles of distant courts, and the need for sturdy woven domestic goods remained constant.

As one travels east from East Turkestan to China, the appearance of rugs begins to differ from those most Westerners think of as "oriental," even though many motifs seen in classical Persian, Turkish, and Indian carpets originated in the arts of ancient China, arriving in the 12th century in the wake of invading Mongol hordes and along the famed silk routes stretching from the Far East to the Mediterranean.

East Turkestan rugs tend to be transitional in type, borrowing colors and designs from rug-making neighbors both to the east and to the west. The best of the Tibetan rugs, a Chinese-influenced art of relatively recent date, possess a unique vigor and charm, especially the so-called tiger rugs.

Although Chinese rugs were not introduced to the West until about 1900, there is reason to believe that pile rug making was an established art there as early as the 12th century. The rather sparse use of unfamiliar symbolic figures and the subdued Chinese palette characteristic of these interesting rugs lacked initial appeal to Western eyes more accustomed to the colorful swirling patterns of the carpets long associated with the term "oriental." In recent years, however, sophisticated collectors have come to appreciate their subtle artistry, and the prices of antique pieces have risen accordingly. Today, vast quantities of both silk and wool rugs are produced in government-controlled workshops in Chinese and Persian designs. Although they provide good value as attractive, reasonably priced furnishing rugs, the slick, cookie-cutter sameness of these modern reproductions virtually rules out any collector interest in the foreseeable future.

European interest in oriental rugs revived in the late 19th century, due largely to the popularity of paintings by Western artists fascinated by the exoticism of Middle Eastern scenes. Unfortunately, the resulting revitalization of the Eastern carpet industry was accompanied by a new and not altogether happy twist. Although earlier rugs had also been commercially produced and exported, the colors, the sizes, and even the designs of this later and much larger production were often dictated by foreign importing firms to suit the needs and tastes of Western buyers. Further, the well-intended systems of quality control introduced by these importers resulted in bale after bale of a uniformly well-made but artistically uninspired product.

This development, although of no particular significance to the buyer of a decorative furnishing rug, contributed to the current collector interest in village and tribal weavings. These homely items produced solely for practical domestic use retained a vitality and relative purity of design well into this century. In fact, although unrest in the Middle East has hampered it, tribal research has been one of the most popular areas of study for rug scholars and enterprising collectors interested as much in the weavers' materials, techniques, design sources, and day-to-day lives as they are in the rugs they make.

For More Information

Until recently, books about oriental rugs were published for the most part in costly limited editions authored by gentleman collectors who acquired their information and rug collections in the course of adventuresome journeys through rug-producing areas. Other books, less expensively illustrated and even more myth-laden, were written by rug dealers more interested in intriguing a naive potential rug-buying public than imparting accurately researched information. As Bernard Berenson wrote in his book *Connoisseurship*, the art historian, in order to perform his task adequately, requires three essential tools: objects, photographs of objects, and contemporary documentation. When it comes to rugs, documentation is apt to be vague, unreliable, or altogether lacking; nevertheless, the level of scholarship vis-à-vis oriental rugs has improved a great deal since I began collecting 20 years ago.

Although the best of the scholarly rug books are expensive, particularly those well supplied with good color plates, there are now available— thanks to the rapid advance in rug scholarship—several reasonably priced, competently written, well-illustrated guides.

An annotated list of recommended titles is included in the Resource Guide. If some of the more expensive titles are beyond your reach, inquire about borrowing them through your state interlibrary loan system before settling for an outdated third-rater gathering dust on the shelves of your local library. There has been a lot of nonsense written about rugs, and if you are just beginning to study them, it will be less confusing in the long run if you start with recognized authorities. They, too, may contradict each other on occasion, but at least their contradictions are based on informed reasoning.

Other sources of information are museum exhibitions and university courses. Gayle Garrett of The Rug Project (see chapter on Contemporary Collectible Rugs) conducts an oriental rug seminar for Georgetown University's Continuing Education Department in Washington, D.C.; George Anavian, a dealer listed in the Resource Guide, does the same at New York University in New York City, and concentrated weekend-long mini-courses are occasionally offered by Sotheby's. Notices about upcoming educational opportunities can usually be found in oriental rug society bulletins. (See the Resource Guide for further information.)

THE MARKETPLACE

The most familiar method of exchange is one in which prices are set by producers and sellers on the basis of known costs of materials, labor, and overhead. In this fixed-price situation, new small rugs will always be less expensive than new larger rugs of the same type and quality, and similar rugs will be available at similar prices elsewhere. (In the context of new rugs, "quality" is a trade term used to describe the fineness of the weave. A rug of lower "quality," i.e. coarser weave, can be a perfectly good rug aimed at a lower price-point segment of the market.)

If you are seeking a decorative floor furnishing to complement an already established color scheme, a well-made new rug or carpet priced on a fixed-cost basis will probably be your best option as long as you avoid the Going-Out-of-Business type of dealership. Typically, GOBs bring in substandard merchandise and tag them with inflated prices which are then discounted 60 percent to 80 percent. If the claims sound too good to be true, they probably are.

The second method of exchange is known as private treaty, in which buyers and sellers negotiate the price. In other words, they bargain. Real estate and automobiles are commonly acquired by private treaty, but the average American consumer is equipped neither by culture nor with easily available consumer information to knowledgeably negotiate the price of an antique oriental rug.

With old rugs, the bargaining process assumes a familiarity with wool, dyes, and weaving techniques; how a particular rug compares with others of similar age and origin; and its current market desirability and availability. Unless both parties share general criteria and assumptions related to these factors, it is not possible to engage in an informed negotiation, and if, out of ignorance, you press too hard, the dealer may decide to save the next prize he acquires for a collector savvy enough to recognize and accept a fair price.

The third form of exchange is the auction, which establishes market standards of an object's worth through the process of bidding. The utility of auctions arises from the fact of its being a social forum for resolving uncertainties and ambiguities concerning the monetary value of objects in a manner acceptable to all participants. The more specialized the sale is, the more useful it is to the community concerned with the type of objects on offer.

Rug-only sales, which are rarely held by other than the major auction houses listed in the back of this book, have a ready-made community of dealers, consignors, and collectors, all of them alert to one another's bids and lack thereof. If an important dealer fails to bid on a seemingly desirable rug, it may raise questions in the minds of lesser dealers and slow the bidding. If prior to offering a wonderful collectible rug the auctioneer tells an amusing anecdote about finding it in a Cape Cod attic, the private buyers are entertained, but his real purpose is to inform the dealers that the rug is fresh to the market. Conversely, an equally wonderful collectible rug known to have made the rounds of the dealers before being consigned to auction will always be treated by them with a certain contempt, deserved or not, and provides private buyers an opportunity for a good buy.

What does this community have to teach you, the beginning collector? When a market is highly dependent on a small group of dealers and experts, a temporary dearth of a currently popular type of collectible rug may lead to higher prices, which in turn prompts dealers and seasoned collectors to profit from selling similar pieces, thus creating a surplus which drives prices back down. For this reason, neophytes should resist the temptation to buy solely for investment.

A shrewd dealer can sometimes transform his embarrassing surplus into an advantage by advancing convincing reasons for distinguishing one quite similar rug from another, thus creating a valuable sub-category. Contrary to popular belief, however, extreme rarity can work against the market since there must be a sufficient number of something to allow for the system of categorization that allows a value to be established.

THE AUCTION HOUSE

Once upon a time, dealers in old and antique rugs were the principal buyers of auctioned goods. The few collectors who prowled the dealers' auction house turf could pick up for peanuts the wonderful tribal trappings, rugs, and kilims that until the late 1970s were of little interest to anyone except the cognoscenti. Decorative carpets, too, especially those with "unfashionable" colors and patterns, could be had at wholesale prices. This is no longer the case. In fact, a dealer who today acquires rugs from an estate or through trade is sometimes able to price them for less than they might bring at auction. There are several reasons for this topsy-turvy situation.

In recent years the major auction houses have taken to wooing the retail dealers' customers: some even allow prospective buyers to see how a particular decorative carpet will look in their homes before deciding whether to bid. Pleased by the opportunity to eliminate the middleman and unbothered by commercial concerns about profit and loss, these customers routinely top the dealers' bids. If a rug becomes the object of obsessive desire, the winning bid may leave the dealers reeling with shock.

Such was the case at Sotheby's in New York on January 20, 1990, when an oversize, palely pretty Persian Sultanabad carpet with an already hefty estimate of $80,000–$120,000 soared in the heat of competitive bidding by private parties to $181,500. Although the victor in such duels is often awarded with applause for providing lively entertainment, astronomical bids fueled by ego rarely affect day-to-day market pricing.

Another class of wild-card bidders are the decorators prepared to pay large prices to get their wealthy clients the "design statement" their newly decorated lodgings require. A third cause of inflated bids is auction fever, a mouth-drying, palm-dampening affliction that compels its hapless victims to bid well beyond a carefully predetermined limit. And finally, there's simple ignorance, such as a novice collector's inability to distinguish a 20th-century version of an antique Caucasian Kazak from the real thing.

It is not my intent to discourage budding collectors from attending auctions. Not only are they fun, but the previews of the rug-only sales held two or three times a year by the major houses provide the only opportunity for hands-on study of as many as 200 to 400 good rugs of all types at one's own pace. Close inspection of museum holdings, no matter how wonderful they may be, is hampered by a universal no-touch policy and a color-conservation level of lighting more suited to owls than people.

For their major sales the big auction houses publish illustrated catalogs, available singly or by subscription, that allow serious collectors to track prices and trends. Sotheby's broke new ground with the addition of widely praised structural analyses of the collector pieces in the front half of their catalogs. Most houses offer rugs at mixed-furnishings sales as well. Few of these are of collectible interest, but alert buyers can sometimes pick up for a bargain price good rugs that either have condition problems or were consigned by owners unwilling to wait for the next major sale.

Each house has its own style; each has an informed—but not infallible—staff of experts happy to provide detailed objective advice, either in person at previews that allow interested parties ample time—from two to six days—for firsthand inspection or over the phone to persons unable to attend them. A selection of additional photos can usually be provided to potential absentee bidders, and many pricey rugs have been acquired in this fashion. But unless I was sure the auction house expert advising me "sees" rugs as I do, I would not be inclined to bid on a rug that I or a collector friend whose eye is similar to mine had not personally inspected. And I never rely on the catalogs alone: catalog descriptions sometimes inadvertently omit significant information about condition; a poor black-and-white photograph can make a rug appear less desirable than it really is, and given the inaccuracies of color reproduction, the full-page plates of major offerings can also be misleading.

Always remember that no matter how posh the setting, auction sales, unlike purchases made through retail dealers, are final. Except in the very rare instance of a grossly inaccurate representation, there are no returns, no exchanges. In fact, Keith Wayne, who steered Christie's rug department through almost a decade of successful sales, told me he prefers uncertain buyers to go the retail route.

OTHER AUCTIONS

Small regional and country auctions pose additional hazards. They rarely have experts on staff, and except for the measurements marked on the tag, the information supplied is sparse at best, and often inaccurate. It is true that wonderful buys of decorative carpets and the occasional esoteric collectible can sometimes be made, especially if a rug ring is operating, but bargains of any kind are unlikely at auctions at which two or more rings compete for the same rugs.

A "ring" or "pool" is an impromptu organization of dealers attending an auction—including "pickers" who supply dealers—who agree not to bid against one another, the purpose being to buy the rugs offered at the lowest possible price. One of the ring's members is chosen to bid for the group; later the ring holds its own postsale auction as a result of which some will receive rugs and others will receive money as their reward for agreeing not to compete. Although rings—rugs, silver, whatever—are illegal in many states, they continue to be an outsize thorn in every auctioneer's side.

On-site auctions of estates at a distance from urban centers offer keen-eyed collectors the best opportunities, but sometimes rugs that local dealers are desperate to unload are accommodatingly placed in parlors and hallways to "round out" sales. Ask the auctioneer if the displayed rugs originated in the estate being auctioned. I have found that a direct question of this sort vests me with sufficient authority to rate a truthful answer.

Lies, however, are the stock-in-trade of the weekend motel sales known as short-notice auctions. Friends are forever calling me up about these events, anxious that I not miss this great opportunity to add to my collection. You've probably seen the ads: Important Public Auction! Shipment Cleared from U.S. Bonded Warehouse to Be Disposed of at Nominal Price for Immediate Cash Realization!

I attended one of those sales once out of curiosity and was fascinated by the techniques employed to lull suspicion and flatter bidders. No preview time was allowed, but early arrivals could hastily inspect rugs as they were carried in, and any attribution one cared to guess at was respectfully accepted and one's knowledge complimented. For the most part, the rugs were either 25- to 40-year-old worn examples of types that were mediocre to begin with or else shoddy new goods.

In the beginning of the sale, one or two rugs were regretfully set aside because the highest bids received for these "fine pieces" were too low. This reassured an audience made up of bargain-seeking but basically decent people that they would not be taking unfair advantage of dealers down on their luck. Winning bidders were occasionally complimented for their sagacity in choosing the "antique" rug they had just bought. "A very good buy, sir," the auctioneer would solemnly say, and oh, how the buyer beamed!

By the end of the sale, half of the audience had made "very good buys," including the rugs set aside at the beginning of the sale and whisked out later to "give away" tearfully at prices half again as high as the usual retail price. Again, no returns and no refunds, not even when you belatedly discover in the cold light of day that a significant portion of the pattern has been touched up with paint to hide the wear and bleeding dyes.

ANTIQUE SHOWS

Weekend antique shows occasionally offer interesting rug-buying opportunities, but if a rug dealer is among the exhibitors, chances are that any attractive rug bargains in other booths will have been snapped up before the public is admitted. On the other hand, the booths of knowledgeable dealers who regularly make weekend forays out of their home turf—Peter Pap of New Hampshire and Lawrence Kearney of Massachusetts, for example—allow busy collectors a wonderful opportunity to see a much better than average selection of rugs close to home. Dealers who participate in antique shows will be happy to supply you with a list of upcoming events and bring to any show you plan to attend rugs suited to your furnishing needs or collecting interests (consult the lists of dealers in the Resource Guide).

Many antique show promoters have a policy of admitting early buyers on payment of from $10 to $60 above the standard entrance fee. For the most part, these premium-paying buyers are dealers able to spot a promising item out of the corner of a practiced eye and make an immediate decision. In this company, he who hesitates is lost. A novice collector who rushes to judgment under these pressured circumstances risks making very expensive mistakes. A bargain prize may later reveal synthetic dyes, unnoticed areas of wear, moth damage, and patches.

FLEA MARKETS AND TAG SALES

Flea markets and garage tag sales are rarely worth a rug collector's notice. In-house estate tag sales sometimes offer treasures, but if the ad you see makes your mouth water, you can be sure dealers and other collectors will be similarly affected.

First come, first served is the order of the day at country estate tag sales.

Numbers are handed out to the prospective buyers in the order of their arrival, and they are usually admitted in small groups to guard against pilferage. Dealers will drive considerable distances if the sale is exceptionally promising, often arriving just before the sale begins, whereupon offers of handsome sums to those first in line—$200 to $400 is not uncommon—allow them to sweep in with their purchased low numbers ahead of scores of outraged standees. In the case of rugs, all it takes is one carload of well-heeled dealers to pick a sale clean in the first 15 minutes.

ORIENTAL RUG DEALERS

Auctions and estate sales deserve a place on the collector's agenda, but the most reliable way to assemble a rug collection worthy of the name is through dealers who specialize in old and collectible rugs. Department stores stock new goods only; the average retail rug dealer does too, although dealers may occasionally receive old rugs through trade or from local estates. Any good pieces thus acquired are usually promptly shipped off to the big metropolitan auction houses, so nearby dealers should be asked to call you when anything interesting comes their way.

Specialty rug dealers tend to cluster on the two coasts and in or near major metropolitan centers elsewhere. Until the mid-1970s, most rug dealers were either immigrants or first-generation Americans whose knowledge of weaving was bred in the bone. Dealers with a Middle Eastern family background continue to dominate the oriental rug market, but they have been joined by a group of art- and scholarship-oriented, collector-cum-dealer Westerners whose first introduction to the glories of oriental weaving was often a result of overseas assignments by organizations like the Peace Corps. The former editor of *Oriental Rug Review*, George O'Bannon, is a notable example of these latter-day, home-grown enthusiasts.

Whatever their background or approach, specialty dealers will first send you photos and descriptions of rugs of the type you express interest in acquiring and then ship to you for firsthand inspection any pieces you are considering buying. If you are unknown to the dealer, a returnable deposit of part or all of the price may be required for this service. (Dealers, unlike auction houses, often absorb the cost of shipment if you purchase the rug sent to you on approval, but if you return it, you should expect to pay the entire cost of shipping and insurance.)

Because their stock consists primarily of one-of-a-kind antique and semiantique pieces, specialty dealers eschew the 60 percent–off sale events beloved of Main Street and shopping mall dealers in new orientals. They consider themselves, and rightly so, as dealers in art rather than floor coverings. If you enjoy bargaining, by all means give it a whirl, but don't expect across-the-board, end-of-season types of reductions.

BUYING RUGS ABROAD

If you are planning a trip to a rug-weaving area, this could be a marvelous buying opportunity if you heed certain cautions:

1. If you buy from a dealer unaccustomed to shipping overseas, try to bring your rug purchases home with you. You'd be amazed at the compact package a determined dealer can make of even a fairly good-sized rug.

2. Unless you are very knowledgeable, you should consider confining your choice to new rugs.

In the Turkish bazaars, old-looking rugs of any age are invariably touted as antiques, and all dyes are sworn to be natural. It is assumed that if you don't know what you're looking at, you deserve to be cheated. Fine antique Turkish rugs exported generations ago can be purchased for less in the United States than in Turkey—and more safely, too, now that countries around the world have become understandably sensitive to the loss of their cultural artifacts to Western museums and collectors. You could be fined and even detained if you attempt to take antiques home with you, and although this is less likely to occur in the case of rugs, why take the chance when the new vegetable-dyed Turkish rugs and kilims are such worthy and economical buys? (See chapter on contemporary collectibles.)

For More Information

In the Resource Guide in the back of this book is a list of dealers either known to me personally or recommended by collectors whose judgment I respect or who regularly advertise in *Hali,* a periodical that specializes in rugs and textiles. Subscription information is included in the Resource Guide.

The members of oriental rug societies can also provide names of dealers likely to have rugs and trappings of interest to you. Membership in these societies is well worth seeking. Experienced collectors enjoy advising beginners, and the newsletters most rug societies publish usually include notices of rug-oriented events and tours and offer the best of the new rug books at a discount price to their members. See the Resource Guide for locations and the addresses to write to for membership information.

THE STRUCTURE OF
ORIENTAL RUGS

The clearest, most succinct definition of handmade rugs I have ever come across and that I doubt can be improved upon is contained in a book called *Hand-Woven Carpets* by A. F. Kendrick and C. E. C. Tattersall, originally published in 1922:

> The whole field of hand-made carpets can be divided into two great classes—those with smooth faces and those with a pile. Both classes are textile fabrics, which means that they consist essentially of two sets of threads—the warp and the weft—which cross each other at right angles and are interwoven so as to make a coherent tissue. The smooth-faced carpets consist of warp and weft alone; the pile carpets have, in addition, short extra pieces of thread knotted to the warp threads so that their free ends stand up and form a surface similar to that made by the blades of grass in a meadow.

THE LOOM

Carpets, like other textile fabrics, are woven on a frame or loom. The degree of complexity of a loom varies according to the type, size, and sophistication of the article to be woven and the domicile of the weaver. Obviously, city workshop weavers will use larger and more elaborate looms than the womenfolk of nomadic tribes, but the essentials remain the same: two stout beams kept apart by sidepieces, or in the case of nomadic weavers, by stakes driven into the ground.

The warp threads, which absorb the greater share of the stress created by the weaving process, are generally thicker and stronger than the weft. They are strung vertically upon the loom and lie parallel to the two side beams and to each other.

Once the warp has been strung, the weft threads may be woven through, over and under alternate warp threads, with each weft reversing the course of the previous weft, just like darning a sock. Unlike darning, however, a one-by-one process of interweaving weft and warp would become tedious in the extreme when translated to the large scale of a carpet. To avoid this, a stout rod is passed through the warp threads just as a weft thread would be, above the area where the actual weaving is taking place. The rod divides the warp threads into two sets, or planes, forming a space called a shed between them, with all of the odd-numbered warps lying in one set and all of the even-numbered warps in the other. This manipulation of the warp threads into two sets allows the weft thread, which may be wound on a shuttle, to be thrust through the shed in one motion.

For the alternate passage, or shoot, of the weft, the position of one set of the warp threads relative to the other must be reversed. To achieve this, all of the warp threads at the back of the shed are attached with short, equal lengths of cord to another rod, an arrangement that, in toto, is known as a heddle. When this rod is drawn forward, the attached warps are pulled in front of the other set to create a reversed space, or shed, through which the next shoot of the weft is passed. (Consult the glossary at the end of this chapter for definitions of unfamiliar terms.)

THE NOMADIC HORIZONTAL GROUND LOOM

Nomadic weavers use the simplest looms because they may have to pack up their work many times during the weaving of a single rug. The horizontal beams over which the warp threads are wound are held in position by stakes driven into the ground rather than by rigid upright sidepieces. The tension of the warp threads is maintained by securing one of the warp beams to the stakes by pairs of stout ropes that can be tightened by twirling a stick placed between them. This far-from-ideal method of control makes it impossible to duplicate even the same degree of imperfect tension at each successive setting up of the loom, which is why the dimensions of nomadic weavings are seldom true. But even the most primitive nomadic looms usually have some sort of device to separate the sets of warp threads to facilitate the passage of the weft from one edge to the other.

The nomadic horizontal ground loom.

THE VERTICAL VILLAGE LOOM

The typical village loom is only slightly more sophisticated than the horizontal type. Constructed from roughly fashioned timbers, they are housed

The vertical village loom.

in family dwellings so that the womenfolk may weave rugs—sometimes for household use but usually for the purpose of adding to a family's meager income—between the daily rounds of domestic duties.

The permanency of its placement and the addition of rigid vertical side pieces make it easier to maintain an even warp tension on these looms, but the length of a rug is predetermined by the distance between the upper and lower beams, a limitation shared with the nomadic horizontal loom.

Rugs are almost always woven from bottom to top: as work on a horizontal ground loom progresses, the weaver sits upon the part she has completed; but a weaver using the simplest type of vertical loom sits in front of the loom on a plank that is raised higher as the work progresses, a distinct drawback if one is working indoors in a poorly ventilated room that is dimly lit at best.

Both of these limitations are ameliorated by the Tabriz loom. Although similar to the village upright loom in its essentials, the warps strung around the upper and lower warp beams are looped so that, as the weaving progresses, the warp tension can be readily loosened and the completed portion drawn up behind the lower beam. This allows the weaver to remain seated at the same level throughout the weaving process and offers the additional advantage of doubling the possible length of the article being woven.

THE ROLLER BEAM LOOM

Commercial workshops in all rug-weaving areas use roller beam looms, albeit with local variations in design and materials. It can be as simple as the type used in western Turkish villages, a crudely cobbled wooden structure whose dimensions are determined by the space in the dwelling chosen to house it. This domestic version is rarely wide enough to accommodate more than two weavers, relatives or neighbors who enjoy an exchange of village gossip as, seated closely side by side, their skilled fingers fly between the warps.

At the other extreme are the Romanian workshop looms made of aluminum and as wide as is necessary to produce carpets that will meet the international market's demands. In both cases the upper and lower beams rotate, and in the more sophisticated versions a constant, even tension is maintained through the use of levers. As work progresses, the completed portion of the rug is wound around the lower beam while additional warp is unwound from the upper, which makes it possible to weave carpets of any length desired.

THE MATERIALS

The materials most commonly used to make oriental rugs are sheep's wool, cotton, silk, camel hair, and goat hair. Linen has great strength and has occasionally been used as warp threads in fine rugs. Hemp or jute occurs only in very cheap, coarse products, made mostly in Southeast Asia, which often have considerable charm but wear poorly.

In the distant past, all rugs were made primarily to insulate against the cold. They were made entirely of wool and were as apt to be felted as woven, as in fact many nomadic rugs still are. Sheep wool is by far the most commonly employed fiber; camel and goat hair are used primarily in nomadic and tribal weavings. The soft, honey-colored ground in many old Baluch rugs is natural camel hair, which is sometimes also used for both the warp and weft yarns in their flat-woven articles. Goat hair is generally too coarse and stiff to be used for knotting, but it is frequently incorporated into woolen warp yarns for strength and is used by several tribes to create distinctive, hard-wearing edge finishes.

Although wool is often used for both warp and weft in tribal and village weavings, handspun in many cases, and is by far the most commonly used fiber for pile in rugs of all types, virtually all 20th-century workshop carpets have been made with millspun cotton warps and wefts. Although subject to dry rot in humid environments, cotton is strong, it can be evenly and finely spun, and it is more stable and lies flatter than wool. Cotton was used in the foundations of antique rugs made in China and Persia and in the wefts of some late-19th-century East Caucasian rugs. Because the presence of cotton as a foundation material is often a clue to both the place and date of manufacture, it behooves collectors to acquaint themselves with the structural specifics of the weavings of most interest to them.

Silk has been used as both a pile and foundation material in very fine carpets through the centuries and is sometimes knotted into wool pile to impart a lustrous accent. Although mercerized cotton may be substituted for silk highlights in small rugs and bags, its principal use is in cheap souvenir rugs misleadingly described as "art silk."

THE PREPARATION OF FIBERS FOR WEAVING

Animal and vegetable fibers have one thing in common: initially, they are all a relatively tangled mass of filaments arranged in random manner and mixed with a good deal of trash. The fibers must first be disentangled and picked clean of burrs and twigs and sorted to separate dark- and light-colored strands. Wool is then combed to remove the shorter fibers and arrange the more desirable longer fibers so that they lie parallel to one another in an orderly fashion so as to produce when spun a strong, smooth-surfaced yarn capable of withstanding the stress of weaving.

Camel and goat hair fibers are usually used in their natural colors with minimal treatment before spinning. Sheep fleeces are normally washed after shearing, although some nomadic groups omit this initial washing, which may account for the extraordinary luster of some tribal pile work.

SPINNING

The spinning of wool in Eastern cultures is usually done by women; sometimes children share the task, and in some weaving groups it is considered an acceptable occupation for men, too. Collectors with firsthand knowledge of rug-weaving cultures always mention spinning as the one constant: the people spin while tending their flocks and herds, riding to and from pasturage, walking to fields and orchards, tending babies—in short, whenever both hands are not required to perform some other task. Hand spinning is usually accomplished with a spindle, a very simple device predating the wheel and used in many forms since before recorded history.

After the initial thread is spun by twisting the fibers into a continuous strand, several strands are twisted together in the opposite direction of the initial spin to form the yarn. The number of combined threads and the tightness of their twist determine a yarn's thickness and strength: two to four stout strands are firmly combined, or plied, for the warp yarns; the weft is thinner and more lightly plied, and the wool used for knotting the pile is even more loosely plied to avoid a crimped appearance and maintain a lustrous surface.

In the past, cotton was rarely used by nomads or isolated villagers because it had to be purchased from the outside, but improvements in transportation have made it more commonly available; an all-wool, vegetable-dyed product is no longer synonymous with tribal weaving. The wool and cotton used in most commercial rug-weaving workshops is cleaned, machine-spun, and dyed under controlled conditions to ensure uniformity.

DYEING

The wool may be washed again after spinning and before dying if enough grease remains in the wool to make it difficult for the dye to be evenly absorbed. Yarns used for the warp are seldom dyed, although threads from different-colored fleeces may be plied together. Weft yarns are sometimes dyed, and while the natural shades of pile yarns are occasionally used for design elements requiring ivory, gray, tan, brown, and black, they are usually colored with dyes. Traditionally, and in a few areas still, dyes were derived from naturally occurring sources, but these have long since been succeeded by synthetic dyes, which more easily fulfill industry requirements in regard to cost control and standardization. (The next chapter will discuss dyes in greater detail.)

THE WEAVING PROCESS

THE WARP

The first step in rug weaving is mounting the warp on the loom. The closeness of the warp threads, which depends on the thickness of the yarn chosen for the warp, determines to a major extent the fineness of the weaving to be done. Usually one or more of the warp yarns at the edges of the rug will be stouter than the others. It is customary to leave these edge warps free of pile knots but strengthened and fastened securely to the body of the rug with extra turns of the weft yarns. After the rug is completed, the edges are further reinforced with wool, goat hair, or cotton yarns, the methods and materials employed for these edge finishes being yet another clue to a rug's origin.

THE WEFT

Before the knotting of the pile threads on the warp threads begins, a section of interweaving of the warp is usually done—at the bottom of the rug, where the weaving commences, and again at the top after the knotted portion is completed—for the purpose of anchoring and protecting the pile knots from erosion. These plain-woven ends may terminate in a simple fringe created by the ends of the warp threads when the completed rug is cut from the loom, or the warps may be knotted, braided, or fashioned into a coarse, decorative netting. In some rugs a narrow band of plain weave is simply turned under and sewn to the back of the rug; on old Turkoman rugs, the red skirts may be up to 10 inches in length and narrowly striped in blue or otherwise decorated. In the case of much old Baluch work, the woven end skirts are elaborately patterned, the pile colors being repeated in traditional geometric designs. These characteristic rug end and edge finishes, whether plain or fancy, deserve the collector's notice and should be respected, insofar as possible, when repairs are undertaken. A later section on repair and restoration will discuss this question in greater detail.

After the initial band of plain weave has been completed and the first row of knots tied to the warps, a weft thread or threads are inserted. If two wefts are used, a common choice, the thread is transported through the shed from one side of the loom to the other in a single shoot, and immediately brought back through the reverse shed. If only one weft is inserted, a technique characteristic of the Hamadan district of Iran, then the reversed-shed weft is returned after the completion of the succeeding row of knots. Rugs like the South Caucasian Kazaks may have three or four red-dyed wefts clearly visible between each row of knots; in others, like the 19th-century Persian Kermans and Bijars, one or more of the wefts are hidden from sight within the structure. To the expert eye, the color, placement, and number of wefts laid in between each row of knots is as distinctive as a fingerprint.

To lay in wefts so that the same degree of tension is maintained throughout requires enormous skill, and although we take a well-made rug for granted and complain of its high cost, most of us would be very hard put indeed to duplicate it with our fumbling Western fingers.

KNOTTING THE PILE

The knots used in creating pile rugs are not tied knots in the same sense as those used by sailors and fishermen to securely attach boats to docks and hooks to fishing line. Rather, they are made by looping around the warp threads lengths of yarn held securely in place, not by the fashion in which they are looped but by the pressure exerted both by the adjacent knots and by the wefts, which are first passed between each row of knots and then pressed down very hard against them with a coarse, comblike tool known as a beater.

Most weavers use their fingers alone to "tie" the yarn, which is then cut with a knife snugged into the palm of one hand to produce the tufts that make up the resilient pile surface. In some Iranian districts a tool known as a *tikh*, which combines a knife with a hooked end, is used first to pull the pile yarn through the warps and then to cut the yarn after the knot is completed. In no case do oriental rug weavers employ short, precut pieces of yarn for their knots. As the knotting progresses, the weaver may roughly shear completed portions to check on the correctness of the emerging design, but the final shearing is saved for a master craftsman to accomplish after the completed rug is removed from the loom.

The two knots used in the majority of oriental rugs are the Persian, an asymmetrical knot known traditionally as the *Senneh*—after a Persian weaving town—and the Turkish, or symmetrical knot, described in older publications and among traditional collectors as *Ghiordes*, the name of a famed Turkish weaving center.

The Turkish knot is employed primarily in Turkey and the Caucasus; both Persian and Turkish knots are used in Iran, and the Persian knot is found in Indian, Chinese, and the majority of Turkoman rugs. The decision to use one or the other of these knots is more a matter of tradition than any inherent advantage one has over the other, although a number of authorities believe it is easier to execute very finely detailed curvilinear patterns with the Persian knot in one of its several variations. With rare exceptions, the same type of knot is used throughout a single rug; occasionally, however, a Persian-knotted Turkoman will be found to have Turkish knots along its edges.

Because of the confusion generated by attaching the names of countries to an element of rug structure that disregards national boundaries, you will find the straightforward descriptive terms, symmetrical and asymmetrical, more and more frequently used in oriental rug publications.

Both knots utilize adjacent warp threads: the yarn in the symmetrical Turkish knot lies across and on top of the pair of warps, the free ends passing around behind the warps and the two ends emerging together between them. In the asymmetrical Persian knot, one end of the yarn completely surrounds one warp thread while the other passes behind the second warp thread and comes up outside of it. Since the Turkish knot is symmetrically looped, the two little bumps or nodes it makes on the back of the rug almost always look about the same, although it may be coarser or finer depending on the particular rug. The space taken by a single Turkish knot is broader than it is high, which means that in a Turkish knotted rug there are fewer knots per inch horizontally than vertically.

Symmetrical or Turkish knot with two wefts of equal tension passing between each row of knots.

Asymmetrical or Persian knot opening to the left, with two wefts of equal tension passing between each row of knots.

Asymmetrical or Persian knot opening to the right, with one weft passing between each row of knots.

Persian knots, because of their asymmetrical structure, may be looped so that the encircled warp thread is either the right or left thread of the pair. Knots opening to the left incline the pile to the right; knots open to the right incline it to the left.

In some rugs the tension of the wefts is deliberately varied so as to markedly displace one thread of the warp pair, thus pulling the emerging tufts of pile closer together. To more easily visualize this, hold up two fingers from one hand to represent the pair of warp threads, their knuckles becoming the two nodes of a single knot. When the fingers are in the same plane, both knuckle-nodes are clearly visible, but if you rotate your fingers from horizontal to the vertical, as if one finger-warp were being displaced by the pressure of a tightly drawn weft exerted upon it, then only one knuckle-node can be seen. Looking at the back of a rug, when one of the knot nodes no longer lies parallel to the other, the result is a series of squares created by one node rather than the rectangles two nodes form. This allows the knot count along the rug's width to equal that of the length, which in turn minimizes distortion of complicated designs worked from an artist's drawing or cartoon.

As we have seen, there's more to the combination of warp, weft, and pile knot than at first meets the eye. The sizes of the yarns, the position of the warp, and the tension of the wefts affect a rug's construction and feel, the amount of detail possible in its design, and its wear characteristics. Is there such a thing as an ideal structure? The answer, of course, depends on the purpose a rug is intended to serve. For example, comparisons of collectible rugs on the basis of the density of the knot count fall wide of the mark, the

Symmetrical knots with two wefts of varying tensions.

Symmetrical knots with two wefts of varying tensions.

Asymmetrical knots with one loose, one tight, weft.

Asymmetrical knots with two tight wefts, one loose weft.

fineness of a rug's knotting rarely being of primary interest to a sophisticated collector.

Three other types of knots are the *jufti*, the Tibetan, and the Spanish. The *jufti*, which is tied over four warps instead of two, is a wool-and-labor-saving variation of either the Turkish or Persian knot. It is sometimes interspersed with regular two-warp knots, but in either case its use is rarely acknowledged by the weavers who employ it and is considered a deceptive practice.

Tibetan weavers employ a unique looping technique in which a full row of loops is made at a time, each loop around a pair of warp threads and in combination with a guide rod that remains in place until wefts are inserted and beaten down, at which time the loops are cut and the guide rod removed. The Spanish knot, which is peculiar to antique Spanish carpets, completely encircles every other warp thread, the encircled thread alternating with each row.

A skilled weaver, working without interruptions, can tie up to a thousand knots in an hour. Rugs may be knotted by a single nomadic woman weaving traditional patterns from memory, by a group of weavers working from an artist's cartoon pinned to the loom above their flying fingers, or in a shop filled with looms of identical rugs woven in sections by teams of weavers following the knot sequence called out to them in a rhythmic drone. Even if each workshop weaver ties an average of 8,000 to 10,000 knots a day in the width of the carpet assigned her, only a few inches of a finely woven carpet can be knotted in a single day, and it can take a month or more to complete it.

As a general rule, very finely knotted rugs are more expensive than those with an average knot count, but the breathtaking impact of superior examples of tribal weaving can induce collectors to part with very large sums to acquire relatively coarsely knotted, often quite small works of textile art.

The number of knots per square inch can vary from about 16 to 1,000, reaching an incredible 2,000 in a few extraordinarily fine Mughal prayer rugs. In the vast majority of carpets the number lies between 50 and 100; a knot count above 300 is uncommon, and little is gained aesthetically by increasing the count beyond 400 knots to the inch. If durability is an important consideration, a well-made carpet of middling coarseness will prove more satisfactory in service than a finely knotted one.

The wide variety of techniques employed throughout the weaving history

Jufti *knot*.   Spanish *knot*.

of carpet-producing countries precludes a uniform knot-counting system. The only constant is that knots should be counted along the width first and along the length second. Always keep in mind, however, that although each pair of bumps in the rows you see across the width of a rug's back ordinarily represents one knot, only one bump will show in the case of a depressed warp structure, which is characteristically ribbed in appearance to a greater or lesser degree depending on the severity of the warp displacement. In written structural analyses of rugs, knot counts are expressed in terms of knots either per square inch or per square decimeter, which is 10 centimeters by 10 centimeters. There are approximately 2.54 centimeters to the inch.

FINISHING

Upon completion of the weaving of a rug, it is removed from the loom and finished either for domestic use or for the market. The warps may be cut and left as simple fringes or they may be knotted into either slender bundles or a band of netting to provide the pile knots additional protection from erosion. The roughly cut pile will then be given a final clipping: a quick once-over in the case of a nomadic weaver, but in city workshops a master craftsman undertakes a precise shearing suited to a rug's style and fineness of knotting. Modern Chinese and Indian pastel floral candy-box designs are commonly embossed by clipping a groove around certain of the motifs to throw them into opulent relief. Clipped, too, is the dark outlining of the traditional designs of much of the new generation of vegetable-dyed Turkish village rugs. The intent, frowned upon by many collectors, is to ape the pleasing three-dimensional look created by the characteristic deterioration over time of acid-dyed black and brown wools.

Washing is the final step in the finishing process. This varies from a simple cleansing with soap and water to treatment with chemicals to "soften" bright colors and to heighten the natural luster of the wool pile. Depending on the type and concentration of the chemicals used, the effect on the appearance and durability of the rug can range from mild to disastrous. A collector may accept a mild chemical wash in a furnishing rug, but any hint of past chemical treatment will adversely affect the desirability of an otherwise collectible piece.

FLAT-WOVEN RUGS

To repeat part of the definition quoted at the beginning of this chapter, flat-woven, or smooth-faced, rugs "consist essentially of two sets of threads . . . which cross each other at right angles and are interwoven."

Although some flat-woven work is very fine and intricately patterned— most notably the exquisite Senneh kilims—and some combine several

Plain weave structure.

techniques in a single piece, the examples most sought after by collectors are slit-tapestry kilims woven in simple, traditional geometric designs accented by bold figures and bands and blocks of brilliant color. They are the graphic art, the posters of the rug world, and enthusiasts consider the average pile rug fussy and insipid in comparison.

Authorities differ widely, sometimes heatedly, on how best to group and describe the various flat-weave techniques. For the beginning collector, understandably confounded by this large, bewilderingly complex class of weavings, I have adapted and updated Valerie Justin's introduction to the subject in her book *Flat-Woven Rugs of the World*, which is noteworthy for its clarity.

PLAIN WEAVE

Plain weave is produced by a simple alternate interlacing of the warp and weft. Depending on the thickness and spacing of the warp threads, the resulting fabric is said to be balanced, which means that neither the warp nor the weft predominates. If, however, either the warp or weft dominates, with one set of threads becoming more visible than the other, the result is known technically as a warp- or weft-faced weave.

TAPESTRY WEAVE

Tapestry weave is a type of weft-faced plain weave used in kilims in which the warp is entirely concealed by beaten-down weft threads woven in color

Tapestry weave used in kilims.

blocks rather than continuously across the width of the loom. These discontinuous colored wefts turning back into their own color blocks create a slit between the warps of one block and the adjoining color areas. This slit may be left open to serve as part of the design; it may be eliminated during the weaving by dovetailing the wefts from adjacent color areas on a single warp, or it may be sewn closed after the weaving is completed. Sometimes an added, or supplementary, weft in a contrasting color or sheathed in gold or silver is used to join and strengthen the slits, thus highlighting the basic design with added color or glitter.

Most flat-woven textiles have geometric designs, but curvilinear designs can be achieved by depressing the wefts unevenly with the beater, tightly pressing them in some areas and leaving them looser in others to express the soft curves of floral motifs. Known as eccentric wefting, outstanding examples of this tapestry-weave variation can be seen in the lovely Balkan-style floral kilims being reproduced today in western Turkey (see chapter on contemporary collectibles).

SOUMAK WEAVE

In this technique, the wefts are not just interwoven with the warps; they actually wrap around them. Sometimes the rows of warp-wrapping wefts alternate with shoots of plain-weave wefts, in which case the wrapping wefts are considered supplementary rather than part of the basic structure.

Soumak warp-wrapping sequences can vary considerably from place to place and are dictated largely by tradition.

BROCADING

The term *brocade*, when applied to flat-woven articles, indicates the addition of discontinuous supplementary wefts or warps to a basic interwoven structure; therefore some soumak weaving in which the warp-wrapping

Soumak weave with shoots of weft alternating with warp-wrapping wefts.

Soumak weave with shoots of weft alternating with warp-wrapping wefts.

technique, alternating with plain weave, is confined to a specific pattern or color area can be considered a type of brocading. Soumak brocade is usually a one-faced fabric in which the ends of the differently colored discontinuous wefts are left hanging loose on the back.

Other forms of brocading used in Turkey are the *cicim*, which often combines weft floats with brocaded accents easy to confuse with embroidery (see below), and the *zili*. The *zili* has many forms, the most distinctive of which presents a ribbed surface appearance.

WEFT-FLOAT

If continuous wefts are used to create a surface pattern, they are temporarily unincorporated into the basic structure by being "floated" on the back between pattern areas. The bands of weft-float decoration often seen on the skirts of old Baluch rugs provide an excellent example of this technique.

EMBROIDERY

The patterning techniques discussed above are employed during the weaving process. If decoration is added with a needle after the woven article is removed from the loom, the rug is said to have been embroidered.

A GLOSSARY OF RUG-WEAVING TERMS

Written descriptions of weaving and fiber manufacture often employ undefined technical terms bewildering to the layman. Below are definitions of the most commonly encountered puzzlers and a review of some of the terms used in this section.

Beating Up, Down, or In The process by which a weft or wefts are forced down tightly against a preceding row of knots. This is accomplished with a large multitined wood or metal forklike tool known as a beater.

Carding The process of brushing out, cleaning, and intermixing fibers with a pair of carders, which are paddlelike implements set with angled teeth of bent wire.

Cartoon A drawing on paper, usually graphed, showing a section of rug design. For large urban workshops, cartoons are prepared to order by artists, but a village weaver can buy cartoons at local markets and adapt them to suit her needs and fancies.

Combing Preparing wool for worsted (see below) spinning by combing out the short fibers and arranging the remaining longer fibers into smooth, parallel order.

Dovetailing To avoid slits in tapestry weaving, the discontinued wefts from adjacent color areas meet and share a common warp.

Fibers Commonly Used in Rug Making

Cotton A soft fluffy vegetable fiber of almost pure cellulose with a flattened tubular structure. Although stronger wet than dry, moisture reduces its elasticity and, if prolonged, invites dry rot.

Silk A protein animal product much finer and stronger than other animal fibers. A continuous silk filament of 400 to 1,000 yards can be reeled from a single silkworm cocoon.

Wool and Hair An animal fiber made up of infinite numbers of small scales that allow it to bend without breaking. The quality of the fiber, whether from sheep, goat, or camel, depends on where the animal was pastured, its breeding and age, from what part of the animal and at what time of year the wool or hair was obtained, and whether it was alive or dead at the time of pulling or shearing.

Animal fibers are stronger when dry than wet and although vulnerable to insect damage are not subject to dry rot.

Flatweave A fabric created by the interweaving of horizontal threads (weft) with vertical (warp) threads in any one of a variety of interlocking techniques.

Fringe The cut warp ends of a rug removed from the loom.

Heddle The rods attached to the loom to which alternate warps are attached and drawn forward and back to create the space, or shed, to facilitate the passage of the weft threads.

Jufti A type of pile-making knot whose looping encompasses more than the usual single pair of warps. Although the resulting product is considered inferior, it is sometimes employed as a labor- and material-saving device.

Knots, Pile The knots most commonly used to loop pile yarns around the warps are the symmetrical Turkish knot, also known as the *Ghiordes*, and the asymmetrical Persian, or *Senneh*, knot. These knots and a few of their many variations are described and illustrated in the text preceding this glossary.

Pick Alternate term for shoot, the passage of one thread of weft through the warp threads. This passage of the pick may also be described as being "laid in the shed."

Ply See *Yarn Ply and Twist* below.

Rove or Roving A drawn out and slightly twisted roll or sliver of fiber ready for spinning.

Selvage The edges formed by the passage of the weft yarns around the bundles of warp threads that bound the sides, sometimes reinforced after weaving is completed by overwrapping with goat hair or overcasting in wool.

Shed The space formed by the separation of the warp threads into two planes and through which the shuttle passes carrying the weft thread. This space can be created either by use of a heddle (see above) or by a more primitive device known as a shed stick (see below).

Shed Stick A long flat stick threaded through alternate warp strings. By turning the stick on edge, a space yielding a reasonably satisfactory shed is formed.

Shoot See *Pick*, above.

Shuttle A device around which weft threads are looped to prevent the yarns from becoming entangled on the floor and to facilitate the passage of the weft through the warp shed. If several colors are used, a shuttle will be required for each.

Skirt The bands of plain weave on the ends of some types of rugs are known as skirts when their length exceeds approximately 3 inches. These skirts may be of a single color or striped or otherwise decorated with either pile or flat-woven motifs.

Spindle, Drop A device consisting, in one common version, of a shaft approximately a foot in length to which, near the bottom, a disk-shaped weight is joined. The shafts are usually wooden; the weights may be of wood or clay or fashioned from metal coins. Light of weight and eminently portable, it is the tool of choice for spinning yarns in the Middle East.

Spinning The process whereby animal or plant fibers are twisted into strong continuous strands suitable for weaving.

Warp The chief foundation thread of fabrics; also, the strong yarns running from end to end on a loom and interwoven with weft threads, which are usually thinner and more loosely spun.

Weft The thread or yarn interwoven with the warp threads and carried on a shuttle through a space, known as the shed, created between them.

In pile rugs, wefts are employed to separate and anchor the rows of pile knots and strengthen the selvedges. In flat-woven textiles, various techniques employ wefts that are discontinuous, supplementary, or floated, terms described in the preceding section on flatweaves.

Woof A term sometimes used for weft.

Woolen Woolen yarns are made from carded and interlaced short fibers, which, when spun, make a light, fluffy yarn unsuitable for rugs because of its inability to withstand the abrasive stress of the weaving process, much less the wear it would receive underfoot.

Worsted A process whereby long fibers of wool are combed parallel and spun into a strong, smooth-surfaced yarn. Oriental rugs are traditionally made from long, lustrous worsted-spun fibers, which acquire a characteristic paintbrushlike tip with wear. The term is also applied to a suiting cloth made from worsted-spun yarn.

Yarn Ply and Twist When fibers are spun into yarn, the twist of the threads is described either as "Z" or "S," depending upon the direction of the slant of the fibers. In the structural analyses supplied for rugs in some publications, the technical descriptions of warp, weft, and pile yarns needed to determine a rug's provenance appear in an abbreviated form. For example, a "Z2S" notation for a warp yarn indicates a makeup of two single Z-spun strands S-plied together.

The initial spun thread is termed a single. Combined singles are a ply; two singles twisted together are 2-ply; three singles, 3-ply, and so on. When yarn singles are plied, the twist is usually opposite to that of the initial twist of the singles. Plied yarns can also be twisted together—in the direction opposite to that of the initial ply—to produce the stout outer warps needed to strengthen the selvedges.

"S" and "Z" spun yarns.

The tightness of the twist imparted to the yarn in the various stages of twisting and plying is determined, in part, by the use to which it will be put. Warp yarn, the principal foundation thread and subject to continual stress during the weaving process, is the tightest and stoutest; weft yarn, less so; and pile yarn, the least tight and thick of the three.

For More Information

A detailed examination of rug structures and the variety of weaving techniques employed in the oriental rug-weaving areas over the centuries far exceeds the scope of an introductory guide. Dozens of books have been written about flatweaves alone. The annotated list of books and periodicals in the Resource Guide will help you choose publications applicable to your particular area of interest.

DYES USED IN ORIENTAL RUGS

Rug enthusiasts can chat about the intricacies of warps, wefts, and knotting with a commendable degree of open-mindedness, and even an exchange of opinion about the provenance of a given rug may provoke only coolly discourteous disagreement. The topic guaranteed to transform discussion into a heated argument verging on naked aggression is natural versus synthetic dyes, probably because to scholars and many collectors the presence of synthetic dyes is *prima facie* evidence of inferiority.

Some respected experts maintain that since it is entirely possible to duplicate synthetically even the most subtle of natural shades, it is rather silly to dismiss a rug as unworthy of collection solely on the basis of synthetic dyes. They point out that when synthetic dyes were first introduced into remote areas, tribal weavers viewed their brilliance as special; the drawbacks as yet unknown, it was only their expense that limited their use to cotton and silk accents. As a clincher, these experts cite the fact that in some cases the only way to distinguish between a natural and a synthetic dye is through laboratory analysis, an expensive procedure sometimes necessary for scholarly research to establish beyond question whether or not a rug was made before the introduction of synthetic dyes into Middle Eastern rug-weaving districts in the mid to late 1870s.

But to the connoisseur, whose interest extends beyond technical minutiae to the historic and ethnic context in which carpets were woven, there is much more to the impression of color than the actual color itself. The shimmering pointillist effect of fine antique carpets is not the result of conscious planning or what we are now pleased to term quality control. Rather, it is to a significant degree a felicitous, accidental by-product of their manufacture.

The subtle shadings of pile color known as *abrash* occur because it is virtually impossible to avoid variations in color from one dye lot to another when using natural materials. Vegetable dye color is the product not merely of a particular plant variety but of the conditions in which it is grown—altitude, soil, moisture provided, and maturity at time of harvest—and the mineral content of the water with which the dyebath is prepared, all of which are largely a matter of circumstance. The qualities of the wool to be dyed—in natural color, degree of oiliness, and the varying thickness of hand-spun and plied fibers—also affect the way dye is absorbed and its color reflected.

In the past, since time was not a commodity, the weaver employing this vegetable-dyed wool could lavish upon each rug the care necessary to knot precisely the symbols and patterns reflecting her tribal or Islamic traditions, often including a few idiosyncratic touches of her own. Then, mellowed by sun and dust and smoke, the pile developed a patina through decades of respectful use. A truly old rug gains thereby an authenticity that, to the educated eye and sensibility, distinguishes one carpet from another no matter how similar they may appear to the layman.

Because the supply of natural dyes has always been limited and uncertain and their successful employment required considerable skill, the availability of synthetic dyes that could be measured and used with a precision impossible with vegetable dyes was not only encouraged but necessitated by the late-19th-century revival of the carpet trade. Carpets had been made for export before then, of course, but largely for a limited, wealthy clientele of discriminating aristocrats. The era of the pretty 9 × 12 designed for Western parlors had yet to arrive.

It was this later commercialization, aimed at an international market of comfortable middle-class folk, that introduced standardization in both carpet sizes and colors. After all, the reasoning went, how could a logical pricing structure be developed unless rugs without "unsightly" variations in color could be supplied to suit Western homes and tastes? Unfortunately, many of the early synthetic dyes were neither light- nor water-fast, and their use in otherwise well-designed, expertly knotted carpets was disastrous to the point where they were temporarily banned from both Persian and Turkish workshops. But synthetic dyes have improved enormously over the years, and both retailers and buyers can be justly satisfied with the choice offered by the variety of competently dyed rugs available in the market today.

Will a new, synthetically dyed carpet maintain its value? Assuming one chooses a quality piece to begin with, it undoubtedly will. Its relationship to an antique carpet made in a traditional context will remain that of a fine reproduction; but as time goes by, this distinction, including the ability to make it, may become blurred as copies more and more resemble the real thing.

I was amused recently to see in a department store a pile of identical scatter rugs that, from a distance, looked extraordinarily like 19th-century Turkoman tribal weavings. The color was the dark browny-red typical of old Yomud rugs; they had a subtle *abrash*, and even the border design was slightly irregular, as it often is in genuine nomadic work. These machine-made Belgian products would not fool anyone upon close inspection and were not intended to do so, but when the Middle Eastern rug workshops attain the sophistication of the Belgian and Dutch copyists and dyers, a new generation of hand-knotted reproductions will surely kindle hotter arguments than ever among future oriental rug enthusiasts.

NATURAL DYES

All dyes have a chemical makeup. The advantage of natural dyes is that even the most brilliant lack the uncompromising quality of modern synthetics as they are commonly employed by Eastern dyers, and time and sun will not appreciably mellow these almost aggressively fast dyes.

Natural dyes, even when expertly made and applied, yield by their very nature imprecise results that successful commercial synthetic dyes, again because of their very nature, do not. Although colors from natural dyes can be vibrant, they are not "pure" colors in the sense synthetic colors are because the decocted plants and insects contain many chemical constituents; therefore, although natural colors can be produced within specific ranges, it is rarely possible to exactly reproduce a particular hue. On the other hand, because of the naturally occurring chemical "overlaps," natural dyes are almost never disharmonious. If one considers this imprecision to be aesthetically superior, then synthetic dyes straightforwardly used will not satisfy, and synthetics manipulated to simulate the honest imprecision of natural dyes will deeply offend.

Part of the charm of natural dye materials lies in the romance of an art that was well developed by 2500 B.C. and in the sounds of names like indigo, saffron, and madder, which echo of the pyramids, Imperial Rome, Persian dynasties, and the black tents of nomads. Below is a list of the more commonly used natural dye materials—some dyestuffs are used universally; others are only locally available—and the metal salts, known as mordants, that are introduced to create a chemical bond between the dye and the fiber, as some dyes do not unite readily with animal fibers unaided. The name comes from the latin word *mordere*, which means "to bite."

INDIGO (INDIGOFERA TINCTORIA; ISATIS TINCTORIA)

Indigo is the most commonly used of all dyes, closely followed by madder. One oriental rug authority has said that these two dyes plus a few mordants and undyed dark and light wools make up the basic range of color. Exquisite rugs have been created from nothing more. Indigo has to undergo a complex process in a fermentation vat because the dye obtained from the leaves, indogotin, is not water-soluble. The natural and synthetic forms of indogotin, both of which may be obtained as a powder from dye supply houses, are chemically indistinguishable.

There are a number of ways of changing the insoluble blue powder to a solution. One traditional method, said to be the secret of the heavenly blue in some antique Turkoman carpets, is to steep the powder in the urine of very young boys. Whether this or a less exotic method is employed, the yarn is first dipped in the resulting greenish-yellow solution, then lifted out and exposed to the air, whereupon the coloring matter deposited on the yarn unites with the oxygen and turns blue. It is an entrancing process. Repeated immersions and airings deepen the blue to any desired shade. To produce greens and purples, indigo-dyed yarns may be mordanted with the appropriate metal salts and overdyed with yellow or red dyes, respectively.

MADDER (RUBIA TINCTORUM)

Another of the most ancient dyestuffs, the plant from which madder is obtained grows both wild and under cultivation. Its color-fastness ranks very high. The dye is obtained from the red material beneath the outer bark of roots at least three years old. The roots are usually dried and powdered in order to release the color readily into the dyebath.

Madder yields a good clear red, varying in hue from orange-red to garnet to violet, depending on the proportion of the color-influencing compounds present in the plants used to make the dye and the minerals used for mordanting the wool. Madder rose is a beautiful clear, light, ruby red commonly seen in old Baluch tribal rugs; in the Melas area of Turkey, a strong pure orange is obtained from madder growing locally in the wild. A blue-toned red found in Chinese rugs is derived from a related plant, *Rubia codifolia*.

COCHINEAL (DACTYLOPIUS COCCUS)

Cochineal is a red dye obtained from an insect cultivated on cactus plants, principally in Mexico and Central America. One pound of cochineal powder contains about 70,000 of the dried insects. The Spanish introduced the dye to Europe in the early 1500s, but it was not used in Eastern carpets to any great extent until the 19th century.

The color, depending on the mordants used, usually has a cooler tonality than madder red and ranges from an orange-toned scarlet red through blue-toned crimson to purple. For a long time, the term *crimson* was applied solely to the bluish-red dye derived from either of two insects: the kermes, or oak shield louse, and the cochineal. Another insect-derived red dye is lac. Lac was used in early Persian carpets and extensively in India, but kermes-based dyes have not yet been found in any Eastern carpet.

WELD (RESEDA LUTEOLA)

Weld, an annual herb growing about 3 feet high, is considered the best source of yellow dye and is almost as fast to light as indigo and madder. All parts of the plant except the roots can be used; approximately 3 ounces of plant material is required for each ounce of wool. Depending on the mordants used, a bright yellow to gold to yellow-green may be obtained, and an indigo overdye results in a lovely medium green.

ISPEREK, OR ISPARUK (DELPHINIUM SULPHURAEUM)

Although this milkwort is widely used as a yellow dye, the color obtained is apt to fade to cream upon prolonged exposure to light.

OAK (QUERCUS, IN VARIETY); TANNER'S SUMACH (RHUS CORIARIA)

Black and dark brown dyes are created when wool mordanted with iron salts are treated with the tannins extracted from these and other plant sources. The disadvantage is that the effect of the combined iron and tannin is corrosive, and wool thus treated tends to become brittle, especially when exposed to light for long periods. This effect is so well known that black-dyed wools used in reproductions of old rugs are often clipped to approximate an antique look.

There are many other plants used for dyeing, and to the very knowledgeable eye the colors they produce are as significant a clue to a rug's origin as its weave and design. Pomegranate, saffron, buckthorn, Persian berries, turmeric, and camomile produce yellows, and henna, a soft yellow-red. A green dye is extracted from ripe turmeric berries and from various combinations of dyes and mordants.

MORDANTS

Mordants, which provide the chemical bond necessary to fix dyestuffs to wool and silk fibers, affect color tones significantly. Tin is used to brighten a color; iron salts to darken or "sadden." Unfortunately, both of these agents can, unless carefully used, render wool harsh and brittle. Many old Baluch rugs exhibit an interesting but unintentional three-dimensional effect because of this corrosive quality, the dark browns and blacks all but disappearing long before the reds and blues show any signs of wear. Other minerals used for mordanting are alum, chrome, tannin, and carbonate of soda. This last, an alkali, can also adversely affect animal fibers.

Whether natural or synthetic dyes are employed, the Middle Eastern dyer traditionally colors the fibers after they have been spun into yarn. If mordants are used, the metal salts, having been dissolved in liquid, are applied first. The yarn is then dried and immersed in large vats of the colored dyeing solutions and allowed to remain for varying amounts of time depending on the shade desired. Succeeding uses of the same dyebath will produce paler and paler hues. When the wool is removed from the vats, it should be rinsed until the water runs clear, as even a normally fast color will bleed from the yarn at a later washing if it is insufficiently rinsed after dyeing. The wool is then dried again before collection or purchase by the weaver.

Natural colors are softened by prolonged exposure to strong light, and Western eyes used to the mellow look of even strongly colored old vegetable-dyed rugs are often jolted by the brightness of new vegetable-dyed wool, not to mention antique rugs, like those in the Black Church in Brasov, Romania, that have been shielded from light for centuries.

In old pieces made by some Turkoman tribal weavers, undyed natural brown wool is often found to have lightened over the years. Among the vegetable dyes, yellows—except those derived from weld—are particularly subject to fading. Greens achieved through an overdyeing of indigo and yellow often revert to blue on the front of the piece, where sun has faded the yellow, while the original green persists on the back. Indigo, which is deposited on fibers rather than bonded with them by mordants, is subject to slight color loss over time through abrasion.

SYNTHETIC DYES

By the end of the 19th century a method for the commercial synthesis of indigo had been developed, and this, coupled with an earlier synthesis of madder—a dye called alizarin—signaled an end to the commercial use of natural dyes in the West. However, although synthetics were used in rug-weaving areas as early as the last quarter of the 19th century, natural dyes were also used in Eastern rugs well into the 20th century, and a revival is well under way, most notably in Turkey.

The color-fastness of dyes to light and water has always presented dyers and chemists with major problems. In fact, the early history of organic chemistry consists largely of investigations of dye-making materials and methods. The first commercial production of a synthetic organic chemical was the dye mauveine, which was more or less accidently discovered in 1856 by a young British chemist, William Henry Perkin, through the oxidation of the coal-tar derivative, aniline. Unfortunately, mauveine and its early successors, all derived from aniline, proved to be notoriously fugitive.

Within ten years of the discovery of mauveine, a group of more brilliant magenta-toned dyes, all generally referred to now as fuchsine (fooks-een), rapidly supplanted the paler mauve. The presence of these dyes in late-19th-century rugs is best detected by their absence: old rugs with areas of pale dirty gray or beige on the face often retain a trace of the original magenta on the back.

When a dye fades, this does not mean the coloring substance vanishes into thin air. Rather, a chemical change, triggered by light or moisture or another incompatible substance, transforms the original dye into a new compound, which may be colorless, less highly colored, or differently colored. The principal objection to the early synthetics is that instead of merely softening to a paler hue, as the natural dyes do, the entire tonality of one or two colors shifted enough to destroy the color balance of the rug as a whole.

These unstable dyes were so unsuited to rug making that by 1910 their use was, as mentioned earlier, banned in Persian workshops and in some Turkish districts, although the policing of these bans was spotty and in remote areas virtually impossible. Nevertheless, large numbers of weavers returned to the use of naturally dyed yarns until later in the century when more reliable synthetic dyes became available.

Unfortunately, the bad reputation earned by the early dyes became unjustly attached to later synthetics as well, all of which became popularly and inaccurately known as "coal-tars" or "anilines" whether or not they were derived from coal tars or shared their undesirable characteristics. Not all synthetic dyes used today are reliable, but the color-fastness of the better varieties is good to excellent. Whether or not one likes the *quality* of the color thus obtained is a subjective judgment best left to individuals to make for themselves, but when cost is an issue, a new, well-made, synthetically dyed decorative furnishing carpet can provide many years of trouble-free service.

The chemical makeup of modern synthetic dyes is extremely complex, and an explanation of the system used to assign them into chemical family groups is not only beyond my ability to convey but unnecessary for the purpose at hand. More to the point is a simplified version of the pragmatic classification system used by professional cleaners and textile conservators charged with solving problems arising from the cleaning and restoration of valuable textiles.

The following definitions apply to animal fibers only. Cotton, or cellulose, presents the dyer with problems quite different from wool or silk; and since the use of dyed cotton as a pile fiber is very limited, it will be less confusing if it is eliminated from the discussion altogether.

DIRECT BASIC DYES

The aniline dyes are basic dyes, not in the "fundamental" sense of the word but rather because the color is absorbed directly from a neutral or weakly alkaline (i.e., base) solution, although sometimes a small quantity of acid is added to very hard water to facilitate absorption. As a class, the basic dyes are powerful, clear, and brilliant in hue and easily applied to wool and silk, but they have only fair to poor fastness to light, some fading so rapidly and markedly as to be known as fugitive. A late and relatively stable dye of this type is Rhodamine B, a bright fluorescent pink found in some late-19th-century Turkoman Ersari tribal rugs. The use of anilines was widespread in all of the traditional rug-weaving areas except among the Turkoman tribes of western Turkestan.

DIRECT ACID AND AZO-DYES

The first acid dyes, in which color is absorbed from an acid solution, were developed in 1862, but they did not become commercially available until the 1880s. They too are brilliant and easily applied to animal fibers, and although some acid dyes present the same problems due to lack of fastness as do the basic dyes, they were widely employed in the latter 19th century and in some areas still are.

Among the acid dyes used in the late 19th and early 20th centuries was Ponceau 2R, also known as Russian Red, which is a clear, bright red used extensively by Turkoman and Caucasian dyers. Although relatively fast to light, it sometimes stains the warps and may run when washed. Other acid dyes in common usage as determined by laboratory analysis were Amaranth, Crystal Scarlet, and Rocceline, a very unstable wine red found in late Yomud work. The dyes Orange II and Croceine Orange were used in the Caucasus and Turkey respectively to produce a fast color whose stridency persists long after adjacent areas of pile dyed with fugitive anilines have faded to beige or gray.

The wide variability in fastness is not surprising in light of the fact that there are three main classes of acid dyes, ranging from those freely soluble in water and possessing moderate fastness to the less soluble, more complex azo dyes with a high degree of fastness. To tribal or village weavers, simplicity of preparation and ease of application may be more desirable than long-range stability.

MORDANT AND PREMETALLIZED DYES

As we have seen, mordanting is employed extensively with dyes made from natural materials to facilitate their absorption and promote fastness, and the same principle applies to synthetic dyes. The azo dyes mentioned above displayed superior fastness when applied to mordanted wool, and in the 1940s a class of superior synthetics known as chrome or premetallized dyes was introduced to Eastern rug workshops. These dyes, which incorporate potassium bichromate as a mordant, are available in a wide spectrum of colors that are fast to light, water, and alkali. Chrome-dyed rugs considered too bright for modern Western tastes are often given a chemical wash to subdue their vibrancy.

Although antique rugs known to be dyed entirely with vegetable colors can also be very vividly colored, it is not the brightness of synthetics that connoisseurs consider objectionable but rather the uncompromising, hard-edged quality that results from their controlled, even, and thorough absorption.

DATING RUGS BY THE PRESENCE OF SYNTHETIC DYES

Many dealers and collectors can date rugs quite accurately by color alone, but this method can lead the overconfident novice badly astray. The following generalizations can be used as a rough guide to determining the age of rugs unless a substantial sum of money is riding on the judgment. In that case, the advice of an objective expert is always to be preferred.

To recapitulate, synthetic dyes were introduced into all of the rug-weaving areas around 1875–1880, except for rugs made by nomadic tribes too isolated to receive the dubious benefits of these wonders of organic chemistry. However, since rugs dyed entirely with natural materials were and are still being made, their exclusive use is not a guarantee of antiquity.

Mauve to Magenta

The earliest aniline dyes produced fugitive colors including a mauve, two magentas, blue, green, and purple. The original color may still be visible on the light-protected backs of areas of dirty gray-beige pile. If this pile is relatively unworn, the color may also be detected at the base of the knots. The presence of these dyes dates a rug to roughly 1875–1900. Purple dyes persisting on the face of a rug may be synthetic, but an aniline dye would have long since faded away.

Bright Orange

The acid dyes Orange II and Croceine Orange are characteristic of some late-19th- and early-20th-century Caucasian and Turkish rugs, particularly a well-made but depressing East Caucasian Shirvan type in which they are seen in conjunction with indigo blue, a faded-to-gray fuchsine or later type of listless purple, and a pale blue-green, the green and orange often staining the warps. Be careful, however, not to dismiss all strong orange hues as synthetic: madder, depending on where the plants grow, yields an authoritative orange, too.

Red

Even if one has had the opportunity to examine hundreds of rugs of all types and ages, there is no foolproof way to distinguish between the many natural and synthetic reds by color alone. Strident reds and pinks are apt to be synthetic, as are dark, dull wine reds, but a more reliable clue is bleaching at the tips of the pile fibers and dye runs ranging from blatant bleeding to faint pink blushes and staining of the warps and fringes. Bleeding red dyes have ruined quantities of carefully woven, handsomely patterned late-19th- and early-20th-century Turkoman rugs. Rugs of good quality made since about 1940 are apt to have stable reds, but inexpensive village pieces should be inspected for telltale blushes and stained fringes.

Blues

Natural indigo blues, as well as those prepared from the chemically identical synthetic indigo, are reliably light- and water-fast; but since they are pigmented colorings, they are subject as they age to partial removal through abrasion, particularly in flat-woven textiles. The process is gradual, and the effect is usually too slight to be considered aesthetically objectionable. A blue that bleeds is sure to be synthetic.

Yellows and Greens

Since yellows and greens obtained from most natural sources are subject to fading to one degree or another, uniformly vivid shades of either color should, as a general rule, arouse suspicion. On the other hand, if weld was the source, the older the carpet, the clearer and purer the yellow is apt to be.

CHEMICAL WASHES

The strident quality of synthetic dyes gave rise to the practice of using chemical washes to soften them. The strong reds in Mahals and Sarouks imported from Iran in the 1920s were first bleached to rose and then sometimes painted by hand to a then popular deep maroon. The candy-box pastels of post–World War II Kerman rugs and the golden Afghans of the 1960s were also created by chemical washes, and the majority of modern synthetically dyed carpets are routinely treated in this fashion to a lesser or greater degree depending on the desired effect. Although in some cases the color-mellowing, luster-enhancing result may be considered an improvement, the process tends to rob wool of its natural lubrication and, depending on the chemicals used, decrease its ability to withstand wear.

Always keep in mind that old rugs in mint condition will have clearer, fresher colors than a rug of the same age and type in average condition, and that the variations in hue characteristic of rugs made with natural dyes are, if not too pronounced, considered desirable.

Before deciding to buy a particular rug, you should view it in daylight. Any retail dealer reluctant to oblige you should be regarded with suspicion. Artificial light enhances the natural beauty of pile knotted with high-quality, lustrous wool, but daylight is preferred for judging the quality of the color and the detection of dye runs. It is not always possible to inspect a rug in daylight at auction previews, but if it is, insist on it even if the staff clearly considers you a nuisance.

For More Information

Several of the books and periodicals listed in the Resource Guide will provide you with additional information about dyes and the approximate dates of the introduction of synthetics into specific weaving areas, but nothing you read will be of much help to you in visually distinguishing synthetic from natural dyes. For this, you will need to see many rugs, preferably in the company of knowledgeable dealers or collectors. If an oriental rug society meets at a reasonably convenient distance from your home, you should apply for membership if only to take advantage of the frequently scheduled postlecture show-and-tell sessions.

ORIENTAL RUG SIZES, FORMATS, AND MOTIFS

Oriental rug formats and motifs are as traditional as the weaving techniques used to incorporate them into useful and decorative textiles. Creativity in the Western sense has little place in a culture that regards innovation as a threat to traditional values, and rugs hailed by Western collectors as unique invariably prove to be unusual variations on very old themes.

A successful rug as judged by Western connoisseurs usually excels in three areas:

1. The choice, clarity, and use of color.

2. The proportional relationship between the size of the rug and the elements within it—field, medallions, spandrels, borders—and of the elements to each other.

3. The selection, execution, and spacing of the motifs.

Until the last quarter of the 19th century, the sizes of rugs made as floor coverings were dictated by traditional manners of furnishing; in fact, size alone can indicate to a knowledgeable collector the probable age and intended use of a rug. In addition to rugs, weavers working at simple wooden looms provided the knotted-pile and flat-woven textiles needed in a variety of shapes and sizes for domestic storage, the transport of goods and crops, and decorative trappings suited to a way of life that was either wholly or seasonally nomadic.

In Persian dwellings, four narrow rugs were arranged in a long rectangle, one across the top with the other three placed side by side at right angles to it, the flanking pair typically narrower than the middle rug. This arrangement allowed for considerably more flexibility than the squarer room-size rug made later for the Western market, and these old rugs—cataloged by auction houses as "long" or "corridor" rugs—are often ideally suited to modern open-plan houses. The large triclinium or audience carpets sometimes seen at auction are a late-19th-century development aping the look of the traditional arrangement of four.

Aside from custom, another reason rugs tended to be long and narrow is that although the length of a carpet woven on a roller-beam workshop loom is limited only by the capacity of the beam, its width is fixed by the width of the loom, which in turn is dictated by the space, rarely ample, available

Traditional arrangement of carpets.

for it. The lengths of the great carpets in museum collections are generally two or three times their widths, and most antique rugs and kilims of Middle Eastern manufacture are similarly proportioned.

The sizes of smaller rugs made by village and tribal weavers were—and still are—determined by domestic as well as market considerations but are usually found to have proportions of 2 to 3—that is, roughly 1½ feet in length for every foot in width.

My choice of the adverb "roughly," by the way, was deliberate. A case in point is the *dozar*, the term long applied in the trade to rugs approximately 4½ × 7 feet—which, incidentally, is about the widest rug a woman weaving alone can comfortably manage. Although the *zar* is a traditional Persian unit of measure—a *dozar* is two *zars*—different villages had *zars* of different lengths, ranging between 41 and 44 inches. This degree of variance may seem odd by Western standards, but measurement in the weaving countries, according to Leslie Stroh, editor of *Rug News*, is like situational ethics:

> If you know that he knows that you know, then you *both* know, and the definition (of size) depends not on some abstract measure, but on the reality that both buyer and seller are confronting. There are small dozars and big dozars; there are dozars that actually measure correctly and dozars that do not . . . [yet all] come into the marketplace with both parties thinking of them as dozars.

Although equating long and narrow rugs with age is usually safe, the reverse is not necessarily true. The shape of some antique Chinese and Turkish rugs and Southwest Persian Afshar tribal rugs approach the square, but it wasn't until the turn of the century, in response to a booming revival of Western interest in oriental rugs, that weavers throughout the rug-producing areas began making the squarer sizes that in terms of rug dimensions persist to this day.

Although it makes much more artistic sense to place a rug in a room so that the design and color, uncluttered by furniture, may be fully appreciated, the Western tendency has always been to blanket the floor with a rug upon which furniture is then plunked. For this reason, although in this country all sizes of hand-knotted floor coverings are customarily referred to as "rugs," the term "carpet" will be employed here for the large room-size rugs popular in Western homes.

This use of oriental rugs as a sort of patterned carpeting required a reworking of traditional designs, not all of which could be happily adapted to the new proportions; attempts to scale down for scatter rugs the dignified, spacious designs popular in room-size carpets were even less successful. In an effort to surmount these problems, artists commissioned by Western entrepreneurs began experimenting with combining traditional motifs in new ways; and once the barrier of tradition was breached, entirely new patterns soon followed. The most successful of these command good prices today: those commissioned by the Ziegler manufactories in Arak, Iran, the old Sultanabad of Persia, are an example of adapted designs; Sarouks featuring detached floral sprays represent new ones.

A bewildering variety of names can be found attached in the oriental rug literature to every size and shape of woven article. No standard terminology exists: each weaving area has its own name for articles whose purpose remains the same no matter where it is made, and further confusion results when these native terms are translated into the languages of Westerners writing about them. In addition, collectors have decided preferences, verging on snobberies, about the terminology used within their specialties.

Once a collector has chosen an area of concentration, a vocabulary of terms appropriate to it can soon be acquired via the literature and rug society lectures and in conversation with specialist dealers and other collectors. Here, in the interest of clarity, I plan to rely with as few exceptions as possible on descriptive and use-specific terms, beginning with rugs woven as floor furnishings. The fact that today's collectors may consider the best and oldest of them too rare or fine for such a plebian function is, for this purpose, irrelevant.

RUG SIZES

The units in which the measurements of a rug are expressed depend, if it is new, upon where the rug was made, or, in the case of old rugs, where the description is encountered. Foreign dealers and publications employ the metric system; American dealers and auction house catalogs supply dimensions in feet and inches, except for Sotheby's and Christie's in which both are given. For simplicity's sake, the sizes of the arbitrary groupings of rugs that follow are given in feet only; but readers should bear in mind that in the case of old rugs variations from exact dimensions are much more the rule than the exception.

MAT

Mats are small rugs, roughly 2 × 3 feet, used as bedside, doorway, and fireside rugs and room accents. Many mats used for these purposes were originally the topsides of covers for long, narrow pillows used on low couches or to support the back when sitting on a floor rug. In some cases the flat-woven backs are still attached. If the borders are unequal in width and if there are plain-woven tabs along one edge and a skirt along the other, the mat was probably the face of a bag used either for the transport or storage of goods.

SCATTER

Larger than a mat and smaller than an area rug, scatter rugs range from 2 × 4 to about 4 × 6 in varying proportions. Most of the old rugs in this category were produced by women weaving alone or with a family member or friend on home looms, and the naive, exuberant charm of the best of them is prized by collectors.

AREA (DOZAR)

Approximately $4^1/_2$ × 7 feet, rugs in this category can make a design statement far surpassing their modest, easily stored size. Included in this group are the enormously popular thick-pelted, boldly colored, geometrically patterned South Caucasian Kazaks as well as low-piled, elegantly detailed, jewel-toned Sarouk Ferahans.

LONG OR CORRIDOR RUG

These are rugs originally made for the traditional layout of four. They range in size from (a) 5–6 feet wide by 10–12 feet long, (b) 6–8 feet by 16–20 feet, and (c) 3–4 feet by 16–20 feet.

RUNNER

Although the narrowest of the long rugs are often used as runners, they are less likely than rugs designed for that specific use to have designs repeated in columnar fashion. Whichever type you choose, rugs used on stairs should be sturdily constructed and in good condition. A glossy, long-piled, loosely woven rug is unlikely to prove satisfactory for that purpose.

ROOM-SIZE

Rugs intended to cover most of the floor area of a given room range in size from a Western-size 8 × 10 or more traditionally proportioned 9 × 11 up to 24 × 14 feet; those exceeding that size are often referred to as palace carpets.

The large majority of older room-size carpets are of Persian manufacture; today they are as likely to be Indian, Pakistani, Romanian, or Chinese.

PRAYER

Prayer rugs always have an arch-shaped element at one end—rarely, both ends—representing the *mihrab* set in the wall of the mosque facing the holy city of Mecca and symbolizing the gateway to paradise. Prayer rugs have for centuries been a popular item of commerce and have been made mostly in scatter sizes in a variety of designs and materials, including extremely finely knotted silks intended as luxurious wall hangings.

Only a minority of the vast number of rugs made with the prayer format have been employed by the faithful for that purpose. Enjoined to use what is defined simply as a clean spot facing Mecca, a length of easily carried sacking or toweling serves the needs of many devout Muslims for the prayers they observe five times daily. Prayer rugs are, however, customarily used as such in mosques, which have been given them over the centuries as tokens of reverence and thanksgiving.

RUG FORMATS

PILE RUG FORMATS

Although the motifs used in oriental rugs can, when their variations are included, number in the hundreds, the ways in which these elements are organized can be reduced to six basic formats. A seventh, notable for its *lack* of organization, ends the listing.

Medallion

The classic court and urban workshop rug design features a single medallion or medallions centered in a bordered field. This format, which according to most authorities was derived from early embossed book bindings, was finely knotted in graceful curvilinear forms. The field may either be open—that is, without additional decoration—or swirled with readily recognizable vines, leaves, flowers, and trees. In the simpler, more coarsely knotted country-cousin versions produced on village looms, the graceful flower shapes assume simpler, more geometric forms; in tribal weavings they often verge on the abstract.

This is perhaps the appropriate place to address the problem presented by dated rugs. Workshop rugs with a curvilinear medallion format frequently have Arabic numerals dating their completion woven into an oblong border cartouche, but rustic rugs too are sometimes dated, with the numbers typically

Medallion format.

SPANDREL

PENDANT

MEDALLION

GUARD BORDER

MINOR BORDER

MAIN BORDER

WARP FRINGE

Sixteenth-century embossed bookbinding.

The dating of old oriental rugs accords for the most part with the Islamic system, which begins with the Hegira, Mohammed's flight from Mecca to Medina in July of A.D. 622. Although the Moslem lunar year is eleven days shorter than our solar-based year, a reasonably accurate conversion can be achieved by adding 583 to the translated Islamic date, as shown above.

Arabic numerals with formula for dating inscribed rugs.
SKETCH AFTER FRANSES.

knotted into the field near the top of the rug as the weaving neared completion. Since age is valued in rugs, if the shape of the figures eludes easy identification, the reading of them will usually favor as early a dating as possible, and forging a date at the time of weaving or a later reknotting is by no means unheard of. A further complication is presented by illiterate weavers imperfectly copying dates they saw only as a filler motif.

As for undated rugs, to paraphrase Steven Price writing in *Oriental Rug Review*, the attribution of a date to a piece that lacks a complete provenance should be the result of careful consideration of the possibilities regarding the period and place most likely to be the one when and where it was made. He goes on to say, "As collectors, we don't like to do this, because . . . we dislike uncertainty in the attribution of our treasures . . . (but) this is the best we can do most of the time. To pretend otherwise is to deceive those who believe us or, even worse, deceive ourselves."

Allover Designs

Removing the central focal point from a medallion format with a decorated field allows what had been a background design to expand into either a latticed or an unregimented pattern, which often appears to extend beneath and beyond the borders that arbitrarily contain it.

Compartment Rugs

In these, the field is divided into evenly proportioned boxed design units containing repeated motifs usually arranged in parallel, checkerboardlike, rows. The static quality of this format is often pleasingly relieved by variations in the size and color of the individual design units and their placement in relation to the others.

Repeat Designs

Turkoman rugs, the red-grounded "Bokharas" long a popular staple of the trade, are prime examples of rugs whose fields are patterned with motifs symmetrically repeated row upon row with little or no variation aside from alternations in color. The geometric figures, or *guls*, peculiar to each Turkoman tribe are more generously spaced in antique rugs than in later versions; and as a rule the later any type of rug with a repeating motif was made, the more cramped the motifs are apt to be.

Striking effects are achieved by strong contrasts in the colors of motifs in succeeding diagonal rows or in stepped patterning extending over the entire field.

Repeat motifs may either be contained within the borders or cut by them, in which case they may be considered to extend beneath and beyond the bounds imposed upon them.

Pictorial

Rugs depicting famous persons and scenes from history and legend have never been made in great numbers, and although often interesting or charming, they are rarely artistically successful. A notable exception is the exquisite 16th-century slit-tapestry silk Kashan piece depicting the Persian legend of Leila and Mejnoon, sold by Christie's in 1990 for the stunning price of $480,000. At least as stunning, in quite a different sense, is the mind-boggling "Maggie and Jiggs" silk Kashan rug, circa 1925, brought to my attention by an article in *Oriental Rug Review* and reproduced here with no further comment.

Prayer

The field below the arch, in which the faithful kneel, is sometimes open, sometimes flanked with pillars, and sometimes decorated with objects associated with religious observance and symbols: incense burners, water

"Maggie and Jiggs" silk Kashan carpet, sold in 1989 for $22,000.
PHOTO COURTESY OF CHRISTIE'S

CROSS PANEL

SPANDREL

MIHRAB

HANGING LAMP

COLUMNS

Prayer rug format.

A variety of prayer rug styles: (a) Persian, 16th century; (b) Daghestan, Caucasus; (c) Baluch, Persia; Afghanistan; (d) Ersari Beshir, West Turkestan; (e) Turkish, stepped form.

jugs, lanterns representing the light of God, and the tree-of-life design beloved by Baluch weavers. The coupled-column Ottoman court manufactory prayer rug given to the Metropolitan Museum of Art in New York by James Ballard is considered particularly fine.

There is a type of prayer rug with multiple niches set side by side in single or parallel rows, which was probably developed for use in mosques: in Turkey, I have seen modern versions stretching the entire width of the interior. Known as *saphs*, they are sometimes referred to in the trade as family prayer rugs, but most authorities doubt they were ever used in a domestic setting.

A prayer rug with a series of stepped arches is peculiar to Turkey and is seen in both pile and flat-woven formats.

Sampler

Designs can pass from one weaving group to another in several ways: by direct observation, through graphed representations, and via sampler rugs, or *wagireh*, in which popular border and field motifs are randomly knotted. Sampler rugs are associated mainly with the Bidjar weaving area, and the best examples are vied for by collectors.

FLATWEAVE FORMATS

Kilims

Turkish kilims are characteristically either very long, in which case they were woven in two strips sewn together, or woven in a prayer format in scatter and area rug sizes.

Persian kilims are usually woven in one piece; the majority are reversible, and medium sizes are more common than the very long pieces associated with Turkey. Runners were made, too, but old examples are a rarity. The exquisite 19th-century kilims associated with the Kurdish weavers of Senneh are in a class by themselves: their intricate, delicate floral designs and relatively small size—many are woven in a prayer format—make them more suitable candidates for wall hangings than floor furnishings.

Old kilims made by Turkoman weavers are not often seen in the marketplace except for a narrow, shortish, tightly woven interlocked type associated with the Yomut tribe; it has red, white, and dark blue geometric motifs arrayed in rather compressed bands.

The more frequently available medium-sized, reversible kilims attributed to Caucasian weavers are remarkable for the clarity of their vivid, saturated colors.

Indian tapestry-woven rugs are known as *dhurries*. Because they are made of cotton, the name has become associated with inexpensive floor coverings of low durability, but quality pieces, some containing silk, have been woven for centuries. They are woven in one piece, and old *dhurries* of interest to collectors are generally of scatter to area size. An interesting group made in Indian prisons in the early 20th century features realistic fish, birds, and crocodiles crowded feathered cheek by scaled jowl in naturalistic settings. Clearly intended as hangings, these pieces have a horizontal format and run about 3 × 4 feet.

Soumak

Soumaks, wherever they originate, are usually of medium size and woven in one piece. Caucasian soumaks are the most frequently seen in the marketplace, and the designs, unlike those used for kilims, are clearly derived from much older knotted-pile rugs. Collectors particularly favor the designs influenced by early rugs with dragon motifs.

MIXED TECHNIQUES

Plain or balanced-weave textiles, in which the weft and warp have equal representation, are as likely as not to be combined with a variety of other techniques into distinctive structures whose names vary according to where they were woven. These include the elegant and somber mixed-technique covers (some one-piece, others made in two pieces later joined) character-istic of some Persian Baluch tribes: a group of large Turkoman rugs with plain-woven red grounds closely covered with a rectilinear repeat in weft-float brocading and a smaller type with stripes in variegated subdued colors alternating with wider bands of a stepped chevron design. Baluch and Turkoman flat-woven rugs usually have long skirts similar to those on their pile rugs.

One-piece mixed-technique rugs in small and medium sizes were woven throughout Turkey and Persia with every variety and combination of flat-weave technique represented; two-piece examples made by some tribal weavers approach the square. In Anatolia, prayer rugs were as frequently flat-woven as knotted in pile.

FORMATS FOR WEAVINGS OTHER THAN RUGS

Tent and Yurt Trappings

In the Middle East, tents used by nomadic and seminomadic tribes are large affairs, generally woven from dark brown or black goat hair and referred to in the literature, appropriately enough, as black tents. Yurts are similarly portable structures in which light-colored felt coverings are

A yurt, a portable domestic structure covered with felts secured by a long, wide flat-woven band. The decorative weaving above the entrance is a kapunuk.

Tent door rug (engsi).   *Door surround.*

wrapped around a round, domed framework and secured by very long flat-woven bands, which are sometimes lavishly decorated with motifs in knotted pile. Yurts and yurtlike dwellings are associated with Turkoman and Shah-savan tribes in northern Iran and tribal peoples throughout Central Asia.

Door Rugs. Because several versions of these interesting Turkoman weavings contain archlike elements, these pile tent entrance hangings used to be mistaken for prayer rugs. The unique layout is similar from tribe to tribe, but what it is intended to represent remains uncertain.

Tent Door Surround. A three-sided, usually tasseled Turkoman weaving whose form exactly follows its function, these are rarely seen in the market. Antique examples in reasonably good condition command high prices.

Meal Cloth. This is a long, narrow flatweave with decorative borders, surrounding a field that is sometimes figured but more often left plain and undyed as a symbol of humility and reverence. To sit or walk on these cloths is frowned upon, as they are intended exclusively for the service of food.

Oven Cloth. In this instance, "oven" refers to a basin containing glowing coals placed under a low, square table covered by an old blanket or quilt on top of which is placed a richly decorated smaller square that may be either entirely flat-woven or ornamented in pile. The family warms itself by sitting around the table and under the heated blanket.

Storage Bags

Whatever the overall size of bags made to store bedding and other household articles, they are customarily longer than they are deep. When fastened along the top edge, they can either be hung from woven-in loops from the tent framework or set side by side lengthwise along the wall or on

Tent framework-hung storage bags are made in a variety of sizes. These are the most common: (a) 1' × 2'; (b) 1½' × 3'; (c) 3' × 4½'.

(a) Chest-type storage bag; (b) salt bag; (c) spoon bag.

low benches, where they serve as pillows. Either entirely flat-woven or with pile fronts and flat-woven backs, these bags frequently exemplify tribal weaving at its best. The faces are usually all that make their way into the market; an entire bag commands a premium.

Four-sided chest-type storage bags are found in all Iranian tribes except the Turkoman and Baluch; they are woven by girls of marriageable age to contain their dowries. Intact bags are rarely available; collectors are usually happy to settle for one beautifully woven side.

Salt Bag. This bag, used to store salt and other loose granular foodstuffs, has a wide body out of which rises a narrow chimneylike extension that serves as a spout and, flapped over, protects the contents from moisture and contamination. Its dimensions vary but are usually between 1 and 2 feet square.

Grain Bag. These bags, similar in shape and size to our flour sacks, are for the storage of grains for both family and domestic animals. Braided wool or goat hair loops at short intervals along the top allow the contents to be secured against rodents.

Spoon Bag. Narrow flat-woven or pile-faced small bags are used for storing spoons and spindles. Loops extending from each top corner allow the bag to be attached to the tent frame.

Bags for Personal Belongings

A variety of small, single-pouched bags are woven to hold combs, money, tobacco, and the like, which can be defined, depending on the size, as vanity bags, satchels, and knapsacks. All bags of this type were made

Single-pouched bag with carrying strap.   *Double-pouched joined bags.*

with a strap or handle, but accessories of this sort, including tassels and beads and decorative fringes, are often worn away over the years.

A bag format encountered with minor variations throughout the rug-producing area is a double-pouched type joined together by a flat-woven strip whose width indicates its use: if made to be carried over a man's shoulder or forearm the strip will be narrower than that on bags intended to be slung across the back of his donkey or horse.

Whatever the purpose, these bags, whether small or large, exhibit a greater variety in both design and weave than any other single class of Middle Eastern weaving. Collectors prize them for their artistry, and their small size allows them to be stored and maintained much more easily than a comparable number of rugs.

Animal Trappings

The bags described above have a practical function, but many of the trappings woven for horses and camels are intended as adornment pure and simple, especially those used at weddings, where they serve much the same purpose—albeit in a grander form—as the crepe paper ribbons seen streaming from American cars honking their way from church ceremony to restaurant reception.

(a) Saddle cover; (b) horse cover; (c) one of a pair of camel-flank trappings used in wedding processions; (d) breast decoration for bride's camel; (e) knee cover for horse or camel.

Saddle Covers. The shape and finish of saddle covers varies widely, depending upon the style of saddle used.

Horse Covers. Horse covers are usually flat-woven, no doubt because a pile textile of sufficient size would be insufficiently flexible. Although the overall size may vary, the shape is generally the same from place to place. A Caucasian type with rows of stylized animals, either brocaded or soumak and usually fringed, are known as *vernehs*.

Camel Trappings. The most sought after are the five-sided bags—rarely, heptagonal—for decorating the right and left flanks of a Turkoman bride's camel.

Aside from the above, there is a wide variety of splendidly belled, tasseled, and shell-decorated trappings for the heads, chests, rumps, and even knees of both camels and horses. Proud indeed must be the rider whose mount is thus caparisoned. Although less commonly seen, the collecting of these artifacts is a pursuit ideally suited to those attracted by weavings both made and used in a tribal setting.

RUG MOTIFS

Scholars and collectors have pondered long and hard about the origins of rug motifs, and over the years various schools of thought have grown up on the subject. The conventional view, enormously simplified, is that oriental rug design originated from two distinct traditions:

1. The elegant, curvilinear floral forms developed by 15th-century Persian court artists, supplemented in the 16th century with designs derived from Chinese porcelains admired by contemporary Islamic collectors, and rendered, finely knotted, by skilled weavers in the palace workshops.

2. The rectilinear, generously scaled latticelike and compartmented Turkish designs, similar to the carvings on early stone buildings, eminently suited to the limitations set by the rather large, square knots typical of Turkish weaving.

The nomadic weaver's idea of design is represented by the geometric infinite repeat, and among simple weavers the tendency to revert to this concept is very strong, even in the case of floral motifs borrowed from more sophisticated carpets.

Skeptics claim that these neat, well-documented theories fail to satisfactorily account for, among other anomalies, the patterning peculiar to the 15th–16th-century carpets produced in Egypt during the second Mamluk dynasty, not to mention the very early, astonishingly sophisticated Pazyrk carpet, which has a border of realistically drawn animals around a field of repeat geometric figures.

Further, although traditionalists claim Turkoman *guls* and the geometric devices on tribal rugs are, for the most part, highly abstracted versions of Persian floral motifs or ancient Chinese symbols, others convincingly interpret them as tribal totems. Out on the far edge of rug studies are the mystically inclined, who are currently engaged in a highly charged debate concerning their efforts to document the identification of tribal rug motifs with prehistoric cult mythology.

Any examination of rug motifs must also give consideration to how the various weaving processes—knotted pile, soumak, slit tapestry, etc.—affect design. In the words of scholar/weaver Marla Mallett, "Design change and disintegration is accelerated as motifs migrate from medium to medium, since different technical constraints apply."

Collectors wishing to pursue the theoretical roots of rug design should consult the Bibliography at the back of this book. Presented here, prosaically and in visually confirmable terms, are the design progressions and variations of the motifs most commonly seen.

CURVILINEAR MOTIFS

Boteh

This pear-shaped or curled-leaf design with the bent-over top is encountered in all types of Persian and Caucasian rugs in an enormous variety of shapes and sizes, but rarely in Turkey, where it has never been part of the design vocabulary.

Boteh is a Persian word meaning "cluster of leaves"; a similar word, *buta*, is the name of a wild plant once used as kindling, and in Azerbaijan the motif

Ten variations of the Boteh motif.

is believed to symbolize the tongues of flame rising from its burning branches. Whatever the root—or roots—of this extremely popular motif may be, *boteh* is the name by which the figure is always referred, including in India, where it appears in the graceful form later popularized in the West by Paisley shawls.

The *boteh* is often used as a filler, or occasional, motif in the field designs of village and tribal weavings, but it is primarily a field motif. Sometimes it appears on the ground of a medallion rug, in which case it is small and its representation modest, as befits an allover secondary element, and sometimes in bold horizontal or diagonal rows in which the bent top may either face always in the same direction or alternate row to row. An interesting variation is found on old Persian Qashqai tribal rugs, among others, in which a flowering plant knotted in a *boteh*-like shape lends a blurred delicacy to a motif that in cruder, geometric forms can be strongly emphatic. In sum, I think it safe to say that no other motif has spawned weaving variations of more collectible interest.

Herati

The name applied to a pattern unit composed of a diamond-shaped floral center flanked by four curved leaves is derived from the city of Herat, which during the flowering of Persian carpet design was the most important urban center in what was then eastern Persia. During the 16th century its workshops produced wonderful carpets, many of which incorporated the leaf-and-flower unit now known as Herati. Stylistic links to the design can

(a) Herati motif; (b) Mina Khani; (c) Harshang motif; (d) Afshan motif.

be found on 16th-century Cairene tiles, Ottoman carpets made in Cairo, Persian Kerman vase carpets, and early stone inlays in India.

The Herati pattern is used either as an allover design or as a medallion rug background and, rarely, as a central figure on a bag face. It is seen at its best when the leaves and flowers are given room in which to flourish; when densely packed and finely knotted in subdued colors, it has about as much verve as a linoleum pattern. It is famously associated with Persian Ferahan rugs; tribal versions are apt to be distorted by compression.

Mina Khani

This name is applied to a lozenge-shaped arrangement of a central open rosette connected by a graceful lattice with four smaller and simpler flanking florettes. A favorite of Persian Kurdish weavers, it often appears in symmetrically repeated field designs on Veramin and Hamadan rugs. A version in which the flanking flowers are knotted in white and the central rosette supplied with a border of serrated leaves is seen on a type of Caucasian Shirvan known in the trade as blossom rugs. An even more striking effect is achieved on some Baluch rugs by floating the flanking white flowers—sometimes stylized, sometimes quite realistic—on a field of dark indigo blue or intense madder red, on which the lozengelike rigidity of the pattern may be loosened and the lattice vines asymmetrically placed.

The Mina Khani is sometimes seen on bag faces, and a pretty variation featuring a spray of three white florettes is used as a border design.

Harshang or Crab Motif

This irregularly bordered flamelike design, seen on Caucasian and Persian rugs and occasionally in rectilinear form on Turkish rugs, derives from a blossom with leaflike projections, which was a staple on the earliest rugs in both Turkey and Persia. Some think the blocklike geometric pattern associated with Caucasian Star Kazaks is, in fact, an abstraction of the Harshang motif. The label "crab" was applied by weavers and dealers unfamiliar with the motif's historical progression.

Gol-Farang or Foreign Flower

This late-19th-century motif incorporating clusters of roses in full bloom was produced in direct commercial response to the French-influenced fashions popular in Czarist Russia. Realistic versions appear on Persian Senneh, Bijar, Baktiari, and Kerman rugs, in which the clusters may either be arrayed in rows as a field decoration or used as the central figure in a compartment design. An Afshar rug I once owned had a field repeat of lush, geometricized roses surrounded by a traditional tribal border.

These interesting rugs, somewhat of an acquired taste, are striking in Victorian settings.

Afshan

A floral motif directly adapted from an open, tuliplike flower presented on a bent stem was used as a flanking element for more important design units on 18th-century Caucasian rugs. An interesting version is seen on 19th-century Caucasian rugs, most notably Perepedils from the Kuba area, in which the flowers are simplified, the stem bent at right angles, and the whole conveying a strangely Chinese look.

Bid Majnun or Weeping Willow

This field design, which features willows, cypress, and poplars as well as vines and flowers, is one of the most appealing of the village weaver's repertoire. Although influenced by symmetrically formatted classic garden carpets, the Bid Majnun is at its best when informally arranged.

This motif is most frequently seen on Bidjar and other Kurdish rugs but is employed throughout the rug-weaving areas. An attractive Indian interpretation sold in 1990 at a Sotheby's auction in New York.

Tree-of-Life

The tree-of-life is a very old and universal motif symbolizing man's yearning reach from base, earthly life to the purity of paradise. In village

Three variations of the tree-of-life motif.

Zil-i-Sultan motif.

and tribal versions the tree is usually reduced to a single vertical trunk stemmed with stylized, three-lobed leaves. A distinctive version found on many Baluch prayer rugs is more rectilinear than curvilinear; on workshop rugs, the artistry expressed in finely knotted and prettily arrayed blossoming naturalistic trees tends to overwhelm the symbolic significance.

Zil-i-Sultan

A classical Persian flower-and-vase repeat rendered either realistically or highly stylized as a field repeat design. Occasionally, the motif is much enlarged to serve as a rug's focal point.

Gerus (Garus, Garrus, etc.)

An elegant allover pattern of interlaced and somewhat angularized vine-and-flower arabesques seen usually on a dark indigo field on large to palace-size carpets. It is associated with Kurdish weaving towns and considered to have been derived from an early group of Kurdish rugs, an example of which, dated 1794, is in the Metropolitan Museum of Art.

Shah Abbas Designs

These represent a variety of motifs derived from the classical Persian carpets designed during the Safavid dynasty in the 16th and 17th centuries. According to A. Cecil Edwards, author of *The Persian Carpet*, these palmettes, rosettes, cloud bands, and vases "appear in the field of the carpet, isolated from each other, evenly spaced and invariably interconnected into a pattern by some sort of stalk or trellis."

OTHER FLOWER MOTIFS

In addition to being incorporated into stylized design units, flowers are also used as recognizable single-blossom motifs. The most realistic are found on classical Indian Mughal carpets, often as growing plants, and include the rose, poppy, tulip, carnation, peony, lotus, chrysanthemum, lily, geranium, and hollyhock. In a later group of Indian prayer rugs known as *millefleurs*, a veritable explosion of mixed blossoms fills the field of the *mihrab*. The tulip and carnation are popular motifs in Turkey, and the peony, chrysanthemum, and lotus are most strongly associated with East Turkestan, Tibetan, and Chinese rugs.

Another widely used botanical motif is the many-seeded pomegranate, a symbol for fertility appearing most frequently on East Turkestan and Far Eastern rugs.

CLOUD BANDS

The cloud-band motif, which appears in both border and field designs, entered the West via Chinese artisans brought to Samarkand in the early 15th century by its Mongol conquerors. From there, it spread to adjacent areas and was soon taken up by Persian artists, whose versions include one that has an arguably *mihrab*-like shape.

Cloud bands are found in Persian, Turkish, Caucasian, Beshir Turkoman, and, of course, Central and Far Eastern Asian weavings.

HUMAN AND ANIMAL FIGURES

Strictly interpreted, the sayings attributed to Mohammed, the Prophet of Islam, in the *hadith* forbid the representation of human figures; in practice, some Muslim societies observe this stricture, and others disregard it. As a general rule, figural motifs are much less common on Turkish and Afghan rugs than on those from other rug-weaving areas. An interesting exception is a small contemporary rug I own of village origin that features a portrait of Turkey's revered father figure, Kemal Ataturk, rendered in the dashed-off style of a pen and ink sketch.

Figures in the realistic round are uncommon everywhere except on pictorial rugs. More usual are cartoonlike or stick figures, and their cheerful appearance helter-skelter in a village rug's field, along with the domestic animals who share their lives, can be counted upon to evoke a smile on a rug collector's face and a covetous wish in his or her heart.

Realistic animals appeared on early classical Persian and Indian carpets and still do on city workshop rugs; on collectible village rugs they are reduced largely to blocky stylizations, stick figures, or abstractions. In fact, except for flowers and trees, which are readily incorporated into a design structure, realistic representations are poor choices for knotted-pile and flat-woven rugs. Textiles are associated with pattern, not pictures; therefore, the more stylized and the more subordinate to the pattern a pictorial motif can be, the better.

Wild animals commonly appearing on oriental pile weavings include lions, an ancient symbol of courage and strength appearing in various

Shah Abbas palmettes.
SKETCH AFTER TAHIR
ZADEH BIHZAD,
THE PERSIAN CARPET,
A. CECIL EDWARDS.

a   *b*

Cloud bands. (a) Classical version used as a field motif; (b) compressed version seen in borders.

Human and animal figures are often seen on village and tribal rugs.

Birds appear in a variety of highly stylized forms, hinting of mythic significance.

guises on rugs of all Persian tribal groups, and tigers—or rather the skins of tigers—on some very early Turkish rugs and on the later Tibetan rugs with which they are currently most associated. The game animal most frequently represented is the antelope, which on the classical Persian and Indian rugs known as "hunting rugs" was portrayed in mortal struggle with a predator.

Camels and horses are popular motifs in all weaving areas, as are birds, which frequently appear in highly stylized forms hinting of mythic significance. The double-headed horned creatures in Turkoman guls are interpreted by some scholars as crested birds. Birds in a more recognizable form, but still far from realistic, are seen on Turkoman camel trappings, Baluch rugs and bags, and Persian and Turkish village rugs, among others. The large, realistic parrots seen on some late-19th-century workshop rugs would seem to lack any significance, including artistic.

A wholly mythic creature is the dragon, whose flamboyant picturization on early Caucasian carpets caused its name to be associated with those rugs as well as with a wide group of pile and flat-woven rugs made since that are considered to have dragon-inspired figures. It is a motif thought to have descended variously from the Chinese winged dragon symbols introduced to Central Asia along trade routes and ancient local myths in which heaven and earth were represented by a bird and serpent.

The Chinese had a design vocabulary all their own, which, although it influenced Western design, was not until much later itself affected by Western notions. The Chinese motifs representing philosophic abstractions and intellectual accomplishments have no counterparts in other rug-producing cultures; the use of animals as symbols for desirable qualities like strength and purity is, however, universal. Included in the Chinese repertoire, in addition to dragons, were the *feng huan*, a roosterlike bird that in combination with a dragon symbolizes peace and prosperity. (In the West, interestingly, the same combination, known as the dragon and phoenix motif, represents conflict.) Bats are symbols for happiness and good luck; cranes, for longevity; deer, for well-being; paired fish, for abundance, prosperity, or fertility. The fierce-looking temple guardians known as fo-dogs and the kylin, a wondrous staglike animal with flaming tail and shoulders and a dragon's head adorned with a single horn, are symbolic of a long and noble life.

GEOMETRIC MOTIFS

If a rug is coarsely Turkish-knotted and produced by a village or tribal weaver from designs absorbed in childhood, the design is much more likely to be geometric than one woven from supplied cartoons in an urban workshop.

As stated earlier, there also seems to be a further, culturally determined division: curvilinear designs are in general associated with Persian-influenced weaving, geometrics with the Turkic tradition. Whether this does, in fact, constitute a fundamental difference is as yet imperfectly understood by scholarly investigators trying to weave coherent theories from a tangle of conflicting ethnic, anthropologic, religious, and aesthetic considerations. All one can say for sure, according to art historian E. H. Gombrich, is that "nothing comes from nothing."

Many of the geometric designs seen on 19th-century rugs can be traced back to floral origins, as exemplified by border motifs, the majority of which were clearly derived from flower, vine, and leaf prototypes. On Turkish rugs, we often see quite realistic tulips and carnations, beloved by Ottoman textile and tile designers, used as both border and field motifs. In short, when it comes to oriental rug design, there are no absolutes.

Examples of early and extremely influential Turkish geometric rug designs are the small and large Holbeins, including their many variations, and a hooked figure used universally but referred to in its Turkish guise as the Memling gul (see Gul, following). Such designs have since been tagged with the names of the 15th-century artists who used the rugs bearing these bold patterns as colorful accents in their paintings.

Geometrically patterned rugs invariably conform to one of the six formats described earlier in this chapter, although ready assignment can sometimes be hindered by an ineptly woven version of a symmetrical design or motifs inserted chock-a-block to fill otherwise empty spaces.

Other motifs associated with the Turkish design tradition and employed elsewhere by weavers with Turkic roots include the following:

(a) Caucasian version of
the dragon motif;
(b) dragon and phoenix
motif on early Turkish rug;
(c) highly stylized version
of the dragon and phoenix
conflict used as a
border motif.

(a) Ottoman carnation-decorated Iznik tankard, mid-16th century;
(b) carnation cluster border motif; (c) carnation and tulip border
repeat; (d) carnation flower-based border motif.

(a) Three medallion
large-patterned
Holbein format,
Turkey, 15th–16th
centuries;
(b) two-one-two
medallion Holbein
format, Turkey,
15th–16th centuries.

(a) Classic 18th-century Turkish Ladik prayer rug with columns and band of tulips;
(b) contemporary Turkish rug with stylized version of Ladik format.

(a) Yun-chien cloud collar, a possible source of the Turkish elibelinde motif; (b) ancient Chinese bronze mirror with yun-chien cloud collar motif; (c) the elibelinde "hands-on-hips" motif; (d) another elibelinde figure seen on Turkish kilims; (e) geometricized yun-chien/elibelinde figure; (f) geometricized yun-chien used as a field repeat motif.

Ram's horn motifs.

Elibelinde

Said to be a symbol of fertility, the motif known as *elibelinde*, which means woman-with-hands-on-hips, is a very old one with many variations.

Ram's Horn

A male fertility symbol, also with many variations, is used as both a field motif—usually as part of a larger design unit—and a border element.

Star

Stars, indicating a wish for happiness, are used both boxed and unboxed, either as a repeat or in combination with other motifs.

Memling Gul

Gul (see below) is a term normally applied to the large tribal emblems on Turkoman rugs; the Memling Gul is a hooked, stepped, Turkoman gul-like

Soumak bag face with Memling gul used as central ornament. PHOTO COURTESY OF CHRISTIE'S EAST

*(a–d) Amulet motifs; (e) stylized prayer rug
lamp; (f) Turkoman necklace pendant.*

figure seen on village and tribal rugs throughout the Middle Eastern rug-
producing region. The name it is known by in the West is that of the 15th-
century Flemish painter, Hans Memling, whose compositions frequently
incorporated rugs with this design.

Amulets

The term *amulet* seems to have become the fail-safe label to apply to
geometric figures whose roots and significance as woven motifs have
become hopelessly confused in a snarl of conflicting interpretations. One
minor example is an hourglass-shaped figure with toothed, comblike ends—
sometimes a major element in a field design, sometimes a filler motif—
known variously as a bridal comb, a stylization of a mosque lantern, a piece
of jewelry (a type of which it does indeed resemble), and an hourglass
meant to remind the faithful of the ephemeral nature of earthly life.

In sum, motifs referred to in the literature as amulets may in fact serve a
specific magical purpose (i.e., warding off the evil eye) or may simply be
figures whose origins and significance, if any, are uncertain.

Gul

Gul is a Persian word for flower applied to the motifs, primarily
octagons of varying proportions, that ornament in a repeat pattern the
woven products of the rugs and trappings made by fierce nomadic
Turkoman tribes who wandered westward from their homeland in remote
Asian steppes about 2,000 years ago. Descendants of those tribes—the
Tekke, Yomud, Salor, Ersari, etc.—today inhabit sections of northeastern
Iran, Turkmenistan in the USSR, northern Afghanistan and, as a result of
the late hostilities there, refugee camps in Pakistan, where they continue to
weave traditional rugs.

Scholars trace the generally lobed shape of the primary guls to a Chinese
design known as the cloud collar, a symbol for the gateway to paradise

introduced through Central Asia along the same route as the cloud band discussed earlier.

The large primary guls identified with the various tribes were knotted as tribal-specific symbols only into rugs, although they were sometimes used decoratively on bags made by other tribes, such as the Salor gul seen on late, elaborately skirted Tekke bags. Secondary guls, of lesser tribal significance, could be used on a variety of tribal weavings. On rugs, these minor guls were placed on the field at the point at which lines would intersect if drawn diagonally through the centers of the major figures in adjacent rows.

It is not possible to present here more than a sampling of Turkoman motifs, so I urge readers whose eyes linger longest on these wonderful red weavings to acquire one or more of the authoritative books listed in the Bibliography. Very high prices are routinely paid for the oldest and rarest examples; also-rans, no matter how decorative, do not count for much among the cognoscenti and therefore make a reasonably priced area for beginners to explore.

Tekke

The Tekke tribal gul is always quartered by dark lines intersecting at right angles. There are two secondary guls, and although (b) is less common it is not indicative of greater age.

Yomud

The Yomud used three primary guls, only one of which, the elaborate *kepse* gul, considered by some authorities to be a floral abstraction, is tribal-specific; it is, however, not quartered like the other two, the *dyrnak* and the animal-ornamented *tauk-nuska*. The use of secondary guls is inconstant, and there is no consistency of type when they are employed. The Yomud tribal output of weaving was, and still is, very large. Anything of a practical nature that could be woven was, and a wide variety of motifs were used for ornamentation.

Ersari

The Ersari were the largest of the Turkoman tribes and the readiest to adopt designs from other sources. For example, although they have a tribal-specific gul, the *gulli-gul*, which contains stemmed cloverleaf-like designs in each quarter, a common border design is a *boteh*-based meander. The Ersari weaving repertoire also includes variations on the Mina Khani, cloud bands, Zil-i-Sultan, and the *boteh* used as a field design.

Chodor

The primary Chodor gul, the *ertmen*, is a lozenge-shaped, stepped gul containing stylized flowers and enclosed in a delicate lattice starred with florettes. This group also used the animal-figured *tauk-nuska* gul (see Yomud above) on rugs.

Tekke guls.
(a) Major gul;
(b, c) minor guls.

Yomud guls.
(a) Tauk-nuska;
(b) kepse;
(c) dyrnak.

Other Turkoman guls.
(a) Ersari gulli-gul;
(b) Chodor ertmen;
(c) Salor gul for carpets;
(d) Salor gul for bags and
trappings; (e) Ersari border
motif based on the boteh.

Salor

This tribal gul is quartered and contains within each quarter three stemmed cloverlike figures and a stylized animal figure. The secondary octagonal figure used in conjunction with it in the typically elegantly spaced Salor format is much smaller and simpler. Another large, crenellated gul appears only on weavings other than rugs.

Weavings that can be unequivocally identified with the Salors are rare; other types that escape easy attribution and for that reason not discussed here are Saryk, Arabatchi, and Kizil Ayak.

MAJOR BORDER MOTIFS

The great majority of designs used for main borders in the oriental rug-weaving cultures are floral-based, with the exception of some figures primarily associated with Turkoman rugs and a Turkish border design group derived from Arabic script and used occasionally by Caucasian weavers. Even a design like the Yomud Turkoman "boat border," at first glance seeming wholly rectilinear, can be traced back through successive stages of stylization to flowering vine and palmette antecedents.

Flowering Vine and Palmette. This classic Persian format appears in many variations. Among them are those illustrated here.

Blossom Repeats. Blossoms used in both realistic and stylized forms include carnations, tulips, garden balsam, narcissus, and, in Far Eastern rugs, lotus and peonies.

Ram's Horn. This motif, used over a wide area, is a very old Turkic symbol, appearing in a variety of guises from a simple hooked "Y" used in minor borders to more complex hooked figures seen in the borders and fields of Turkoman, Turkish, and Kurdish village and tribal rugs. The ends of the hooks are sometimes elaborated into a crested shape some scholars identify as birds.

Ashik. This steeply stepped ornament used by many Turkoman tribes, primarily in borders but also as a field design, is considered variously to be a stylized rosette or bird with spread wings. *Ashik*-like motifs are also seen on Turkish rugs.

Kufic Variations. These are geometric main border designs based on a very old rectilinear Arabic script known as Kufic.

Other Geometric Motifs

The geometric border motifs pictured here are commonly seen: three are identified with Turkoman weavings; the other three are universally used.

Cloud Bands. The Chinese cloud band discussed in connection with field motifs was also a popular border motif, often used in a humped version like a looped ribbon bow.

Trefoil. Thought to be derived from the lotus blossom, this very old three-lobed reciprocal figure is widely used in both major and minor borders.

Yomud rug with so-called boat border. PHOTO COURTESY OF GROGAN & COMPANY

Left: *stylizations of palmette and flowering vine border motif including (c) Yomud "boat" and (d) 20th-century Soviet version, with tanks and airplanes.* Right: *three classical flowering vine and palmette borders.*

Floral motifs used in borders. (a–e) Flowering vine and leaf variations; (f) tulip and serrated leaf, known as "cup and leaf." (g) Four flower and leaf stylizations; (h) Turkoman "curled leaf" motif; (i) Caucasian flower and leaf stylization; (j) four stages of a Turkish floral geometricization.

Left: *Kufic border motif variations. (a, b) Turkey, 13th century; (c, d, e) Turkey, 16th century; (f) Turkey, 19th century; (g) Caucasus, 19th century.* Right: *other geometric motifs include the six pictured here. (h) "Tuning fork" repeat, Turkoman; (i) "running dog," universal; (j) aina-kochak, Turkoman; (k) universal; (l) ram's horn, universal; (m) a variant of the stepped Ashik figure, Turkoman.*

MINOR BORDER MOTIFS

Floral and leaf forms on minor borders are typically highly conventionalized, even on workshop rugs. However, although a sort of generic rosette is the rule, a realistic pink carnation motif is often seen in the minor borders of some low-piled rugs woven in northeastern Caucasian districts.

Among the many simple geometric repeats universally used for minor borders and guard stripes are diagonal barber pole stripes, reciprocal sawtooths, angularized vines, and hooked, wavelike patterns frequently labeled "running dog" or "latch hook."

FLATWEAVE MOTIFS

The designs seen on flat-woven articles made for domestic use are in most cases peculiar to the weaving tradition of the village or tribe of which the weaver is a member. These motifs, passed down through the generations, comprise an artistic vocabulary whose combination into woven phrases subtly varies from weaver to weaver and rug to rug; accordingly, although the old flatweaves of a given village will be similar, they are never identical.

Three versions of the reciprocal trefoil motif.

*A sampling of minor border motifs. (a, b) Persian. (c, d, e) Caucasian.
(f, g, h) Turkoman.*

"S"-based border repeats.
(a, b, c) Turkoman;
(d) Caucasian;
(e) Persian;
(f, g) Turkish.

Collectors enjoy arguing about the roots of these designs—some researchers insist they can be traced to Neolithic art forms—but all agree on the importance of the role tradition plays in flatweave design, especially kilims. In fact, knowledgeable kilim collectors not only can assign a piece to a particular village or tribe on the basis of its design and coloration but can date them by subtle variations most of us would fail even to notice. The growing interest in flatweaves has sparked the publication of numerous books devoted to them, with some limited to specific types and weaving areas. You will find recommended titles in the annotated book list in the Resource Guide.

Flatweave formats tend to be dominated by repeat geometric patterns in horizontal, vertical, or diagonal rows. Banding is much more common than on pile rugs, and the size of individual design units often approach the monumental, especially on very old Turkish kilims.

Although curvilinear patterning is certainly possible, as evidenced by floral 16th-century Persian and Ottoman kilims and 19th-century Persian Senneh and Bidjar kilims, it is uncommon.

Stylized figures of animals and birds are frequently depicted on mixed-technique bags and other domestic articles. The brocaded plain-weave covers known in the trade as *vernehs*, on which camels and horses parade row upon row, are particularly popular with collectors of "folky" weavings. Another sought-after type, the Caucasian soumak flatweave known as a *sileh*, features large S-shaped compartment figures said to be derived

Dragon-based figures seen on flat-woven Caucasian silehs.

from the dragons on much earlier knotted rugs, which, depending on the age and type, they more or less resemble.

Collectors, with the exception of those drawn to austerity, are generally attracted by animal figures on a village or tribal weaving, a fact lost on neither dealers nor auctioneers. All other factors being equal, dragons, camels, or crested birds can be expected to exact a premium roughly proportionate to their visual appeal.

For More Information

I know of no books devoted entirely to oriental rug motifs, but many of those in the annotated book list in the Resource Guide, particularly P. R. J. Ford's *The Oriental Carpet*, provide useful information. *Hali* and *Oriental Rug Review* frequently publish articles on the sources and variations of a single motif; reasonably detailed indexes of both publications are now available.

BEGINNING YOUR COLLECTION

BEFORE YOU START

When it comes to acquiring rugs, the interests of collectors do not always coincide with those of the dealers and auction house experts supplying their needs. This is hardly surprising. Nevertheless, the advice given me for beginning collectors by knowledgeable representatives of all three groups can be distilled into one well-worn phrase: look before you leap.

If you intend to buy no more than two or three good old rugs to enhance the interior decor of your home, you need not look very far. The color, type, and size of rugs employed primarily as furnishing accessories usually complement what is already in place. One would not, for example, expect to see a silk and metallic-thread *souf* Kashan in a remodeled New England barn or a coarse, long-piled Turkish bedding rug in a Louis IX drawing room. But although an existing decorating scheme may limit one's choice, it in no way makes it less deserving of serious consideration.

At the very least, a thorough reading of the two books discussed below and visits to museum collections in your area should precede investigations of dealer stocks and auction house offerings. As your eyes become accustomed to rugs with unfamiliar patterns and palettes, you might find yourself drawn to something quite different from what you originally had in mind, like the Tabriz remembered from your grandparents' house or the mellow Heriz seen at a friend's. If the visual pleasure you experience is strong enough, you may soon find yourself seeking out more of the same, and even though floor covering remains the primary purpose of the rugs you eventually purchase, the first step up the collecting ladder has been taken.

The cornerstone of any budding collector's reference library should be the two titles heading the recommended reading list of everyone I interviewed: Murray L. Eiland's *Oriental Rugs*, third (or latest) edition, and *Oriental Carpets* by Jon Thompson. (Ordering information for publications recommended in this chapter will be found in the annotated book list in the Resource Guide.)

Dr. Eiland has traveled often and widely in the rug-producing areas. He believes in drawing his conclusions from personal experience and study, and his thorough, hands-on knowledge of rugs is straightforwardly communicated in this reliable, information-packed, conventionally organized collector's guide to 19th- and early-20th-century Persian, Caucasian, Turkoman, and Turkish rugs. Although short on historical background information and woefully below par as far as color plates are concerned—there are many useful black and whites, however—its virtues far outweigh its shortcomings.

Jon Thompson's *Oriental Carpets* has been described by one internationally respected scholar as "the best-written, best-researched . . . best illustrated general book on oriental carpets available." It has also proved to be a trend-setter in terms of organization of the material, differing from all that preceded it by discussing carpets not in the usual country-of-origin context but in terms of technical achievement. In other words, rather than grouping rugs geographically as Persian, Caucasian, Turkish, and Turkoman, he has defined four new categories based on weaving skills, which in fact closely parallel the interests of most collectors. They are tribal weaving, cottage industry rugs, workshop or town carpets, and court carpets. For the beginner seeking to define his or her own rug interest, Jon Thompson's sumptuously illustrated book is without question the place to start.

CHOOSING AN AREA OF CONCENTRATION

Let us assume you have read Eiland and Thompson and have visited one or more of the rug collections listed in the back of this book. Let us assume further that you have not become discouraged by your realization of how large and complex the collecting field you have chosen is. You could, at this point, go one of two ways: adopt the one-of-this, one-of-that, assorted cookie approach or continue looking and reading until you find yourself being consistently drawn to one type of rug or weaving above all others. It could be the color or the feel of the wool; it could be the technical excellence of the weaving; it could even be the challenge posed by uncertain attributions. Whatever it is, wait for that mental click that brings your predilection, probably already recognized at gut level, into sharp focus.

Mind you, there is nothing *wrong* about wanting to own examples of a variety of rugs; in fact, most collectors do, including the late Wilton Mason of North Carolina, who once wrote me, "I will probably never own any of the classic rugs that look so lovely in the glossy books, but this [realization] has had a liberating effect. Within what I can afford, I now buy only the rugs that move me, that bring comfort and joy through their intrinsic beauty and uniqueness, whatever their type."

Wilton Mason, however, was blessed with an unusually discerning eye.

On average, unless one has a great deal of time to devote to one's collecting, it is very difficult to learn enough about all classes of rugs not only to unerringly choose good typical examples but to spy out the shining lights, the unique, out-of-the-ordinary rugs that challenge comfortable assumptions.

TWO CASE HISTORIES

Rod Griffith, a Connecticut-based contractor who specializes in laboratory casework, grew up with the oriental rugs his grandparents had acquired from a dealer who traveled each spring from New York City with a carload of rugs for customers in far outlying areas. Rod says he took those rugs for granted until he and his wife acquired a large old house. Deciding that oriental rugs would be the appropriate furnishing for the wide board floors, they began to visit the dealers in their area, but the rugs, their prices, and the dubious lore offered them persuaded him to postpone buying until he knew more. "I read a lot, subscribed to *Hali* and *Oriental Rug Review*, started going to auctions, and sought out knowledgeable collectors at rug society meetings and conferences." Finally, after taking a weekend-long university seminar in oriental rug appraisal taught by leading experts, he decided he was ready to take the plunge.

With two young children to educate, Rod Griffith admits he is unlikely ever to be a collector of world-class rugs, but that hasn't dampened his enthusiasm. As a carpenter, he has always been intrigued by how things are put together, and in six short years he has acquired an impressive familiarity with the structure of a wide variety of oriental rugs, thanks in large measure to his own painstaking, hands-on observations.

Like Wilton Mason, Rod Griffith isn't a specialist collector. But suppose you decide to focus on, say, the bold, colorful rugs of the southern Caucasus. These cottage industry rugs, woven in long-established patterns for almost two centuries, are a good choice for beginners. Thanks to their enduring popularity, there is a large, well-documented and -illustrated body of literature about them; it is relatively easy to distinguish one from another; and attractive examples are not hard to come by. The downside of popularity is that stellar examples, even those with "problems," command six-figure prices from the international trade. The cost factor is further exacerbated when collectors who haven't taken the time to educate themselves unjustly inflate prices by paying up to $25,000 for mediocre rugs in mint condition, having mistaken flash for substance.

Every dealer has at least one story to tell about proudly displayed collections of garish, mechanically designed turn-of-the-century Caucasian rugs with nothing to remark kindly about except condition. This could never be said about the rugs selected by Rosalie Rudnick, a Boston-based collector who, admittedly knowing nothing at the start, ten years ago began the slow, painful, yet gratifying process of self-education that has allowed her to acquire from dealers, at auction and by trading with other collectors, a distinguished group of Caucasian rugs, almost all of which predate 1850. Condition does not control her decisions. Having seen the wonders a skilled hand can work on a worn rug with an inspired design and wonderful color, Ms. Rudnick has gone most collectors one better by taking lessons from the best restorer of village and tribal rugs in New York City. She is now able to restore her own rugs with a near-professional level of skill.

Few have that degree of dedication to collecting; most of us hope for shortcuts. There are none. It is only by looking at, comparing, touching—in short, by *studying*—many, many rugs, both in and out of our area of specialization, and by asking the right questions of knowledgeable scholars, dealers, and collectors that we may hope always to be able to tell good rugs from bad ones, and, eventually, the best from the good.

That's where looking before you leap comes in again. Early in my collecting career, which by chance began in the great rug boom of the late 1970s, I was like a kitten in a swarm of butterflies, wanting everything that caught my fancy. Lacking the authoritative books and periodicals available today to guide my education, as well as a mentor to counsel restraint, I made mistake after impulsive mistake. Once I knew enough to be embarrassed by my ill-chosen excesses, I couldn't shed them fast enough, but it was an expensive lesson even in that rising market.

New York collector DeWitt Mallary, who specializes in Turkoman and Baluch tribal weavings, advises the beginner to resist "buying to buy." Wells Klein, who divides his time between Manhattan and Vermont, says collectors should guard against allowing the desire for a particular type of rug to override their aesthetic judgment. "Don't be desperate," he says, "another, better rug will come along." Both caution beginners about setting collecting goals beyond their financial reach. Collectors will always make mistakes— it's part of the learning process—but fewer will be made if most buying is postponed until after an area of specialization is chosen and study undertaken. (Interestingly, Mr. Klein's collecting focus has changed from the Caucasian rugs cited in the first edition of this book to Turkoman weavings, whose design and structural subtleties have provided him a new, stimulating, and intellectually challenging area of study.)

Collectors who lack easy access to museum collections and major auction house previews should consider buying one or two of the catalogs prepared by Eberhart Herrmann, a dealer with perhaps the most discerning eye in the world rug trade. These are primarily very expensive picture books— the text is German—but what pictures! What rugs! In conjunction with the Eiland and Thompson books mentioned above, they provide an unparalleled visual index of collector aspirations.

Another indispensable library acquisition is the periodical *Hali*, which covers the rug world at home and abroad, including previews and reports of auctions and news of dealer and museum exhibitions. *Hali* is published in generally excellent color, and the advertisements, unlike those in most periodicals, provide additional useful information about current offerings on the market.

APPROACHING THE STARTING GATE

As was remarked earlier in connection with Jon Thompson's book, *Oriental Carpets*, collectors tend to specialize within categories defined roughly by the intent of the weaver and the circumstances in which the weaving is done. In the pages that follow, all collectible weavings have been assigned to one of five categories of weaving skills, within which they are further grouped geographically, starting with Turkey and proceeding east to China.

The ability to identify rugs with reasonable certainty is not easily acquired; fortunately, the illustrated, annotated catalogs of the major auction houses provide identification for us. They are not always right, as dealers and experienced collectors are quick to point out, but they are more apt to be so than the average collector. Auctioneers encountered down the scale, from smaller regional houses to country barns, either depend on a local dealer for attributions or supply nothing but the size and an implied caveat. Dealers in new orientals may know less about old rugs than a well-read novice.

Thus set adrift, as it were, beginning collectors are often reduced to attempting rug identification on the basis of design. If the rug is a traditional type, of respectable age, and if one is content to have a general rather than specific identification, the odds for making a reasonably good guess are in your favor. Late-19th- and early-20th-century rugs whose designs were dictated by commercial interests are another matter altogether. European companies like Ziegler, The Persian Carpet Company (PETAG), and Oriental Carpet Manufacturers, Ltd. (OCM)—the last organized production in Turkey and India as well as Persia—supplied their weavers with wool, dyes, and designs and sparked the great oriental rug revival at the turn of the century. The results can be seen in dealer stocks and auction rooms today. However, the designs given the weavers were not necessarily indigenous, and it was under OCM aegis that the washing of rugs with chemicals to produce instant mellowness was institutionalized, although rarely taken to such extremes as the "Golden Afghans" popular in the 1960s.

Further complicating the problems of identification is the fact that even isolated village and tribal weavers, unaffected by wide-ranging entrepreneurs, were sometimes influenced by patterns seen on rugs brought to market by weavers from other areas. Because of the ease of imitating or adapting surface designs, authorities agree that the most reliable way to assign a rug to an already defined weaving group is through a close examination of the weave pattern visible on the back. These weaving techniques, absorbed by children as they work at the loom alongside their mothers, emerge through the weavers' fingers in a linked series of habitual motions strongly resistant to change.

The weave characteristic telling the most about which weaving group is likely to have produced a rug is the weft: the color and spin of the material of which it is composed, the thickness and firmness of the ply, how many times and with what degree of tension it passes between the knots, and how firmly it is beaten down against them.

The knot, too, is a distinguishing feature—not only the kind of knot used, but the spin and thickness of the knot wool and the tightness with which it is looped around the warps. To determine whether a knot is symmetrical (Turkish; Ghiordes) or asymmetrical (Persian; Senneh) the rug should be "broken open" by folding it back parallel to a line of wefting. If the horizontal bridge of the revealed knots covers both warp threads, with the pile ends coming up between them, the knotting is symmetrical; if one of the warps can be seen *between* the emerging ends of the pile it is asymmetrical (for details see the chapter on rug structure).

Finally, the back may be relatively flat in appearance or slightly or markedly ribbed due to the depression—more accurately, displacement—of alternate warp threads. Other useful clues are the edge and end finishes—assuming they are original—the colors used in the pile design; the handle—the rug's relative firmness or floppiness—and the appearance and length of the pile wool.

Committing a dozen or more weave patterns to memory is one thing; applying that knowledge amid the distractions of a crowded auction preview is quite another. Limiting one's collecting focus is probably the best way to minimize confusion: the differences between classes of weavings are often subtle, the variations sometimes encountered within them even more so.

What if the rug one wishes to identify eludes ready assignment? Pinning down an ambiguous weave pattern to a specific time and place is an exacting yet enthralling challenge for many scholars and collectors. Dealers often consider the process more exasperating than anything else, but since large sums of money can be riding on the outcome, they too are often drawn into the controversy.

Friends are made and lost in wrangles over provenance. According to Joseph Alsop in *The Rare Art Traditions*, "in all forms of collecting, the collector's category is always controlling since all collectors require their prizes to belong to the correct category . . . [which] is another way of saying that the object collected is what it is claimed to be and not something else."

Since rug weavers seldom kept records of their work, many firmly held opinions about rug provenance are necessarily subjective: Enthusiasts are given to constructing elaborate theories based on flimsy evidence involving dyestuffs listed on ancient bills of lading, imperfectly translated journals written by travelers of uncertain reliability, and fragments of Neolithic art reported but never verified.

In recent years, however, oriental rug studies have become more rigorous, with graduate-level degrees being awarded. As a result, a generally accepted body of knowledge is fast taking shape, and thanks to its publication in a veritable torrent of books and the periodical mentioned above, a novice has a much better chance of making accurate identifications today than as few as 15 years ago.

GET READY, GET SET . . . CONDITION

The factors that most affect dealer pricing and auction estimates are age and condition. The ability to accurately estimate the age of a rug, like an eye for natural versus synthetic dyes, comes only with experience. Chemical washing and hard usage can produce a mellow antique look, and a smoothly worn back, which occurs naturally over many years of use, can be artificially achieved with a blowtorch and elbow grease. Deliberate fakery is uncommon but becomes a possibility whenever prices soar to tempting highs. Some of the classical carpets collectors vied for early in this century were later judged counterfeit; today new flat-woven bags woven with old materials are reaping the rewards of the collector demand for tribal artifacts. An antique rug in mint condition is rare enough to demand confirmation as such by a qualified expert.

Determining a rug's condition, however, requires no more than a close and careful examination of the features discussed below. This can be accomplished by the rankest of beginners and had better be, unless one has no concern for one's pocketbook or the possibility of eventual resale.

Pile worn evenly low, which can enhance the clarity of the design of finely knotted carpets, will affect value less than uneven wear. If wear is so pronounced as to require repiling for a rug to become serviceable for normal floor use, its price should either reflect its damaged condition or, if a dealer rug, include the cost of repair.

A rug reduced from its original size, whether to fit a particular space or eliminate damaged areas, should be priced less than a similar unaltered rug, even if the new dimensions suit the place you have in mind for it. Look for missing borders and truncated designs, but be warned: reductions can be accomplished so cleverly they may be almost impossible for an untutored eye to detect.

Other common problems affecting a rug's value are:

1. Rebound or added edges, particularly if the original weft wrappings have been cut.

2. Damaged or missing fringes or plain-woven skirts.

3. Wear creases and moth damage.

4. Holes.

5. Stains.

6. Unsightly repairs.

7. Bleeding or strident synthetic dyes and washed-out colors, whether synthetic or vegetable.

8. Painting to disguise exposed foundations or conceal faded, bleeding, or harsh colors.

9. Dry rot in cotton foundations.

10. Glued-on backings.

11. Ripples and uneven dimensions, although the latter, if moderate, is tolerated in tribal rugs.

Taking all of the above into account, before making a final judgment you should be sure what your primary interest is in acquiring a particular rug. The need for a purely decorative furnishing rug to retain its original structural integrity is much less compelling than it is for a collectible weaving. One might well prefer a Heriz carpet purchased for a dining room to have tightly rebound edges even if the color and texture bear no relation to the original. A Baluch tribal rug, however, will lose some value if edges that should be overwrapped in goat hair have been reworked with new wool, no matter how careful the workmanship or exact the color match.

Speaking of color, the character, application, and balance of color in rugs, qualities often underappreciated by beginners, are, in combination, more important than physical condition to many collectors and specialty dealers. In fact, one well-known dealer, when asked what qualities he looks for in a rug, routinely answers, "Three: color, color, and color." A faded rug may suit your decorative scheme, but it should be priced for less than a like piece with clear, rich colors. Similarly, although good chrome dyes are acceptable in decorative rugs, vegetable-derived colors are preferred in collectible old rugs; to the purist even a trace of a synthetic dye is anathema.

ABOUT THE PRICES

The following listings of the pile and flat-woven rugs and other articles available in today's market are intended to be no more than an overview. Almost all were sold at auction.

I have not included a range of dealer prices along with the auction house estimates. All dealers in old rugs are affected by the auction process to one degree or another: as a source of stock, as a means of selling locally acquired rugs of world-class quality or of disposing of long unsold stock, and as a guide to what's currently hot, what appears to have fallen out of favor, and the average prices realized for both. But unless the factors determining dealers' prices are carefully spelled out—assuming I knew what all of them were—they can be misleading.

Some dealers in old rugs will, if they acquire a rug at a good price, pass on part of their savings to the buyer; others mark all rugs at what they consider the going price to provide a cushion for rugs they may be unable to sell for enough to cover their cost. Pricing also depends on how easily an old rug can be replaced in a dealer's stock by one of reasonably similar age and quality. And finally, even a dealer able to flintily resist the hardest-nosed bargainer will sometimes give a price break to a novice who takes his or her fancy.

The auction arena is a public marketplace supplying not so much a baseline of prices as a level playing ground. Oriental rugs do not attract the high-flying investors who periodically push the fine arts market to such absurd heights. In fact, in December 1990, just after the bottom fell out of one such market, Sotheby's held a rug sale more successful than any held there in recent years, selling almost 90 percent of the lots offered, some at more than double the high estimates. On average, however, rug collectors are the Scrooges of the collecting world: buyers of fine art appear to pride themselves on how much they pay; rug buyers, on how little. Accordingly, they tend to strongly resist house-hyped estimates.

Rugs offered at auction must sell within minutes of their appearance on the block. Since an unsold rug exacts a handling charge, it is in the consignor's interest to agree to a realistic range of estimates and reserve figure below which it will not be sold. According to Jo Kris, the head of the rug department at Skinner in Massachusetts, realism usually prevails, collectors' grumbles to the contrary.

Auctiongoers intending to bid are required to register and are assigned numbers. In New York State auctioneers must by law indicate the failure of a lot to sell; elsewhere, lots that fail to reach the reserve price are often "knocked down" to numbers the auction house has assigned to itself. When lots whose final bid is below the low estimate are consistently awarded to the same two or three numbers, it can be assumed these are the house numbers for that sale. Buyers interested in rugs that fail to sell during the auction can sometimes arrange to purchase them postsale at attractive prices.

As you read through the following pages, be wary of drawing hasty conclusions if a pictured rug appears similar to one seen at a dealer's shop priced below or for more than twice the realized auction price. Beginners are often hard put to distinguish a new, chemically washed, vegetable-dyed Anatolian village rug from its 19th-century prototype, but a dealer will justly tag such pieces with very different prices. Even if the rugs compared *are* similar, price alone should not determine whether you buy at auction or from a dealer.

Buying at auction is well suited to decisive, cool-headed types who know exactly what they're about—no returns, remember? But many collectors, including the very sophisticated collectors interviewed for this guide, prefer the flexibility inherent in buying from sympathetic dealers. At this point, however, it is important to mention how the collecting of rugs differs from other kinds of art collecting and how this difference affects the attitudes of collectors vis-à-vis the marketplace.

Rugs, unlike other art objects, appeal to the tactile sense as well as the visual, and the handle of a rug provides experienced collectors with an important clue to its probable origin. Short of renting a warehouse, however, rug dealers are unable to display their wares as dealers in porcelain, fine art, and even furniture can.

The collector, not trusting the dealer to always know what might catch his fancy, would, ideally, like to see every rug in stock. "How can I tell what I want," he says, "until I see what you have?" But most of the dealers I interviewed are not thrilled, understandably, by the prospect of spending two or three hours with collectors more interested in indulging their passion for looking at rugs than in buying one, reducing the dealer's gallery to a shambles in the process.

Dealers in small tribal pieces—The Hazara Gallery and Adraskand in California come to mind—can usually afford to allow collectors to browse through their stock, but large decorative rugs are heavy and awkward to roll out and roll up again, and area rugs, stacked in piles of 30 or more, require many to be lifted and moved to extract the one or two that catch a collector's eye. In short, we have here a classic conflict of interest. Auction buying will never, *should* never, replace the rewarding relationship many collectors have with dealers, but at auction previews we can look and touch to our heart's content, providing ourselves with both pleasure and instruction at the same time.

The prices that follow were realized for oriental rugs and other weavings selected from dealer rugs and a total of about 2,030 sold at auction from December 1994 through December 1995 in New York and Boston. All prices include the buyer's premium, it having become customary not only to charge the consignors commission rates based on the amount lots sell for—the higher the hammer price, the lower the rate—but to add a flat 15 percent of a winning bid to the buyer's invoice.

The listings begin with classical carpets and early tribal rugs, proceed through later tribal weavings, rustic loom production, and flatweaves, and conclude with commercial workshop rugs. Readers should bear in mind that although no foreign auction results are included here, the oriental rug market is an international one. In fact, Krikor Markarian, a New York City dealer in world-class collectible weavings, sorely regrets the steady transfer of the best American-consigned antique rugs to Europe, where the appreciation of oriental rugs as an art form is much more widely developed than it is in the United States. Prices in the United States are affected by worldwide demand, by changing tastes in rugs, and by the fluctuation of the dollar on the world exchange. In other words, the prices listed here are temporary guides, not gospel.

Remember, too, that when a winning bid soars well beyond the high estimate, it can indicate either that (1) the auction house experts under-valued the merits of that particular rug, or (2) the high bidder, for whatever reason—ego, ignorance, home decor needs—was willing to pay an inflated price to get it.

FAKE ALERT

As mentioned in the introduction to this edition, there have been reports of small tribal artifacts, currently popular with collectors, being expertly copied in old, natural-dyed wools salvaged from worn-out flatweaves. Deliberate fakery of this sort is rare compared to its incidence in, say, collectible glass or scrimshaw, but contemporary Turkish copies of antique rugs are sometimes touted as the real thing by unscrupulous dealers. Be suspicious of mint condition, ecru-dyed machine-spun warps, wool pile clipped to approximate the corroded effect of black and brown pile in old rugs, and a muted tonality characteristic of a chemical wash. Obviously no one wants to buy a new rug for the price of a rare antique, but the best of these copies, knotted with hand-spun lustrous wool and dyed with glowing vegetable colors, are well worth buying for their true retail value of about $60 to $110 a square foot.

QUALITY AND CONDITION KEYS

Although the quality and condition of an object determine its collectible and monetary value, these terms have little meaning unless one has seen a great many examples—good, bad, and indifferent—of the object in question. Desirability is also affected by fashion, and it is this that makes the application to collectible rugs of the first two terms less straightforward than one might at first think.

As was mentioned earlier, although very finely knotted rugs (over 300 knots per square inch) are generally more expensive than those with an average knot count (50 to 100 knots per square inch), fineness of knotting has little bearing on the *collectible* value of a rug. In the following listings, therefore, the terms Coarse, Average, and Fine refer only to the number of knots per square inch. Coarse indicates a KPSI of 50 or less; Average, 50–100; Fine, 100 plus.

Please also bear in mind that although the synthetic dyes found in rugs made in the last half of this century are reliably fast and produce a wide variety of colors, serious collectors have yet to accept them in anything but "furnishing" rugs. ND means that all dyes appear to me to be natural; SD indicates traces of one of the garishly colored or unstable early synthetic dyes.

In the lists that follow, rug descriptions are tagged with the one-word keys defined below. No rugs of less than good quality are listed, but a very old classical rug fragment tagged as superior quality is more likely than not to be in poor condition.

Good quality: Good example of type with clear, stable colors pleasingly incorporated into a balanced but stereotypical design.

Very Good Quality: Wool, colors, and rendering of the design distinguish it from others in its class.

Superior Quality: The exceptional drawing and balance of the design elements together with the use of vivid natural-dye colors enhanced by lustrous wool serve to make other rugs of whatever type look ordinary.

Poor Condition: Foundation exposed by extensive wear; holes and tears unrepaired or inexpertly repaired; extensive moth damage; dry rot (cotton foundations only); major losses to ends and/or edges; large areas of obvious repiling; design-destroying reductions.

Fair Condition: Low pile showing uneven wear but with no warps or wefts visible; edges and ends in need of repair; loss to end borders; small areas of moth damage; stains; obvious repiling and repairs.

Good Condition: Slight, even wear; repiling and repairs noticeable only on close inspection; edges restored to near original condition, and if end fringes or skirts are missing or reduced, the ends have been stabilized.

Fine Condition: Pile nearly full and unstained; edges and ends original and intact; repairs and/or repiling minor and of restoration quality.

PLEASE NOTE: The spelling of terms applied to oriental rugs and trappings is subject to many variations. I have supplied some of the variants commonly encountered in the literature and auction and dealer listings, but until a standard terminology is universally accepted, collectors must continue to muddle through the confusion as best they can.

CLASSICAL CARPETS AND TRIBAL WEAVINGS, 1500–1800

To connoisseurs of Eastern rugs, quibbles about the distinction between fine and decorative arts are rendered irrelevant by the design, beauty, and historical interest of great early carpets, but the fact of the matter is that first-rate examples of the rugs woven in the court-sponsored workshops of the Safavid, Ottoman, Mughal, and Mamluk dynasties can be acquired for less than a third-rate painting.

Because of the scarcity of fine classical carpets and early tribal weavings, dealer stock is very limited and their prices determined by other than purely market forces. Dealers more likely than others to have such pieces are noted in the resource listings; but for the most part, they are consigned from distinguished collections or as deacquisitions from museum holdings to whichever of the major auction houses offers the best terms and widest presale publicity.

A fairly representative selection of early examples of wide-ranging quality was sold at auction in 1994–95, with a spectacular Mughal Star-Lattice Carpet, c. 1700, establishing a new world price record at Christie's. Some of the Turkoman weavings may date to as late as the first quarter of the 19th century, but in the context of tribal weaving—which was long undervalued and for the most part wore out in daily use—this is considered very old.

When reading the accompanying descriptions please bear in mind that because of their extreme rarity, the condition of very old carpets and tribal artifacts affects prices differently from rugs woven in the later 19th and early 20th centuries.

TURKISH CARPETS

Ladik Prayer Rug, Central Anatolia (c. 1800, 5' × 3'6"). Beneath the unornamented madder red *mihrab* is a band of the inverted tulips typical of late examples of this classic design, bordered in this case with a highly stylized vine and blossom meander on gold. Average, sym.; ND in red, blue-green, medium blue, gold, ivory. Good quality; poor condition..Est. $300/400; sold for $517

"Transylvanian" Prayer Rug, Western Anatolia (18th century, 5'4" × 4'4"). Once believed to have originated in Eastern Europe because of the many examples—donated as thanks offerings—found in churches throughout the Transylvanian region. Despite its worn condition and the awkward corner resolutions of the palmette/cartouche border, the rarely seen open *mihrab* format of this rug allowed

Ladik Prayer Rug, Central Anatolia, c. 1800, 5′ × 3′6″, $517. PHOTO
COURTESY OF SKINNER, INC.

its sale at near the low estimate. Average, sym.; ND in red, light blue, mustard, pale
green, pale yellow, ivory, brown-black. Very good quality; poor condition............
....Est. $4,000/6,000; sold for $4,600

Ottoman Cairene Carpet, Cairo, Egypt (16th century, 10′11″ × 23′5″). This elegant carpet's floral vinery, graceful leaves, and refined blossom motifs combine the
weaving and artistic traditions of both the Egyptian Mamluks and the Ottoman
Turks, who conquered the Mamluk Sultanate in 1517. Average, asym.; ND in

*"Transylvanian" Prayer Rug, Western Anatolia, 18th century, 5'4" ×
4'4", $4,600.* PHOTO COURTESY OF CHRISTIE'S

cherry red, gold, green, medium and pale blue, yellow, brown. Superior quality; fair
condition. ....Est. $70,000/90,000; sold for $123,000

Star Oushak Carpet, mounted fragment, Western Anatolia (late 16th century, 5'4"
× 4'5"). Although worn, this large fragment contains a complete eight-lobed blue
star filled with red-accented gold tracery, on a madder red field ornamented with
delicate floral tracery and bordered with similarly delicate flowering vine repeats.

Average, sym.; ND red, dark and light blue, blue-green, yellow, ivory, brown. Superior quality; poor condition..........................Est. $5,000/7,000; sold for $4,600

"Bird" Oushak Rug, Western Anatolia (17th century, 4'2" × 6'3"). Often seen in European paintings of the same period, the so-called perching bird motifs are actually clusters of four stylized leaves radiating from a geometrized blossom. Typical of this group is the rather wan palette and the bold but awkward drawing and spacing of the field motifs and cloud-band border. Coarse, sym.; ND in pale cherry, ivory, tan, light yellow, brown. Very good quality; fair condition. ....
Est. $5,000/7,000; sold for $32,200

........ia (18th century, 3' × 4'3"). ....is enlivened by the precisely ....ordered by a narrow brown-........:oral, dark and medium blue, ...on..
$3,000/5,000; sold for $4,312

........0'7"). This striking flatweave ....milar to the archaic *elibelinde* ....ows of 3 on an ivory ground, ...d stylized carnations. ND in ....lmon, ivory, brown. Superior ....$3,000/4,000; sold for $8,625

CAUCASIAN CARPETS

........× 12'9"). Despite extensive ....:a, the spectacular purple and ....l motifs bordered with a linked ....ND in purple, red, blue, ivory, ...$4,000/6,000; sold for $3,737

........11'8"). Bold but stiffly drawn ....rdered with a vine and blossom ....ge, red, yellow, ivory, brown. ....$2,000/3,000; sold for $3,727

PERSIAN CARPETS

........× 13'8"). Graceful variegated ....n a rose red field bordered with a large-scale stylized palmette and leaf repeat on dark blue. Average, asym.; ND in cool red, rose, dark and light blue, blue-green, dull orange, yellow. Superior quality; fair condition. ....Est. $7,000/9,000; sold for $31,050

Isphahan Carpet, Central Persia (c. 1750, 6'5" × 9'8"). A variety of large palmettes on a rose field with a lattice composed of vines and cloud bands, within a very bold palmette and flowering vine repeat on a wide blue-green border. Average, asym.; ND in rose, blue, blue-green, yellow, ivory, brown. Very good quality; poor condition. ....Est. $5,000/7,000; sold for $5,520

"Polonaise" Carpet, Central Persia (17th century, 5'10" × 13'8"). The name given this group of carpets arises from the mislabeling as Polish a similar carpet shown at the 1878 Paris International Exhibition. Variously attributed to Isphahan and Kashan, the design is derived from earlier Persian carpets and is typically knotted in silk and gold/silver-wrapped silk threads on a cotton foundation. This example, which has an elegantly rendered palmette and vine border enclosing the worn field's palmette-decorated swirl of vinery, has been cut and pieced. Fine, asym.; ND in tans, greens, blue-green, dark blue, pale cherry, ivory, charcoal gray. Superior quality; poor condition............................Est. $10,000/15,000; sold for $40,250

"Vase" Carpet, Central Persia (early 18th century, 5'4" × 11'8"). A variety of polychrome palmettes punctuate a delicate lattice of flowering vines on a cranberry red field enclosed by a graceful flowering leafy vine meander on an abrashed blue border. Fine, asym.; ND in madder reds, dark and pale blue, blue-green, pale green, yellow, ivory. Superior quality; good condition. ....
....Est. $50,000/70,000; sold for $54,625

TURKOMAN TRIBAL CARPETS AND WEAVINGS

Yomud Main Carpet, West Turkestan (c. 1800, 5'1" × 8'4"). An overall repeat of polychrome Kepsi guls on a liver red ground bordered with a stylized serrated palmette and "Turkoman line" vine meander on ivory. The wide pile skirts are dissimilar: one bears an "S" motif; the other, stylized flowering plants. Fine, sym.; ND in dark and brick red, dark and medium blue, blue-green, pale yellow, ivory, black. Very good quality; fair condition. ....Est. $6,000/8,000; sold for $7,475

Salor Wedding Trapping, Central Turkestan (c. 1800, 2'8" × 7'6"). The rich saturated colors and precise drawing of these finely woven camel trappings make them the most desirable of Turkoman tribal artifacts. The three large crimson-silk enlivened guls are a rare feature, this previously unknown example being one of only seven published examples. Fine, asym.; ND in madder red, cochineal crimson, deep and light blue, green, gold, ivory, brown. Superior quality; good condition......
....Est. $30,000/50,000; sold for $46,000

INDIAN CARPETS

Mughal Carpet, Lahore, Northwest India (c. 1750, 7'9" × 14'8"). Realistic large-scale cypress trees and flowering plants are arranged in horizontal rows on a typically crimson field, enclosed by a leaf, palmette, and flowering vine border. Fine, asym.; ND in crimson, rose, green, blue, blue-green, yellow, ivory. Superior quality; poor condition....................................Est. $12,000/15,000; sold for $12,650

Mughal Carpet, mounted fragment, Lahore, Northwest India (18th century, 5'1" × 3'7"). Dark blue serrated leaves enclose repeats of clusters of polychrome floral sprays, single blossoms, and palmettes on a crimson ground. The wide dark blue border features a rigid vine meander with white floral sprays and crimson carnations. Fine, asym.; ND in crimson, rose, saffron, yellow, green, white/ivory, dark blue. Very good quality; good condition............Est. $8,000/10,000; sold for $8,050

Mughal Millefleur "Star-Lattice" Carpet, North India (c. 1700, 12'8" × 13'6"). This extraordinary carpet, which once graced Vanderbilt residences in New York City and Newport, RI, brought a well-deserved record-breaking price at Christie's in 1995. A starlike lattice composed of ivory stylized leaves both

TRIBAL WEAVINGS, 1800–1925

Although many tribal weavings are flat-woven, only knotted-pile articles are included under this heading. Flatweaves, whose collectors tend to concentrate on them exclusively, are dealt with separately.

As a class, tribal weavings have the distinctive, strongly traditional character associated with kinship groups and closely knit isolated communities that have developed over time a tribal-like culture. Some were woven for sale or barter; most were made for personal domestic use. Among the pieces listed here are examples from the Central Asian Turkoman tribes of Afghanistan and Turkestan, now northeast Iran and Soviet Turkmenistan and Uzbekistan; the Baluch in northeast Persia and western Afghanistan; the Yürüks in eastern Turkey; and several Persian groups, including Kurds, Shahsavan, Lurs, Qashqai, Bakhtiyari, and Afshars.

Today few tribes are wholly nomadic. Many live in villages during the winter, taking their flocks to pasture in the highlands in summer. In eastern Turkey, I have seen these groups "going to the *yayla*," their faces alight with pleasurable anticipation. And they still weave. True, much of the present-day output is garishly colored with synthetic dyes, but occasionally a weaver's creative response to his or her environment vividly surmounts the shoddiness of the materials. Prime examples are the little mats embellished with tanks, grenades, helicopters, and Kalishnikov rifles that were woven during the USSR-Afghanistan conflict.

Collectors of tribal weavings accept the fact that because the looms used are both primitive and transportable (see chapter on rug structure), minor distortions are unavoidable. They see them as a sign of authenticity rather than poor workmanship. You might not want a deformed rug for furnishing purposes, but in January 1990 a notably skewed Star Kazak sold at Sotheby's to Eberhart Herrmann, the premier European dealer in world-class rugs, for $286,000.

Awkwardnesses abound: the corner resolution of border designs, for example, is often less than perfect. Sometimes the weaver distracts attention from her errors by the sly addition of a blossom or a funny little animal in what would otherwise seem a clumsy gap in the design sequence. In a professionally designed commercial workshop rug, this sort of thing is rightfully considered a defect; in the context of nomadic and village weaving, it lends the singularity that admirers of these weavings look for. Mark Hopkins, a distinguished collector and current president of the New England Rug Society, put it this way: "The sought-after rug is the one that sparkles with freshness. Nearly all rugs are conceived as symmetrical, whether by centralized or repetitious design. But in most of the best, it is the subtle counterpoint of spontaneously inspired asymmetry—an altered dimension ... a surprising cascade of animal or floral figures, an unexpected twist of line or form just at the point of tedium—that transports a weaving to subjective pinnacles of greatness."

TURKISH

According to the distinguished ethnographer Josephine Powell, who has devoted many years to the documentation of tribal life in Turkey, governments have traditionally discouraged nomadism because of the difficulty of counting populations and collecting taxes. In mainland Turkey the last recorded traditional migration, of the Saçikara Yürüks in the Taurus Mountains, took place in 1983, and the replacement of horses and camels by motorized transport has discouraged the weaving of storage and saddle bags and fabrics for the decoration of animals.

Because of the increased cost of housing and lack of nonagricultural employment, more black tents are seen in the countryside now than five years ago. But although there may be a continuing minor role for seminomadic herders in an economy that provides few new job opportunities, Ms. Powell believes that among tribal women the role of weaving, both for use and peer competition, is all but played out. If this be the case, the bags and trappings woven years ago in a genuine nomadic context will undoubtedly rise in value.

The majority of the items made by the Taurus Yürüks, a Turkoman-related people, are flat-woven. The Kurds weave small rugs—prayer formats are common—and large, boldly patterned runners, both employing distinctive shades of orange-red and violet-shaded brown. Like Baluch work, Turkish Kurdish rugs were undervalued in the past. They are not commonly seen in the market; when they are, they are apt to be badly worn or are late examples disfigured by poor-quality synthetic dyes.

Yürük Rug, East Anatolia (late 19th century, 4'6" × 7'6"). Latchhooked muted polychrome diamonds arranged in a lattice on a sky blue field within a polychrome geometric repeat border enclosed by guard borders with an "S" repeat, all knotted in glossy wool. Average, sym.; ND in medium and sky blue, apricot, rust, violet, brown. Very good quality; fine condition.............Est. $3,500/4,500; sold for $6,670

Kurd Rug, East Anatolia (early 19th century, 4'7" × 7'4"). Seven rows of pairs of joined gul-like devices, alternately red and copper, within a latchhooked stiff royal blue lattice on a dark brown ground, bordered with a highly stylized palmette and leaf meander on dark blue. Fine, sym.; ND in red, dark and medium blue, copper, ivory, corroded brown. Superior quality; good condition...
....Est. $15,000/20,000; sold for $16,100

Kurd Prayer Rug, East Anatolia (c. 1880, 3'3" × 4'6"). Stepped cochineal-dyed

Yürük Rug, East Anatolia, c. 1890, 4'6" × 7'6", $6,670. AUTHOR'S PHOTO

Kurd Prayer Rug, East Anatolia, c. 1880, 3'3" × 4'6", $3,220. AUTHOR'S PHOTO

crimson *mihrab* containing numerous geometric devices on a similarly ornamented blue-green field enclosed by four narrow borders with simple geometric repeats. Average, sym.; ND in cochineal crimson and madder red, medium blue, blue-green, gold, copper, ivory, brown. Good quality; fine condition. ....Est. $2,000/3,000; sold for $3,220

Yürük Rug, East Anatolia (dated 1871, 2'10″ × 6'11″). Brilliant red and blue squares contain bold polychrome cross- and diamond-shaped devices enclosed by a wide ivory border with a repeat of large latchhooked cruciform motifs. One row of very long brown hair (probably goat) crosses through the lustrous shaggy pile. Coarse, sym.; ND in red, dark and medium blue, blue-green, gold, ivory, brown. Very good quality; fine condition. ....Est. at $2,000/3,000; sold for $2,300

PERSIAN

QASHQAI

Although the rugs in this group can be ascribed to various subtribes in the Qashqai Confederacy of southwest Iran, for simplicity's sake I have chosen to follow the auction house policy of grouping them together. The

Qashqai Bags, Southwest Persia, c. 1900, each 1'10″ × 2', $1,100. PHOTO COURTESY OF SKINNER, INC.

Qashqai Rug, Southwest Persia, c. 1890, 4' × 5'6", $1,995. PHOTO COURTESY OF SKINNER, INC.

Qashqai are accomplished weavers, favoring rather densely patterned rugs distinguished by a wide range of jewel-like colors. There is considerable variation in weaving structures within this group; generally, however, the older the piece, the more likely it is for the warps and wefts to be wool.

Bags (c. 1900, each 1'10" × 2'). A hexagonal ivory medallion filled with polychrome floral motifs on a blossom-decorated medallion flanked by spandrels filled with geometrized shrubs, all within a floral meander border. Fine, prob. asym.; ND in red, gold, dark and medium blue, blue-green, ivory. Very good quality; good condition...Est. $700/900; sold for $1,100

Rug (late 19th century, 4' × 5'6"). Two large and two small skewed diamonds on a dark blue field closely packed with randomly placed polychrome diamonds, *boteh*, rosettes, and a few small animal forms; polychrome *boteh* march around a narrow red border. Average, prob. asym; ND in red, dark and medium blue, rust, gold, ivory and reddish brown. Good quality; fair condition...
....Est. $800/1,200; sold for $1,955

Runner (c. 1880, 3'7" × 10'4"). Flower-filled vases and a sprinkling of *boteh* and blossoms decorate the rich gold field of this cheerful rug. The salmon border has a repeat of latchhooked medallions. Average, prob. asym.; ND in red, blue, gold, salmon, green, ivory. Very good quality; good condition...
....Est. $3,500/4,500; sold for $4,025

KHAMSEH

The Khamseh confederation of five southwestern tribes lies to the west of the Qashqai Confederacy. According to one expert, the reds and blues of the Khamseh rugs are unusually intense and a sprightly bird motif, known as the *morgh*, or chicken design, is characteristic of the group.

Rug (late 19th century, 3'6" × 5'10"). I still regret not bidding on this delightful rug whose dark blue field has an overall pattern of blossoming plants and stylized trees within an ivory border with a repeat of well-drawn birds. Average, prob. asym.; ND in red, dark and medium blue, blue-green, gold, ivory. Very good quality; good condition......................................Est. $1,000/1,500; sold for $1,000

Khamseh Rug, Southwest Persia, c. 1890, 3'6" × 5'10", $1,000. PHOTO COURTESY OF SKINNER, INC.

Khamseh Rug, Southwest Persia, c. 1900, 5'9" × 9'4", $6,325. PHOTO
COURTESY OF SKINNER, INC.

Rug (c. 1900, 5′9″ × 9′4″). Although the size of this rug suggests a village origin, the motifs are typical of Khamseh tribal weaving: three joined dark blue medallions placed vertically on an ivory field, all densely packed with bird motifs, within three narrow borders. Average, prob. asym.; ND in red, dark and medium blue, blue-green, ivory, brown. Very good quality; good condition................Est. $1,200/1,500; sold for $6,325

AFSHAR

The inclusion of Afshar work among tribal weavings is complicated by the fact that many rugs made by Afshar weavers are in fact village workshop rugs, often of large size, influenced by designs originating in Kerman, south of which many Afsharis settled in the 19th century.

One curious but seldom mentioned characteristic of Afshar rugs is their tendency to approach the square. Many have decorative flat-woven ends; their wefts, usually double, are dyed orange, and alternate warps are depressed so as to produce a greater or lesser degree of ribbing on the back. Tribal Afshar

Afshar Rug, Southwest Persia, c. 1900, 3′ 5″ × 4′ 5″, $1,265. PHOTO COURTESY OF SKINNER, INC.

weaving is knotted symmetrically; Afshar village workshop rugs usually have asymmetrical knots.

Bag Face (early 20th century, 1'9" × 3'). Serrated leaves flank stepped polygons on a dark blue field bordered with a pretty polychrome blossom repeat on ivory. The tabs at the top of the bag face are decorated with weft-wrapped diamond-shaped patterns. Average, prob. sym.; ND in red, dark and medium blue, blue-green, olive, ivory, reddish brown. Very good quality; good condition...Est. $700/900; sold for $1,495

Rug (c. 1900, 3'5" × 4'5"). Eight rows of staggered *boteh* interspersed with a variety of filler motifs on a dark blue field, bordered with a flower and vine meander on ivory. Average, asym.; ND in dark and royal blue, blue-green, red, rust, ivory. Good quality; good condition............................Est. $700/900; sold for $1,265

Pair of Bags (late 19th century, 2'6" × 3'10"). Each bag face has six large *boteh* containing floral motifs on a dark blue field within a narrow ivory border with a stylized leaf meander. Average, asym.; ND in dark and light blue, blue-green, red, gold, ivory. Good quality; good condition. ....Est. $1,000/1,200; sold for $977.50

KURDISH

Kurdish groups, both weaving and nonweaving, live throughout the large area in northwest Iran known as Kurdistan, to the south in the vicinity of Kermanshah, and in the northeast above Khorasan. Some of the most famous old Persian rug names, like Senneh and Bidjar, belong to the distinctive products of long-settled Kurdish weavers.

The assignment of tribal Kurdish rugs to particular groups has just begun, but in general we are speaking of lustrous all-wool small or runner-size rugs, often heavy and shaggy, with edges double-overcast in dark brown wool. The tribal variety is typically somewhat misshapen but hard-wearing and boldly colored with rectilinear versions of a variety of medallion designs. A common bag face pattern is composed of polychrome interlocking diamonds.

Bag (last quarter 19th century, 1'8" × 1'10"). Hooked diamond-shaped devices within a polychrome diamond lattice characteristic of Jaff Kurd bag faces, enclosed by two borders with octagonal devices, and including a striking brocaded flat-woven back. Average, sym.; ND in dark and royal blue, blue-green, red, gold, green, ivory. Very good quality; fair condition. ....Est. at $300/400; sold for $460

Pair of Bags (late 19th century, each 1'4" × 1'6"). Each small bag has a single off-centered Memling gul on lustrous ivory further decorated with numerous small filler motifs. Appealingly "folky." Average, sym.; ND in dark and light blue, blue-green, red, apricot, ivory, brown. Very good quality; fair condition. ....
....Est. $700/900; sold for $1,092.50

Long Rug (early 20th century, 3'6" × 8'9"). The polychrome lattice of hooked diamonds usually seen on Jaff Kurd bags was knotted into this short runner and enclosed with three narrow floral meander borders. Average, sym.; ND in dark and light blue, blue-green, red, rose, gold, aubergine, ivory, corroded brown. Good quality; good condition...Est. $1,200/1,500; sold for $2,070

*Kurdish Long Rug,
Northwest Persia, c.
1910, 3'6" × 8'9",
$2,070.* PHOTO COUR-
TESY OF SKINNER, INC.

Paired Bags (late 19th century, 1'10" × 5'1"). Another example of the diamond-lattice pattern knotted in particularly lustrous wool, including the skirt decorated with stylized plant forms. Handsomely worked flat-woven backs. Average, sym.; ND in dark and royal blue, blue-green, red, aubergine, gold, ivory. Superior quality; fair condition..Est. $700/900; sold for $690

BALUCH (BALUCHI, BALOUCH, BELUCH)

The tribal assignment of the rugs known generically as Baluch (the term Baluchi refers properly to the language, not the people) presents many of the same difficulties as Kurdish weavings. Northeast Persia and western Afghanistan was home to the nomadic Baluch and related tribes for whom, when they settled in villages there, weaving became a source of income.

The classic Baluch rug is knotted asymmetrically of wonderfully silky wool in shades of red and blue and touches of white on a wool foundation with brown goat-hair edge finishes. On old examples, decorative flat-woven ends are seen more often than not. Camel's hair is often used for the ground of prayer rugs. A number of other tribal groups tend to be herded under the Baluch umbrella, and although their rugs often have format and pattern similarities, the structure and coloration can be quite different. The weaving of the nomadic Baluch in Baluchistan, a province of present-day Pakistan, is limited to flatweaves that are virtually unknown in the American market.

Bag Face (c. 1875, 2'4" × 2'7"). This early and elegant variation of a popular Baluch tribal pattern features an ivory-outlined star device within a quartered octagon on a dark blue ground with a variety of well-spaced stylized blossom and shrub forms, enclosed by an ivory border bearing a very stylized branched tree repeat. Fine, asym.; ND in dark, medium and light blue, rust, red, brownish aubergine, ivory. Superior quality; fair condition. ....
....Est. $1,500/1,800; sold for $1,725

Kurdish Bags, Northwest Persia, c. 1890, each 1'4" × 1'6", $1,092.50.
PHOTO COURTESY OF SKINNER, INC.

Kurdish Bags, Northwest Persia, c. 1890, 1′10″ × 5′1″, $690. PHOTO COURTESY OF SKINNER, INC.

Rug (c. 1875, 3′6″ × 6′). A diamond-shaped lattice encloses quatrefoil floral motifs bordered with a graceful Mina Khani–derived white flower and vine meander on madder rose. Average, sym.; ND in rose, cochineal crimson, rust, dark blue, ivory, corroded brown. Superior quality; fair condition...
....Est. $1,000/1,200; sold for $1,092.50

Bag Face (c. 1875, 2′2″ × 2′4″). Three rows of the Baluch birds coveted by collec-

Baluch Bag Face, Northeast Persia, c. 1875, 2' 4" × 2' 7",
$1,725. PHOTO COURTESY OF
SKINNER, INC.

Baluch Rug, Northeast Persia, c.
1875, 3' 6" × 6' 6", $1,092.50.
PHOTO COURTESY OF SKINNER, INC.

Baluch Saddle Cover, Northeast Persia, c. 1920, 2' × 3'2", $920. PHOTO
COURTESY OF SKINNER, INC.

tors topped by a fourth row of eight smaller birds, and enhanced by the subtle 3-D
effect courtesy of the corrosion of the cinnamon brown field. The ivory border has
the stylized branched tree repeat often seen on old Baluch bags. Very lustrous wool.
Fine, sym.; ND in dark blue, brick red, ivory, corroded brown. Superior quality; fair
condition. (See color section.) ....Est. $3,000/4,000; sold for $4,600

Rug (late 19th century, 2'5" × 4'). Small *boteh* march up narrow vertical stripes
separated by a barberpole stripe, all within a simple "S" repeat decorated border.
Close inspection of the back of this appealing tribal piece revealed that the original
color of the ivory wool on the face was magenta-pink. Average, prob. asym.; ND in
dark blue, pale gold, rust, light brown, SD in fugitive magenta faded to pink. Good
quality; good condition..Est. $500/700; sold for $977.50.

Saddle Cover (1st quarter 20th century, 2' × 3'2"). Four Turkoman-style octagonal guls on a dark blue field with ivory sawtooth edgings and "running dog"
border. Average, asym.; ND in dark blue, red, aubergine, ivory. Good quality; good
condition. ....Est. $700/900; sold for $920

OTHER PERSIAN TRIBAL RUGS

Long Rug, Northwest Persia (late 19th century, 2'7" × 8'). Rows of widely spaced,
crudely drawn small animals and birds interspersed with occasional filler motifs
and two human figures on a heavily abrashed rust to dark red ground, bordered with
a star repeat on ivory. Average, prob. sym.; ND in rust, red, dark blue, blue-green,
gold, ivory, black. Good quality; fair condition..
....Est. $1,500/2,000; sold for $2,300

Veramin Bag Face, North Persia (early 20th century, 1'2" × 3'2"). Of the half-
dozen or so Veramin bag faces seen at auction in 1994–95, this example was the
standout. The single large Turkoman-style gul, which is characteristic of these
pieces, is flanked by small polychrome octagons that glow against a lustrous dark
blue field bordered by star-centered octagons, all within a minor border of pre-

cisely drawn interlocking polychrome triangles. Fine, prob. sym.; ND in dark and light blue, blue-green, red, apricot, ivory, reddish brown. Superior quality; good condition. ....Est. $600/800; sold for $977.50

Gabbeh, Southwest Persia (early 20th century, 4'4" × 6'). This coarsely woven and lushly piled traditional rug was probably made by a Qashqai weaver. All but unknown in the West until about 20 years ago, the bold geometric patterns and rich saturated colors of the best gabbehs recommend them to collectors of tribal art. In this example, concentric stepped diamond medallions are flanked by simply drawn human figures, one in each gold spandrel, and enclosed by three narrow borders: two of them interlocking triangle repeats and one arrowhead repeat on ivory. Coarse, prob. asym.; ND in dark blue, blue-green, red, gold, ivory. Very good quality; fine condition. ....Est. $1,500/1,800; sold for $2,070

TURKOMAN

Among the Turkoman tribes, weaving is a female occupation that relies on the weaver's ability to recall from memory the knotting sequence required to translate their sometimes elaborate tribal patterns into rugs and domestic trappings. Comparisons are often drawn between Turkoman motifs and those on very old Turkish carpets, which is hardly surprising given the tribes' Turkic origin on far Asian steppes. Despite their similarities of origin and culture, however, the weaving done by the tribes differs significantly from one to another in structure, form, and coloration, although to the uninitiated they may seem en masse to be a veritable sea of red.

It is virtually impossible to attach exact dates to Turkoman rugs made before 1880, when synthetic dyes began to be used by Turkoman weavers. No records were kept, and the designs changed very slowly over a long period of time. For that reason ranking Turkoman weavings in order of age and tribal type depends almost entirely on a determination of the natural dyestuffs and color-affecting mordants used by the various tribal groups and the gradual alterations in the forms and arrangements of the traditional motifs. (See the chapter on sizes, formats, and motifs for further information.)

TEKKE, WEST TURKESTAN

The acclaimed red Bokhara is the trade name for Tekke tribal rugs, the best known of the Turkoman weavings. Synthetic dyes played havoc here as elsewhere in the late 19th century, but the best Tekke rugs and bags boast a glowing madder red and velvety handle. The colors used are reds varying from ruby to liver, blues, ivory, green, brown, and some yellow; occasionally cochineal-dyed silk is used for special details. The asymmetrical knotting is the finest of the Turkoman group; the foundation is wool; the back is flat, and the pile is low.

*Long Rug, Northwest Persia, c. 1890,
2'7" × 8', $2,300.* PHOTO COURTESY OF
SKINNER, INC.

Door Surround *(Kapunuk)*; (early 19th century, 3'2" × 3'9"). Although cut and pieced, the velvety pile and precise drawing of the curled leaf motif on this rare early piece energized the bidding of dealers and collectors. Fine, asym.; ND in liver and brick red, dark blue, ivory. Superior quality, fair condition, with the above-noted reservation...Est. $6,000/8,000; sold for $12,650

Bag Face *(Mafrash)*; (early 19th century, 11" × 2'3"). *Ashik* guls and stylized floral elements in two large squares knotted in ivory cotton within a liver-red border of stylized ascending trees and enclosed by another border of connected geometric devices on ivory cotton surrounded by a strip of plushy reddish brown wool. Fine, asym.; ND in brick red, red-brown, dark blue, blue-green, brownish yellow, smoked ivory. Superior quality; fair condition. ....
....Est. $7,000/9,000; sold for $8,050

Bag Face *(Chuval)* fragment; (c. 1875, 1'8" × 3'5"). The tightly woven glowing mahogany pile is decorated with a flattened version of the *marguls* and the boxed-

Veramin Bag Face, North Persia, c. 1910, 1'2" × 3'2", $977.50. PHOTO
COURTESY OF SKINNER, INC.

Gabbeh, Southwest Persia, c. 1910, 4'4" × 6', $2,070. PHOTO COURTESY
OF SKINNER, INC.

Tekke Kapunuk, *West Turkestan, c. 1840, 3′2″ × 3′9″, $12,650.* PHOTO
COURTESY OF SKINNER, INC.

Tekke Mafrash, *West Turkestan, c. 1840, 11″ × 2′3″, $8,050.* PHOTO
COURTESY OF SKINNER, INC.

Tekke Chuval, *West Turkestan, c. 1875, 1′8″ × 3′5″, $2,300.* PHOTO COURTESY OF CHRISTIE'S

star minor gul associated with Salor weaving, within a latchhooked rosette border. Fine, asym.; ND in bright brownish-red, dark blue, ivory, crimson cochineal-dyed silk. Superior quality; fair condition.....................Est. $2,000/2,500; sold for $2,300

YOMUD (YOMUT), WEST TURKESTAN

Yomud weaving displays a greater variety of motifs and bolder coloration than other tribal work, and since it is also one of the largest and most diverse groups, a wider choice of their old and antique rugs, bags, animal trappings, etc., is usually available on the market. Early Yomud work may have either symmetric or asymmetric knots, sometimes both, on a wool foundation; the density is finer than the robust look of the firm-handled pieces would lead one to expect. The Yomud red varies from brick to brown to a distinctive purple-brown. White, yellow, turquoise, green, brown, and a range of blues were generously used.

Tent Pole Cover *(Okbash)*; (late 19th century, 1′9″ × 2′). Serrated polychrome zigzags within a red reciprocal trefoil border. Fine, asym.; ND in dark blue, red, green, ivory. Good quality; good condition...........Est. $800/1,200; sold for $546.25

Camel Trapping *(Asmalyk)*; (last quarter 19th century, 2'7" × 4'2"). *Ashik* gul variants within a variegated diamond lattice, with a compressed version of the same lattice on the dark blue-green border. Average, asym.; ND in red, dark blue, blue-green, ivory, brown. Very good quality; good condition. ....Est. $1,000/1,200; sold for $2,185

Main Carpet (c. 1870, approx. 5' × 10'). Eleven rows of three precisely drawn *Tauk Nuska* guls on a lustrous brownish red field with an unusual minor gul, knotted in a beautiful robin's egg blue, that is reminiscent of the serrated-leaf "C" guls seen on very early Yomud carpets. The wide ivory-grounded "boat" borders on each side are connected top and bottom by narrow *Ashik* gul borders; the skirts are missing. Fine, asym.; ND in brick red, brown-red, dark, medium and light blue, pale yellow, ivory, brown. Superior quality; good condition. (See color section.).....
....Dealer rug, $15,000

Main Carpet (late 19th century, 6' × 9'9"). Staggered rows of *Dyrnak* guls on an aubergine field bordered with a stylized "Turkoman line" vine and blossom meander on ivory. "Pole tree" columns decorate the pile skirts. Fine, asym.; ND in dark and royal blue, blue-green, red, apricot, aubergine, ivory. Good quality; good condition. ....Est. $3,000/4,000; sold for $3,450

Main Carpet, fragment (c. 1850, 4'8" × 5'8"). Precisely drawn *Dyrnak* guls in staggered rows on an evenly worn aubergine ground, bordered with an elegant version of the "boat" border motif on ivory. Fine, asym.; ND in dark and light blue, blue-green, red, gold, ivory. Superior quality; good condition. ....
....Est. $200/400; sold for $632.50

SALOR, WEST/CENTRAL TURKESTAN

The Salor is the oldest and most respected of the Turkoman tribes; the ornamentation of its weaving is refined, elegantly spaced, and beautifully drawn. Although a wide range of colors was used in combination with the dominant clear red, Salor weavers employed them with much less abandon than did the Yomud. The finest pieces often include areas of cochineal-dyed silk. Salor goods are knotted asymmetrically on a wool foundation almost as finely as Tekke work; the back has a ribbed look due to the strong depression of alternate warps.

Bag Face *(Torba)*; (late 19th century, 1'4" × 3'8"). The classic tribal *Kejebe* design enclosed by a boxed geometric repeat and bordered in plain red. Fine, asym.; ND in madder red, crimson cochineal-dyed silk, dark blue, blue-green, ivory. Very good quality; fine condition...Est. $1,500/1,800; sold for $2,760

Door Rug *(Ensi* or *Engsi)*; (c. 1850, 4'5" × 6'5"). One of only eight known of this format, this one shares the dark purple-brown field coloration and the use of starred octagons as a border motif of four of the other examples. Fine, asym.; ND in red, purple-brown, dark and light blue, rust, dark green, dull yellow, ivory, brown and crimson cochineal-dyed silk. Superior quality; fine condition....................................
....Est. $80,000/120,000; sold for $90,500

Main Carpet, mounted fragment (early/mid 19th century, 1' × 1'). A single, elegant main carpet gul on a glowing red field. Fine, asym.; ND in red, dark and light blue, aubergine, ivory and crimson cochineal-dyed silk. ....
....Est. $400/600; sold for $546.25

Yomud Okbash,
West Turkestan,
c. 1890, 1'9" ×
2', $546.25.
PHOTO COURTESY
OF SKINNER, INC.

Yomud Asmalyk, *West Turkestan, c. 1885, 2'7" × 4'2", $2,185.* PHOTO
COURTESY OF SKINNER, INC.

Salor Carpet Fragment, Central Turkestan, c. 1840, 1' × 1', $546.25.
PHOTO COURTESY OF SKINNER, INC.

ERSARI

The sturdy red rugs with the large so-called elephant's-foot gul are known in the trade as Afghan rugs and are woven by the Ersari, the largest of the Turkoman tribes, who have settled for the most part in Afghanistan. Although the classic brown-red "Afghan" is a coarsely knotted workhorse rug characterized by huge, closely spaced guls, the Beshir, a settled sub-tribe, weave rugs of considerably more sophistication, which may be found in the rustic rug category.

The red ground of old Ersari work is warm and clear; blues, turquoise, coral orange, brown, white, and yellow complete the color range. The hard-wearing pile is knotted asymmetrically on a wool foundation; dark brown goat hair is used for the side finishes. Maroon-red used as a ground color is an indicator of post–World War II manufacture.

Beshir Rug, Southeast Turkestan (c. 1875, 4'1" × 4'11"). Thirteen rows of nine irregularly spaced, alternately faced *boteh* on a red field within a red barberpole-edged border containing crudely drawn and spaced smaller *boteh*. Average, asym.; ND in dark and medium blue, red, rose, gold, plum, ivory. Very good quality; fair condition. ....Est. $10,000/12,000; sold for $11,500

Door Rug *(Ensi* or *Engsi)* West Turkestan (late 19th century, 4'9" × 6'6"). The rust red field is divided by a column of stylized shrub forms bisected in turn by three rows of candelabra-like plant motifs, which also decorate the four quarters of the field. There is an inner border of boxed hexagons, a main border of geometric

Ersari Ensi, *West Turkestan, c. 1890, 4'9" × 6'6", $1,495.* PHOTO COURTESY OF SKINNER, INC.

devices, and a narrow flowering-vine meander outer border. Average, asym.; ND in dark blue, rust red, apricot, ivory. Good quality; good condition. ....
....Est. $1,500/2,000; sold for $1,495

Bag Face *(Mafrash)* Southeast Turkestan (c. 1880, 1'9" × 2'9"). A largely open, richly saturated red field with an unusual design of bold ivory-bordered serrated figures flanked by lightninglike zigzags. Fine, asym.; ND in red, dark blue, blue-green, rust, yellow, brown. Superior quality; fair condition. ....
....Est. $7,000/8,000; sold for $8,050

CHODOR, WEST TURKESTAN

Very old Chodor pieces have a characteristic purple-brown ground color and a distinctive main gul. The wool warps are dark brown; the knots, asymmetrical; and the wefts either wool or cotton. The density is moderately fine. Other colors used are clear red, salmon, dark brown, blues, green, yellow, and white. Old Chodor work is not as commonly available as Ersari, Tekke, and Yomud.

Bag Face *(Chuval)*; (last quarter 19th century, 2′6″ × 3′7″). A characteristic jagged lattice encloses polychrome *Ertmen* guls on an aubergine field bordered by a *kotchak* border and ending in an ornamented skirt. Fine, asym.; ND in red, dark blue, blue-green, aubergine, ivory. Good quality; fair condition. ....
....Est. $800/1,200; sold for $1,150

Chodor Chuval, *West Turkestan, c. 1885, 2′6″ × 3′7″, $1,150.* PHOTO COURTESY OF SKINNER, INC.

RUSTIC RUGS, 1800–1925

The vast majority of rugs of collectible interest fall into this category, but the assignment of particular rugs to it is accompanied by a good bit of collector push and pull.

The patterns of commercial carpets, adapted from traditional designs by professional artists, may or may not have anything in common with the traditions of the weavers employed to produce them. Conversely, the forms seen on tribal rugs were chosen from a reservoir of motifs that evolved within a kinship unit and passed through the generations from mother to daughter.

The best commercial carpets, substantial numbers of which were made on village looms, are both skillfully woven and highly decorative; so too are the finest tribal weavings, which in addition have been accorded the status of icons. This being the case, it is hardly surprising that honest rustic rugs of respectable age are increasingly being borne up on the wings of collector—and dealer—wishful thinking into the rarefied realm of tribal art. However, although the weavers of these rugs were indeed in many cases settled members of formerly nomadic tribes, design purity on a village level is always threatened with dilution by "foreign" influences, perhaps introduced via intertribal marriages, perhaps seen and admired on market days on products from other villages.

Commercial carpets are contract-woven for profit; the old rustic rugs being collected today were—although made in a domestic setting and certainly used there—also a significant source of family income. Originality was neither expected nor rewarded, but few weavers could resist enlivening the traditional patterns with personal touches: an unusual juxtaposition of colors, a borrowed field motif adapted for a border repeat, or a traditional medallion skewed in an untraditional way. Whatever it might be, it allowed the weaver of a completed rug the satisfaction of saying, if only to herself: *this is mine*.

Toward the end of the 19th century the demands of merchants for designs of proven salability tended to discourage woven expressions of creative play; accordingly, rugs of that era whose color and choice and spacing of motifs are deemed superior to an otherwise look-alike crowd are sometimes claimed to be dowry pieces, the prideful weaving of which was never affected by economic considerations. Romantic notions of this sort abound in the rug world and in fact are sometimes justified, but budding collectors would be well advised to keep several grains of salt always at the ready.

Please bear in mind as you read through these listings that some collectors value condition much more highly than others do. Put another way, although a wonderful rug in wonderful condition invariably commands a high price, a good rug in wonderful condition often sells for more than a wonderful rug in fair condition.

TURKISH RUGS

Collectors accustomed to the coloration of Persian and Turkoman rugs are sometimes slow to cultivate a taste for Turkish village rugs, but once acquired it often takes over.

Except for Yağcibedir and some Bergama rugs limited to an almost exclusive use of red, dark blue, and white, Turkish rug colors are generally as vivid as those seen on Caucasians, but the palette is quite different. The reds are hotter—except for an exception mentioned later—and the greens more springlike. Salmon and bright copper are favored over mahogany and plum; the lighter shades of blue are used more often than the dark shades, and Turkish dyers excel at purple-toned colors ranging from aubergine to a clear, limpid lavender. Late-19th-century examples often have a blue-toned cochineal red—rugs made in Kirşehir, for example—of a brighter shade than that found in Persian Kermans.

As one proceeds from west to east in Turkey, the colors take on a browner tone, perhaps because of the greater abundance of brown-fleeced sheep in the flocks kept by the seminomadic Kurdish peoples who inhabit those wilder regions. According to Werner Brüggemann and Harald Böhmer, authors of *Rugs of the Peasants and Nomads of Anatolia*, "All Anatolian rugs show red and blue . . . [but] as far as surface area is concerned, yellow is the outstanding colour in Central Anatolia." They go on to say that only half of the East Anatolian rugs they surveyed contained all three primary colors, and not one of them contained all three of the secondary colors: violet, green, and orange. In West Anatolia, on the other hand, "10% . . . contain all three secondary colours, whereas this figure is 60% for Central Anatolia."

The typical honest, sturdy Turkish village rug is symmetrically knotted on a wool foundation with a density that rarely exceeds 60 knots per square inch. The edges consist of from two to four bundles of warps secured and protected by an overcasting with the weft threads alone or strengthened by a second overcasting with a yarn that may or may not match the weft. The plain-woven band used as an end finish is usually red and itself ends in a simple fringe. It may be ornamented with motifs meant to identify the weaver or to ward off the evil eye or both.

In this section we will be looking at a selection of rustic rugs made in western and central Turkey. In recent years, good examples have begun to command prices worthy of their untutored charm and graphic power. If I lived in a far northern clime deprived of winter sunlight, I would save my pennies to buy one if only to remind me of the colors of summer during the long drear days of winter.

BERGAMA, WEST ANATOLIA

Weaving has been carried on here near the Aegean Sea for centuries, and rugs made in the 19th and early 20th centuries have much in common with earlier prototypes. The larger and more colorful rugs woven in the nearby stone villages of the Yuntdag and near Ayvacik are often labeled by the trade and auction houses as Bergama, although they are quite different in both look and handle. A weaving cooperative begun ten years ago to reintroduce the use of vegetable dyes and hand-spun wool has sparked a revival of quality weaving in the entire area. Some of these projects are described in the chapter on contemporary collectibles.

Rug (c. 1880, 4'8" × 6'2"). A pair of latchhooked-lobed gold octagons derived from 16th-century "Holbein" carpets and flanked by latchhooked triangles on a plum-brown ground. Across one end are the gabled boxes more commonly seen on yastiks; the other end, which is dissimilar, is partially missing. The border is a stylized blossom-centered four-leaf cluster repeat on ivory. Average, sym.; ND in red, medium blue, gold, gray-green (indiosulphonic?), ivory, corroded brown. Very good quality; fair condition. ....Est. $4,000/6,000; sold for $6,037

Prayer Rug (c. 1875, 3'4" × 3'7"). Village version of the classic Ladik prayer rug format consisting of simple geometrized columns on ivory and stylized tulips on blue, within a polychrome border repeat of diagonal bars. Average, sym.; ND in red, coral, dark blue, gold, green, ivory, and corroded browns. Very good quality; good condition. ....Est. $3,000/5,000; sold for $6,900

Rug (last quarter 19th century, 4' × 4'7"). Evenly spaced small polychrome octagons on a stepped coral ground flanked by red spandrels. The coral main border has a repeat of octagons and star figures and is enclosed by star-centered polychrome diagonals. Average, sym.; ND in red, coral, blue, blue-green, aubergine, ivory, corroded brown. Good quality; good condition...
....Est. $1,000/1,200; sold for $1,495

KIRŞEHIR, CENTRAL ANATOLIA

In the latter 19th century, the Kirşehir weaving district produced rugs, prayer rugs, *yastiks*, and some runners with a distinctive palette of light turquoise blue, cochineal-dyed crimson, and a spring green that was also chosen for the wool used to finish the double selvages. A lobed diamond-shaped medallion is characteristic of this group of weavings, as are the detailed *lappets* on the ends of the *yastik* described below.

Yastik (last quarter 19th century, 1'9" × 2'6"). Large turquoise-blue medallion within a hexagon flanked by quartered diamonds on a rose red field. The ivory border has a floral repeat; polychrome lappets decorate the ends. Average, sym.;

Bergama Rug, West Anatolia, c. 1885, 4' × 4'7", $1,495. PHOTO COURTESY OF SKINNER, INC.

ND in turquoise blue, rose red, gold, aubergine, light olive green, corroded black. Very good quality; fair condition. ....Est. $800/1,200; sold for $1,380

Prayer Rug (second half 19th century, 4'8" × 6'4"). Stepped crimson *mihrab* beneath a cloud-band traversed cross panel, all within numerous borders with star, flower, and "S" repeats. Average, sym.; ND in red, cochineal-dyed crimson, light turquoise blue, blue-green, gold, aubergine, black. Good quality; good condition. ...
....Est. $2,000/2,500; sold for $3,565

KONYA

The 13th-century Seljuk rugs found in the Central Anatolian Konya mosques suggest a weaving tradition of greater antiquity than that of any other area in Turkey. For that reason, perhaps, the Konya name is a conveniently prestigious one to attach to old rugs made in nearby towns as well. The prayer rug format is often seen; green and gold are used with mellow reds to great effect. Boldly patterned runners were also made in this area, as were pile pillow covers known as *yastiks*, which, when removed from their backing, are used as decorative mats. The row of roofed boxes known as *lappets*, commonly seen along the ends of *yastiks*, were meant to indicate the thickness of the pillow within; similar rows at the ends of some Turkish rugs are purely ornamental.

Yastik (last quarter 19th century, 1′8″ × 2′6″). A single bold medallion on an ivory ground bordered with a highly stylized flower and leaf meander. Average, sym.; ND in red, royal blue, blue-green, gold, violet, corroded aubergine. Very good quality; good condition. ....Est. $2,000/2,500; sold for $2,300

Prayer Rug (third quarter 19th century, 3′7″ × 4′4″). A simple red *mihrab* on a blue ground, both with stylized ascending flowering branches, enclosed in an ivory border with a well-drawn polychrome geometric repeat within two narrow polychrome geometric guards. Average, sym.; ND in dark and medium blue, blue-green, red, apricot, gold, ivory, corroded browns. Very good quality; good condition. ....Est. $4,000/6,000; sold for $5,175

Rug (c. 1880, 3′4″ × 6′7″). Twelve rows of three polychrome latchhooked lozenges on an ivory ground within a similarly decorated abrashed gold border

Konya Yastik, Central Anatolia, c. 1885, 1′8″ × 2′6″, $2,300. PHOTO COURTESY OF SKINNER, INC.

edged with two narrow guards with a stylized polychrome blossom repeat. Average, sym.; ND in dark and medium blue, red, rose, pale yellow, dull gold, tan, corroded brown. Very good quality; good condition. ....
....Est. $6,000/8,000; sold for $8,625

Runner (c. 1875, 3'9" × 11'3"). A yellow field with pairs of well-spaced polychrome octagons containing "Memling" guls, all in richly saturated colors. The ivory border has a repeat of polychrome triangle-armed small squares. Average, sym.; ND in yellow, red, medium blue, green, purple, ivory, corroded browns. Superior quality; good condition. ....Est. $5,000/7,000; sold for $10,350

Prayer Rug (second half 19th century, 3'6" × 5'). In this vividly colored format based on an earlier court design, the columns have been reduced to stubs and the row of floral figures eliminated. The red *mihrab*, which has an inner border scalloped and hooked in blue and gold, is ornamented with a branched flowering plant. The ochre border has a latchhooked Memling gul and rosette repeat, and is enclosed by simple zigzag guards. Average, sym.; ND in medium blue, red, abrashed olive green, deep gold, aubergine, ivory. Very good quality, good condition. (See color section.)...Est. $7,000/9,000; sold for $8,050

LADIK, CENTRAL ANATOLIA

Another well-known village prayer rug format is associated with the town of Ladik in Central Anatolia north of Konya. These rather long and narrow small rugs with their distinguishing row of stiffly erect tulips have been made since at least the 18th century. On early examples a panel of tulips crosses above the *mihrab* and spandrels; on later rugs the tulips bloom upside down in a panel crossing below the niche. The fields of early Ladiks are apt to be an unornamented rich, glowing red. Later, filler motifs were added to fields, spandrels, and cross-panels, and the well-spaced early rosette-and-vine borders became squashed and poorly resolved at the corners.

Prayer Rug (1st half 19th century, 4'8" × 6'4"). An open rusty red, ivory stepped *mihrab* beneath a row of tulips within a highly stylized leaf and blossom meander on ivory. Fine, sym.; ND in red, blue, pale yellow, green, ivory. Very good quality; poor condition..Est. $3,500/4,000; sold for $5,525

MELAS, SOUTHWEST ANATOLIA

The rugs associated with this Aegean town have a prayer rug format featuring a rather narrow *mihrab*, usually red, with a broad diamond head nipped in at the neck. Palmettes decorate ivory spandrels, and the broad gold borders bear stylized palmettes together with leaf and flower figures. Good examples sparkle with well-balanced color.

Prayer Rug (c. 1875, 3'11" × 4'10"). A brick red, ivory-edged *mihrab* decorated with two finely drawn diamonds beneath a floral ornamented ivory arch within a wide, awkwardly resolved yellow border with a stylized flowering leaf cluster repeat, and enclosed by star-blossom repeats on ivory guards. Average, sym.; ND in red, medium blue, gold, green, aubergine, corroded brown. Very good quality; good condition. ....Est. $3,000/4,000; sold for $8,050

CAUCASIAN RUGS

The scatter, prayer, and area rugs made in the Caucasus in the 19th and early 20th centuries have an enduring appeal. Although woven largely for export sale, their striking designs and vivid coloration symbolize for many collectors mythic origins rooted in semibarbarism. The truth is a good deal less extravagant. Most Caucasian patterns have links to Persian, Turkoman, and Far Eastern designs, as typified by those seen in the monumental 17th- and 18th-century Caucasian carpets whose size stamps them as workshop productions.

Caucasian rugs have no need of romantic myths to bolster their vitality, and their vegetable dyes need not be brewed in mountain fastnesses to be beautiful. They are generally divided into two main classes. The first, exemplified by South Caucasian Kazaks, Gendjes, and Moghans, is a symmetrically and coarsely knotted wool fabric with a medium to long pile. Large-scale motifs dominate relatively open fields, which allow blocks of color to be boldly juxtaposed. The second group, exemplified by Eastern Caucasian Shirvans and the Northeastern Kubas, has densely packed short pile, also symmetrically knotted; finely spun yarns; and fields covered more often than not with elaborate small-scale ornamentation. Think of the first type as firecrackers; the second, sparklers.

The place names attached by the trade to the various types of Caucasian rugs don't have a great deal to do with where they were actually made, but this is not a forum suitable for pursuing the subject. Should you decide to collect within this group, reports on the ongoing research concerning Caucasian attributions will be found in *Hali* and *Oriental Rug Review*. Here, the rugs will be listed under the names familiar to most dealers, auction houses, and collectors and under which they are indexed in most currently available books. One caution: Because Caucasian designs are so distinctive, it is tempting to assign rugs an attribution on the basis of their design alone; as always, however, structure is the final arbiter.

LONG-PILED, COARSELY KNOTTED CAUCASIANS

Kazak

Bordjalou, Borjalu, Southwest Caucasus. Vertically arranged, latch-hooked medallions usually dominate the fields of these long-piled, almost shaggy rugs, in which a lavish use of ivory sets off the vivid reds, blues, and golds. Latchhooked figures are also used in the wide primary borders. Other Bordjalou field designs are often accompanied by a main border bearing a reciprocal trefoil motif in ivory and brown.

Rug (c. 1875, 4′10″ × 8′2″). Small randomly placed starlike motifs enliven the upper third of a narrow rich field within bold latchhooked polychrome pyramids on a wide ivory main border. The abrashed brown guards have a polychrome starred

Bordjalou Kazak Rug, Southwest Caucasus, c. 1885, 4' 4" × 6' 9", $8,050. PHOTO COURTESY OF SKINNER, INC.

Bordjalou Kazak Rug, Southwest Caucasus, c. 1860, 4' 11" × 9' 1", $4,600. PHOTO COURTESY OF CHRISTIE'S

repeat. Average, sym.; ND in red, dark and medium blue, blue-green, gold, salmon, ivory, corroded brown. Superior quality; good condition. ....
....Est. $6,000/8,000; sold for $17,825

Rug (last quarter 19th century, 4′4″ × 6′9″). Three latchhooked diamonds placed vertically on a narrow red reserve edged in bright gold and bordered with bold latchhooked green-red and slate blue triangles on ivory within an outer border of a reciprocal trefoil repeat on slate blue. Average, sym.; ND in dark and slate blue, red, green, gold, ivory, corroded brown. Very good quality; good condition.............
....Est. $8,000/10,000; sold for $8,050

Rug (mid 19th century, 4′11″ × 9′1″). Within a particularly felicitous brown and ivory reciprocal trefoil border is a red and blue cruciform medallion flanked by Akstafa birds, two horizontal rows of lozenge-shaped shields and numerous evenly spaced geometric fillers on a worn red ground. Average, sym.; ND in red, medium blue, aubergine, gold, ivory, corroded brown. Superior quality; fair to poor condition...Est. $4,000/6,000; sold for $4,600

Chelaberd Karabagh (Eagle, Sunburst), Southwest Caucasus Two, sometimes three, large striking medallions derived from an early Persian floral-based palmette motif dominate this design, which was mentioned in a 1907 OCM catalog as "a variety of modern rug . . . being made by Tartars in the province of Kazak." The ground color is usually red, occasionally blue.

Rug (late 19th century, 4′6″ × 6′8″). Two flower-ornamented cruciforms within ivory "sunbursts" on a red ground with a scattering of small geometric fillers,

Eagle Kazak (Karabagh), South Caucasus, c. 1875, 6′9″ × 4′5″. PHOTO COURTESY OF GROGAN & COMPANY

bordered with a stylized flower meander. (Similar to photo.) Average, sym.; ND in red, dark and medium blue, gold, ivory, corroded browns. Very good quality; good condition. ....Est. $5,000/7,000; sold for $10,925

Rug (last quarter 19th century, 4'7" × 6'11"). A single flower-ornamented cruciform within an ivory "sunburst" flanked top and bottom with large stylized curved leaves on a red ground enlivened with blossom clusters, branched tree forms, and animal figures. The ivory border has a graceful running dog motif. Average, sym.; ND in red, dark, medium, and royal blue, gold, green, ivory, corroded browns. Superior quality; good condition. ....Est. $10,000/15,000; sold for $13,800

Rug (early 19th century, 4'11" × 5'10"). Distinguished by the precise drawing of its design elements, centered on the rare blue ground of this almost square rug is a single flower-ornamented ivory "sunburst" cruciform flanked top and bottom with bold stylized plant and palmette figures. A narrow flower meander border is guarded by an unusual, highly geometrized and well-spaced pair of rosette and leaf repeats on ivory. Average, sym.; ND in red, medium and light blue, blue-green, gold, ivory, dark brown. Superior quality; fair-poor condition..................................
....Est. $20,000/30,000; sold for $17,250

Karachov, Karachopt, Karachopf, Southwest Caucasus. This format of one large central rectilinear medallion with two pairs of similar, smaller medallions above and below is seen on early Anatolian carpets. The field's filler motifs and border designs vary from rug to rug. Collectors prize the wonderful color, balance, and texture of the best examples.

Rug (c. 1850, 6'6" × 7'8"). A variation on the standard format described above, the red field contains plain and latchhooked boxed figures evenly spaced around a central blue-grounded square with a large ivory octagon containing a latchhooked red rectangle and two geometric device–filled squares. The ivory border contains a bold, highly stylized leafy vine meander. Average, sym.; ND in red, dark and medium blue, blue-green, gold, mustard, ivory, corroded black. Very good quality; fine condition. (See color section.) ....Est. $6,000/8,000; sold for $13,800

Rug (c. 1850, 5'11" × 7'2"). An ivory octagon on a red square whose corners are filled with small diamonds, all on a dark slate blue ground and flanked with star-filled, latchhooked ivory boxes and other smaller geometric devices. Polychrome shieldlike palmettes are used as a repeat motif on the ivory main border. The colors lack the saturated richness preferred by collectors. Average, sym.; ND in red, dark blue, blue-green, mustard, ivory, corroded black. Very good quality; fair condition. ....Est. $7,000/10,000; sold for $8,050

Lori Pambak, Southwest Caucasus. A hexagon-enclosed cruciform medallion, whose horizontal members resemble tulip blossoms, is displayed in threes, twos, or singly on a field that otherwise is usually lacking in ornamentation. The proportions of the medallion differ from rug to rug: when well drawn it can be elegant; too often it is ill-defined and squat.

Rug (late 19th century, 5'4" × 6'8"). On a red field, a somewhat compressed rendering of the latchhooked central medallion and its two pendant minor medallions, surrounded in this example by a scattering of geometric devices within a highly

Lori Pambak Kazak Rug, Southwest Caucasus, c. 1890, 5'4" × 6'8",
$8,050. PHOTO COURTESY OF SKINNER, INC.

stylized leaf and flower meander on ivory. Average, sym.; ND in red, dark and light
blue, blue-green, gold, reddish brown, ivory. Good quality; fair condition................
....Est. $2,000/3,000; sold for $8,050

Rug (late 19th century, 6'1" × 9'4"). This late but handsome example boasts a
well-drawn and proportioned green cruciform within an ivory, blue-latchhooked
octagon flanked by polychrome pendants on a red ground enlivened by evenly
spaced polychrome geometric devices. The four narrow borders include a stylized
leaf and flower meander on ivory. Average, sym.; ND in dark, medium and light
blue, rich blue-green, red, gold, ivory. Superior quality; fine condition.....................
....Est. $15,000/20,000; sold for $19,550

Pinwheel, Southwest Caucasus. The so-called pinwheel motif can be
traced to two possible sources: one is the stylized flower-and-leaf motif

seen in many variations on many rugs over the centuries; the other is a 15th-century Iznik tile design adapted as a textile pattern on early rugs. It is usually centered with a rosette of contrasting color and flanked by serrated-leaf diagonals. Prime examples command high prices; average examples in very good condition also do well.

Rug (early 19th century, 6′ × 9′). On a red ground with a scattering of animal and human figures is a vertical row of large blue "pinwheels" filled with gold rosettes and other geometric devices, flanked by stylized leaves and outer rows of white-rosette centered smaller pinwheels. Interlocking polychrome triangle minor borders guard the ivory main border, which has a diamond and latchhook repeat. Average, sym.; ND in red, dark and medium blue, green, gold, ivory. Very good quality; poor condition. ....Est. $10,000/12,000; sold for $8,912.50

Rug (c. 1900, 6′3″ × 9′6″). Although a late example of the type, the saturated colors, near mint condition, and the handsome, well-balanced pair of reciprocal tre-foil borders—brown on ivory and olive green on red—no doubt energized the bidding. Average, sym,; ND in red, royal blue, olive green, gold, ivory, corroded brown. Very good quality; fine condition.......Est. $10,000/15,000; sold for $15,525

Sewan, Southwest Caucasus. This very large shieldlike, keyhole-shaped medallion, another borrowing from the Turkic design pool, is lent delicacy in some versions by snowflakelike dots of white or gold on a red or green field.

Rug (late 19th century, 5′4″ × 7′11″). In this example the large ivory-edged shield has an inner shield of green and a gabled red center medallion with latchhooked pendants on a red field with poled curved tree branches. Brown and ivory reciprocal trefoil minor borders guard an atypical royal blue main border bearing a poly-chrome leaf-cluster repeat. Average, sym.; ND in red, royal blue, blue-green, green, gold, ivory, corroded brown. Very good quality; fine condition................................
....Est. $15,000/25,000; sold for $21,850

Tree, East Caucasus. Branched trees-of-life in blue and ivory are arranged freely on what is usually a red ground. Sometimes the trees are the major design figure; in Gendje variations they are often used to fill the space around a vertical row of medallions. Although not as colorful as most rugs in this group, good examples have the same appeal as the Kurdish willow and cypress tree carpets.

Rug (1st half of 19th century, 2′6″ × 7′5″). Three rows of two well-drawn and spaced stylized trees, alternately dark blue and ivory, on a worn red field divided by a vertical row of rosettes and hexagons. Zigzag guards enclose the unornamented blue main border. Average, sym; ND in red, dark and medium blue, gold, ivory. Superior quality; poor condition.........................Est. $2,500/3,500; sold for $10,350

Gendje (Genje), South Central Caucasus

Gendje rugs are not easily distinguished from others of the coarsely knotted, long-piled type on the basis of design, except for a distinctive pat-

"Pinwheel" Kazak, Southwest Caucasus, c. 1885, 8'2" × 5'8", $15,525.
PHOTO COURTESY OF SKINNER, INC.

tern of polychrome diagonal stripes figured with small floral designs sometimes alternating with rows of *boteh* figures. A stylized flower, leaf, and
palmette border motif known as "crab" is frequently used to great effect
with these colorfully striped fields. Runners are commonly seen.

Rug (late 19th century, 4'3" × 8'4"). Two polychrome columns of stripes
containing small hooked boxes radiate diagonally from a central vertical strip of

Gendje Rug, South Central Caucasus, c. 1890, 4'3" × 8'4", $3,795. PHOTO COURTESY OF SKINNER, INC.

interlocking triangles, all within an ivory main border with a highly stylized leaf and vine meander. Average, sym.; ND in medium and light blue, blue-green, red, gold, ivory, corroded brown. Good quality; fair condition. ....Est. $3,000/4,000; sold for $3,795

Long Rug (late 19th century, 3'2" × 9'4"). Polychrome diagonal stripes with repeats of small plants within three narrow flower and vine meander borders and a reciprocal trefoil outer border. Average, sym.; ND in dark and light blue, blue-green, red, coral, aubergine, gold, green, corroded brown. Good quality; fair condition. ....Est. $2,500/3,000; sold for $2,300

Karabagh (Qarabagh), South Caucasus

Karabagh rugs were made in larger sizes than most Caucasian rugs; many have obviously commercial designs, two examples of which may be found in the commercial listings. Workshop rugs are apt to have the cool red associated with cochineal-based dye; village rugs have the warmer

*Karabagh Prayer Rug,
South Caucasus, c. 1885, 3'
× 4'3", $1,495.* PHOTO
COURTESY OF SKINNER, INC.

*Karabagh Rug, South Caucasus, c.
1875, 4'6" × 8', $2,070.* PHOTO
COURTESY OF SKINNER, INC.

madder red. A wide variety of designs were made, and most authorities now assign the "eagle" or "sunburst" design rugs discussed above under Kazak to Karabagh weavers. Some late Karabaghs are disfigured by garish and unstable synthetic dyes.

Prayer Rug (last quarter 19th century, 3′ × 4′3″). A barberpole-edged, geometric device–filled arch on a striking ground composed of narrow vertical polychrome stripes within a dark blue border with a simple geometric repeat. Average, sym.; ND in dark and light blue, blue green, cochineal-dyed pink, red, gold. Good quality; fair condition..Est. $1,500/1,800; sold for $1,495

Rug (2nd half 19th century, 4′6″ × 8′). Three bold serrated diamond medallions on an abrashed red field flanked by evenly spaced geometric fillers. Two narrow reciprocal trefoil borders guard an ivory main border with a striking flower and double-ended arrowheadlike leaf repeat seen on early Caucasian carpets. Average, sym.; ND in dark and light blue, blue-green, red, gold, brownish aubergine, ivory. Good quality; fine condition..Est. $2,000/2,500; sold for $2,070

Zakatala (Zakataly), Northern Azerbaijan

The pile rugs of Zakatala, almost unknown in the West as recently as three years ago, have quickly attracted collector attention. Typically relatively coarsely woven, with longish pile and a rich, mellow palette, the designs range from local variations of traditional Kurdish, Turkish, and Anatolian patterns to a bold simplicity similar to the gabbehs of Southwest Persia. The striking, barbaric-looking example discussed here is a dealer's rug (as of this date these rugs are rarely seen at auction) whose prices for Zakatalas generally range from $7,500 to $16,000. Newer pieces are said to be replete with synthetic dyes; this one is not.

Rug (c. 1900, 3′10″ × 6′8″). Centered on a long-piled, extremely lustrous ivory field is a gold rectangle bordered in red-edged blue, above which is a row of red, black-edged smaller rectangles. The only other decoration are two rows of three triangles, one row gold edged in black; the other gold, blue, red, and black. The shaggy border along the top and sides is black, ivory, and gold; the end border is russet edged in dark gold. Coarse, sym; ND in red, medium blue, bright and dark gold, ivory, black. Superior quality; fine condition. (See color section.)...................
....Dealer rug, $20,000

SHORT-PILED FINELY KNOTTED CAUCASIANS

Daghestan, Northeast Caucasus

This name is often applied to a type of delicately lattice-patterned Shirvan (see photo) that usually has a white ground.

Prayer Rug (c. 1850, 4′6″ × 3′2″). A variety of polychrome flowers within the dark blue serrated leaf lattice on the *mihrab*'s ivory ground below a dark blue arch framing a shieldlike device and ivory spandrels containing a variety of amulet motifs. The red main border has a polychrome stylized leaf repeat. Fine, sym.; ND in dark and medium blue, red, gold, green, ivory. Superior quality; poor condition. ....Sold in 1991 for $6,050; est. in today's market, $4,500/5,000

Daghestan Prayer Rug, Northeastern Caucasus, c. 1860, 4'6" × 3'2", $6,050. PHOTO COURTESY OF CHRISTIE'S EAST, 1991

Prayer Rug (late 19th century, 3'7" × 5'2"). This example's field design is less graceful and more compressed than the pictured older rug discussed above. Fine, sym.; ND in red, rose, dark and light blue, blue-green, gold, ivory. Good quality; fair condition...Est. $1,200/1,500; sold for $1,380

Kuba, Northeast Caucasus

A variety of old rugs produced in the Kuba district in the Northeastern Caucasus not only have a similar structure but were made by weaving groups whose identity is in many cases conjectural. The better-known trade names, which are associated largely with particular designs, are Konagend, Perepedil, Seychour, Chichi, and Karagashli. It is hoped that rug researchers will in time be able to supply collectors with the hard information needed for proper attributions.

The Kuba's knot density falls into a range like that of the Shirvans, but unlike them the wool warps are more or less depressed. The wefts are more likely to be wool than cotton; the edges are double-corded and often overcast in blue or white. The end finish usually consists of a narrow strip of flatweave followed by multiple rows of tightly knotted or braided warps.

Kuba Rug, Northeast Caucasus, c. 1885, 3'10" × 5', $3,220. PHOTO COURTESY OF CHRISTIE'S

Kuba Long Rug, Northeast Caucasus, c. 1885, 4' × 9'3", $3,737. PHOTO COURTESY OF SKINNER, INC.

Runner (dated 1876, 4' × 13'8"). Polychrome "snowflake" rosettes interspersed with small animals and geometric fillers cover a dark blue ground. The main border, which is guarded by the pretty repeat of realistic carnations often seen on Northern and Eastern Caucasian rugs, is a precisely drawn—if poorly resolved—bracketed Kufic repeat on ivory. Fine, sym.; ND in dark, medium, and light blue, blue-green, red, pink, dull gold, yellow, ivory, corroded brown. Very good quality; good condition. ....Est. $12,000/15,000; sold for $11,500

Rug (last quarter 19th century, 3'10" × 5'). A column of three Lesghi ivory and dark blue stars on an abrashed red ground with numerous geometric fillers. The handsome but awkwardly resolved Kufic repeat on the ivory border is enclosed by a carnation repeat. Fine, sym.; ND in dark and light blue, blue-green, red, gold, ivory. Good quality; fair condition. ....Est. $3,000/4,000; sold for $3,220

Long Rug, probably Konagend district (last quarter 19th century, 4' × 9'3"). A column of nine hexagons and octagons within a bordered long red "keyhole" medallion on a dark blue field filled with small animal and geometric figures. The ivory main border's blossom and vine repeat is enclosed by carnation-repeat guards. Fine, sym.; ND in dark and light blue, blue-green, red, gold, ivory. Good quality; fair condition. ....Est. $3,000/4,000; sold for $3,737

Seychour (Seichour) Long Rug (2nd half 19th century, 3'4" × 8'4"). A column of three stiff, club-ended cruciform figures (which are exuberantly floral in older examples) and scattered geometric fillers on a dark brown field within a main border with the complex blue and ivory running dog–type repeat associated with Seychour rugs. Fine, sym.; ND in dark and light blue, blue-green, red, rose, ivory, corroded brown. Good quality; poor condition. ...Est. $1,800/2,200; sold for $1,495

Shirvan, East Caucasus

As a class, the Shirvans are relatively finely knotted, with a count ranging from 90 to about 200. Wefts are wool in early pieces, but cotton was being used by the turn of the century, and a narrow double-corded edging finished in white cotton is typical of late-19th- and early-20th-century examples. The colors are very good but less boldly used than those on long-piled Caucasians.

The format popularly associated with this group has a vertical row of lozenge-shaped medallions on a field liberally supplied with geometric filler motifs and, to a lesser extent, stylized animals. Many other designs are also seen: allover repeats, compartmented florals, vertical or diagonal stripes bearing floral or geometric motifs, Mina Khani florals, etc. A densely ornamented type featuring facing pairs of flamboyantly tailed birds is known as Akstafa; the Marasali subgroup employs a distinctive *boteh* variation on the field and a highly stylized *boteh*-like form in the primary border. The dark blue–fielded Marasali prayer rugs are particularly popular with collectors.

Runner (c. 1880, 3' × 12'8"). A latticed column of eight dark blue diamonds edged with gold and containing a variety of palmettes and geometric figures on a dark blue field. The interstices of the lattice are filled with flowers and small Akstafa-type birds; the well-resolved ivory Kufic border on red is enclosed by carnation repeat guards. Fine, sym.; ND in dark and royal blue, blue-green, red, gold, ivory. Superior quality; good condition..........Est. $10,000/12,000; sold for $10,350

Prayer Rug (last quarter 19th century, 3'3" × 5'2"). A gold zigzag-edged lattice on a dark blue *mihrab* containing a variety of geometric devices and a centered pair of human figures under an ivory prayer arch. Poles of polychrome "pinwheels" ornament the ivory main border. Fine, sym.; ND in dark and medium blue, blue-green, red, gold, ivory. Good quality; fair condition..........Est. $800/1,200; sold for $1,495

Rug (last quarter 19th century, 3'9" × 4'10"). A column of three boxed latch-hooked medallions flanked by polychrome stylized blossom and tree motifs and an appealing display of large and small animals, all on a red ground. The gold main border has a stylized leaf and flower bud repeat; the guards have blossom repeats on blue. Fine, sym.; ND in red, dark and medium blue, blue-green, gold, ivory. Good quality; fair condition. ....Est. $2,000/3,000; sold for $2,530

Marasali Prayer Rug (2nd half 19th century, 3'3" × 3'10"). Gold "lightning"-edged polychrome *boteh* on a lustrous blue *mihrab* beneath an ivory prayer arch containing the highly stylized red *boteh* repeated in the ivory main border. The precise drawing,

Shirvan Rug, East Caucasus, c. 1885, 3'9" × 4'10", $2,530. PHOTO COUR-
TESY OF SKINNER, INC.

spacing, and jewel-like colors of this example propelled the bidding well above
the modest high estimate. Fine, sym.; ND in dark and medium blue, red, green,
gold, ivory, corroded black. Superior quality; fair condition. (See color section.)
....Est. $2,000/3,000; sold for $17,250

Talish, Southeast Caucasus

The Talish weavers live in villages near the Caspian Sea and the city of
Lenkoran, which is the name given to a type of rug, usually a runner, that
one authority ascribes to them. The Lenkoran design is dominated by large
clunky medallions that resemble sea turtles more than the palmettes from
which they were probably derived.

Konya Prayer Rug, Central Anatolia, c. 1850, 3′6″ × 5′, $8,050. PHOTO COURTESY OF SKINNER, INC.

Baluch Bag Face, Northeast Persia, c. 1875, 2′2″ × 2′ 4″, $4,600. PHOTO COURTESY OF SKINNER, INC.

Marasali Prayer Rug, Shirvan, East Caucasus, c. 1870, 3'3" × 3'10", $17,250. PHOTO COURTESY OF SKINNER, INC.

Karachov Kazak, Southwest Caucasus, c. 1870, 6'6" × 7'8", $13,800. PHOTO COURTESY OF SKINNER, INC.

Talish Long Rug, Southeast Caucasus, c. 1885, 3'2" × 10'3", $6,612.
PHOTO COURTESY OF SKINNER, INC.

Khotan Carpet, East Turkestan, c. 1850, 6' × 11'2", $19,500. PHOTO COURTESY OF CHRISTIE'S

Qashqai Corridor Carpet, Southwest Persia, c. 1890. 7'3" × 13' 5", $20,700. PHOTO COURTESY OF CHRISTIE'S

Kirman Prayer Rug, Southeast Persia, c. 1870, 4'6" × 5'8", $4,830. PHOTO COURTESY OF CHRISTIE'S

Chinese Carpet, c. 1830, 6'9" × 13'11", $17,250. PHOTO COURTESY OF CHRISTIE'S

Mughal Dynasty Star-Lattice Carpet, North India, c. 1700, 12'8" × 13'6", $992,000. PHOTO COURTESY OF CHRISTIE'S

Bidjar Carpet, North Persia, dated 1896, 10′ × 15′ × 9″, $16,100.
PHOTO COURTESY OF CHRISTIE'S

Beshir Corridor Carpet, Turkestan, c. 1885, 5′8″ × 10′10″, $24,000. PHOTO COURTESY OF PE-
TER PAP ORIENTAL RUGS, INC.

Zakatala Rug, Northern Azerbaijan, c. 1900, 3' 10" × 6' 8", $20,000. PHOTO COURTESY OF PETER PAP ORIENTAL RUGS, INC.

Yomud Carpet, West Turkestan, c. 1870, approx. 5' × 10', $15,000. PHOTO COURTESY OF PETER PAP ORIENTAL RUGS, INC.

Serapi Carpet, Northwest Persia, c. 1880, 11' × 15', $65,000. PHOTO COURTESY OF PETER PAP ORIENTAL RUGS, INC.

Azeri Carpet, Turkey, contemporary, 9'9" × 13', about $12,000. PHOTO COURTESY OF WOVEN LEGENDS

The typical Talish rug is a long, narrow rug of great elegance with a red or dark blue field that is either entirely open or displays two or three judiciously placed, precisely drawn rosettes. Fields with more ornamentation are occasionally seen. The inner border is often a delicately drawn reciprocal arrowhead motif; the primary border, usually white, alternates rosettes of the type used in the field with squares made up of four smaller and more highly stylized rosettes. Wefts are wool in the oldest examples; in later rugs, cotton.

Long Rug (last quarter 19th century, 3'2" × 10'3"). A pair of arm-in-arm human figures, a seated dog, an amulet, and a bird perched atop a stylized tree lend charm to the long narrow abrashed blue field further decorated with an inner border of polychrome stepped triangles instead of the more standard trefoil motif. The wide ivory border has a generously spaced blossom and leaf repeat. Fine, sym.; ND in

Talish/Lenkoran Long Rug, Southeast Caucasus, c. 1860, 3'2" × 10'2", $5,462. PHOTO COURTESY OF SKINNER, INC.

dark blue, red, gold, green, ivory. Very good quality; good condition. (See color section.)...Est. $3,000/4,000; sold for $6,612

Lenkoran Long Rug (mid 19th century, 3'2" × 10'2"). Three large ivory-bordered tulip-shaped medallions separated by armed rectangles on a dark blue field with a scattering of geometric fillers, all within a striking red and ivory reciprocal trefoil main border guarded by narrow "S" repeats. Fine, sym.; ND in dark and light blue, blue-green, red, rose, aubergine, ivory, corroded brown. Very good quality; poor condition. ....Est. $3,500/4,000; sold for $5,462

PERSIAN RUGS

Some names familiar to you may not be included in the following listings. This could *either* be because as a class the rugs bearing these names lack sufficiently distinctive designs and coloration to be classed as collectible, or because examples of good quality were not offered at auction during the two years under consideration, or because they are listed in another category.

AFSHAR, SOUTH PERSIA

Perhaps the reason Afshar rugs took so long to catch on as collectibles is the confusing variety of design influences seen in their weavings. Some Afshars live in northeastern Iran near Meshed, others near Bidjar, and a large number live south of Kerman. In short, it's hard to collect something one can't easily define. But even though the designs of some old Afshar rugs were obviously influenced by contemporaneous commercial Kerman rugs, a distinctive group of rustic Afshars has begun to establish itself in the collectors' hall of fame.

Afshars woven in a rustic setting have an all-wool foundation on which the lustrous pile yarns may be knotted either symmetrically or asymmetrically. According to dealer-scholar James Opie, the former is associated with the tribal work discussed in the tribal weavings listings, the latter with the village rugs listed below. The wefts are usually dyed orange; double wefting is the rule, and the warps are noticeably depressed. Afshar rugs frequently have highly decorative flat-woven end finishes; the side finishes vary, often displaying barberpole overcastings in two or more colors.

Rug (last quarter 19th century, 3'9" × 4'9"). The field consists of a polychrome chevron design with tiny geometric repeats on each narrow stripe within numerous narrow geometric-repeat borders and a flower meander on dark blue. Fine, prob. sym.; ND in dark and light blue, blue-green, red, rust, gold, ivory. Good quality; fair condition...............................Est. $1,500/1,800; sold for $2,185

Rug (c. 1900, 3'5" × 4'5"). Eight staggered rows of alternately facing *boteh* on a dark blue field with numerous small geometric fillers, within a pretty flowering vine meander on ivory, and guards with polychrome interlocking triangles. Fine, prob. sym.; ND in dark and royal blue, blue-green, red, rust, gold, ivory. Good quality; good condition. ....Est. $700/900; sold for $1,265

Afshar Rug, South Persia, c. 1885, 3'9" × 4'9", $2,185. PHOTO COURTESY
OF SKINNER, INC.

Rug (last quarter 19th century, 3'2" × 4'). A stepped lobed medallion and pendants, the latter separated by blossom clusters, on a dark blue field with clumsy
stepped spandrels containing a variety of animal, geometric, and leaf figures. The
ivory main border has a repeat of polychrome ram's horns. Fine, prob. sym.; ND in
dark and light blue, blue-green, red, ivory. Good quality; good condition.................
....Est. $1,000/1,200; sold for $1,092

Rug (last quarter 19th century, 4'7" × 5'9"). Five rows of three cream floral-
bordered squares contain well-drawn polychrome gabled medallions within a handsome floral-ornamented dark blue main border. Fine, prob. sym.; ND in dark,
medium, and light blue, red, rust, gold, cream, ivory, corroded browns. Superior
quality; good condition...Est. $5,000/7,000; sold for $5,175

BAKHTIARI (BAKTIARI), WEST PERSIA

According to C. E. Edwards, the author of *The Persian Carpet*, the area
and room-size rugs known in the trade as Bakhtiari were not woven by

members of the tribe of that name. Rather, they were made in villages in the Chahar Mahal area east and south of Isfahan. Old examples were symmetrically knotted of good lustrous wool on a wool foundation.

Pictorial Rug (early 20th century, 3′9″ × 6′4″). Similar to pictorial rugs attributed to village Afshar and Baluch weavers, this one displays a trio of men standing in tribal dress below a fourth on horseback on an ivory ground with a centered floral-ornamented diamond and scattered stylized plants. The dark blue main border features a flowerhead, palmette, and serrated leaf meander. Average, sym.; ND in dark blue, blue-green, red, gold, ivory. Good quality; fair condition. ....Est. $1,000/1,200; sold for $1,955

Gallery Carpet (late 19th century, 5′3″ × 14′7″). This refined rug has 23 rows of 4–5 polychrome flower-filled urns on ivory within a similarly ornamented dark blue border guarded by narrow gold borders with *boteh* and flower meanders. Average, prob. sym; ND in dark blue, blue-green, red, coral, gold, ivory. Very good quality; good condition. ....Est. $6,000/8,000; sold for $6,900

Bakhtiari Rug, West Persia, c. 1925, 3′9″ × 6′4″, $1,955. PHOTO COURTESY OF SKINNER, INC.

BAKSHAISH (BAKSHAYESH), NORTHWEST PERSIA

Rustic in look as well as production, these symmetrically and rather coarsely knotted all-wool rugs are similar to others made in the Heriz area and enjoy the same popularity with collectors and decorators. A frequently seen pattern is a stylized animal-peltlike medallion on an open field ornamented with sinuous pink figures, probably derived from the cloud-band motif. The corner joinings of the bold patterns on the characteristically wide main borders are invariably poorly resolved. A camel-color outer edge is common.

Rug (last quarter 19th century, 3′ × 4′). Boldly presented, highly stylized polychrome ascending tree branches on an abrashed blue ground bordered with crudely drawn blossoms and diamonds on brown within a plain camel band. Coarse, sym.; ND in blue, red, rose, gold, tan, camel, light and dark corroded brown. Very good quality; fair condition. ....Est. $4,000/6,000; sold for $13,800

Carpet (last quarter 19th century, 11′2″ × 15′). Well-spaced and drawn Bid Majnun tree pattern on a worn rusty red ground within a striking stylized blossom and serrated leaf repeat on midnight blue. Average, prob. sym.; ND in dark and medium blue, rust red, gold, green, ivory. Superior quality; poor condition.............. ....Est. $15,000/20,000; sold for $20,700

Carpet (last quarter 19th century, 10′2″ × 17′9″). A gabled rose-bordered and pendanted gold octagon centered in a dark blue "pelt" with a narrow rose stepped border. The ivory field has a polychrome floral-vinery within rose, blue-green, and

Bakshaish, Northwest Persia, c. 1885, 11′2″ × 15′, $20,700. PHOTO
COURTESY OF SKINNER, INC.

gold spandrels. A narrow floral repeat on dark blue is the only remaining border. Average, sym.; ND in dark and medium blue, blue-green, red, rose, pink, gold, tan, ivory, brown. Superior quality; fair condition. (See color section.)............................
....Est. $15,000/20,000; sold for $17,250

Carpet (late 19th century, 9′8″ × 12′2″). This cheerful, very colorful rug features an ivory-stepped red triangle containing an Herati-filled abrashed blue triangle on an ivory field with an all-over repeat of *boteh*-like small figures within a bold highly stylized polychrome palmette/vine meander on gold. Average, prob. sym.; ND in medium and light blue, red, coral, green, gold, aubergine, ivory. Superior quality; good condition...................................Est. $25,000/30,000; sold for $25,300

BIDJAR (BIJAR), NORTHWEST PERSIA

Old Bidjars are densely packed, well-nigh indestructible rugs knotted symmetrically by Kurdish weavers on a wool foundation with hand-spun yarns dyed with beautiful vegetable colors. Collectors esteem the variety of appealing floral and tree designs seen on rustic examples and the handsome rectilinear medallion format associated with old rugs with a slablike handle. (Also see the commercial rug listings.)

Sampler (Wagireh); (last quarter 19th century, 4′8″ × 8′4″). Large-scale palmettes and arabesques on a reddish tan field and a portion of a palmette, blossom, and vine border design on dark blue within a flower and vine meander on ivory. Average, sym.; ND in muted reds, rose, dark and light blue, blue-green, gold, ivory. Good quality; poor condition...Est. $700/900; sold for $3,737

Rug (last quarter 19th century, 5′1″ × 7′9″). Polychrome variant of the flower and arabesque Gerus design on dark blue within a poorly resolved palmette and blossom vinery repeat on ivory. Average, sym.; ND in red, dark and medium blue, blue-green, gold, ivory. Very good quality; fair condition. ....
....Est. $3,000/4,000; sold for $6,325

Carpet (dated 1896, 10′ × 15′9″). A classic rectilinear Bidjar format featuring a palmette-pendanted triangular medallion, in this case ornamented with the Herati motif, on a subtly tan-striped camel field with small Herati-filled camel spandrels. The dark blue main border has a beautifully drawn palmette and flower vine meander; the two guards have a floral meander and a reciprocal trefoil, all within a plain camel band. Average, sym.; ND in brick red, dark, medium, and light blue, gold, tan, ivory, camel. Superior quality; good condition. (See color section.)..........
....Est. $10,000/15,000; sold for $16,100

BALUCH (BELOUCH, BALUCHI, BELOUCHISTAN), NORTHEAST PERSIA

Rugs made by the settled Baluch weavers in the Khorasan region of northeast Persia share the rather limited palette of nomadic examples, but the weave and finish tends to be finer and the motifs are frequently village versions of classical Persian motifs like the Mina Khani, Herati, and Harshang.

The knotting is asymmetrical on a wool foundation; old rugs frequently have ornamental skirts, and the edges are invariably overcast with brown goat hair.

Bidjar, Northwest Persia, c. 1885, 5'1" × 7'9", $6,325. PHOTO COURTESY OF CHRISTIE'S

Rug (early 20th century, 3'2" × 5'6"). A popular design featuring large and small blossom heads in ivory, red, and aubergine on an ivory sawtooth-edged dark blue field. The red border has a blue "Turkoman line" meander within an ivory running-dog repeat. Average, asym.; ND in red, aubergine, dark and medium blue, ivory, corroded brown. Good quality; good condition..........Est. $800/1,200; sold for $862

Rug (last quarter 19th century, 4'9" × 6'8"). Eleven rows of nine polychrome *boteh* crowd a dark blue field within a red, dark blue, and brown interlocking triangle repeat. Fine, asym.; ND in dark and medium blue, blue-green, red, gold, ivory, corroded brown. Added fringe. Good quality; fair condition...
....Est. $1,500/2,000; sold for $1,725

Carpet (mid 19th century, 6' × 7'4"). A pattern once thought rare, five rows of staggered, well-spaced delicately bordered rectangles filled with geometric motifs glow against a lustrous dark blue ground with numerous fillers, including *boteh* and stylized tree forms, within an ivory-edged geometric repeat on red. Fine, asym.; ND in dark, medium and light blue, blue-green, red, apricot, aubergine, gold, ivory, corroded brown. Superior quality; fair condition. ...Est. $8,000/10,000; sold for $9,200

Baluch Rug, Northeast Persia, c. 1920, 3'2" × 5'6", $862. PHOTO COURTESY OF SKINNER, INC.

HAMADAN, NORTHWEST PERSIA

The weaving villages surrounding the city of Hamadan in northwest Iran have, over the years, produced vast quantities of rugs, almost all of which have only one weft passing between each row of symmetrical knots. The foundation, which was wool in older rugs, has been cotton since about World War I. Sturdy and serviceable, few are collected save for the finer-quality Malayers, which are comparable to Ferahan Sarouks (see the commercial carpets listings), and the very beautiful camel-ground carpets made in the 19th century. The latter are often mistakenly tagged as Serabs (see below), most of which were made in runner sizes.

The Hamadan area production was not only large but extremely variable. Unfortunately, all rugs made there have become unfairly burdened with the reputation of the lesser examples. I recently purchased a lovely old vegetable-dyed, village-made scatter whose glowing cypress-tree design has spurred me to seek examples of similar quality. Bearing in mind that the road less traveled is often the most rewarding, perhaps other open-minded collectors will be encouraged to do the same.

Rug (1st half 20th century, 3'8" × 6'7"). Flower heads and blossom clusters on a dark blue field with two floral borders—a narrow floral meander on ivory and a stylized flower and octagon repeat on red, all within a plain camel band. Average, sym.; ND in dark and light blue, blue-green, red, gold, green, ivory, camel. Very good quality; good condition. .... Est. $1,200/1,500; sold for $1,100

HERIZ AREA, NORTHWEST PERSIA

A rectilinear medallion format is popularly associated with rugs woven in the Heriz district in a range of qualities from coarse to relatively fine, variously labeled Heriz, Gorevan, and Serapi, the latter name usually reserved for the more finely knotted examples. One expert is of the opinion that the rugs known in the trade as Bakshaish (see p. 153) should also be included

Hamadan Rug, Northwest Persia, c. 1925, 3'8" × 6'7", $1,100. PHOTO COURTESY OF SKINNER, INC.

here. The older Heriz-area rugs are adaptable to a variety of settings, and their inventive variations on the medallion theme commend them to collectors seeking noncommercial-looking floor coverings.

Allover patterns are also seen—the large-scale Herati designs are particularly noteworthy—and although room-size rugs are the norm, runners and area rugs are also occasionally seen, the latter more apt to be square than rectangular. The border designs on village rugs are usually poorly resolved at the corners.

The foundations have been cotton for about the last hundred years, and the symmetrical knotting ranges from 30 per square inch to 80 in the finer

Heriz Carpet, Northwest Persia, c. 1895, 9'4" × 13', $14,900. PHOTO COURTESY OF SKINNER, INC.

grades. There are two wefts, often dyed blue, and the double selvage has a sturdy, serviceable finish.

Carpet (last quarter 19th century, 9'4" × 13'). A pretty and relaxed overall pattern of palmettes, serrated leaves, and vinery on an ivory ground within a palmette, blossom, and vine repeat on dark blue, and a vine meander on ivory. Average, sym.; ND in dark and light blue, blue-green, rose, tannish-gold, ivory. Very good quality; fair condition. ....Est. $5,000/7,000; sold for $14,900

Carpet (late 19th century, 9'10" × 12'2"). A rather mechanical rendering of the Bid Majnun tree pattern on a red field bordered by a poorly resolved palmette and jagged leaf meander on dark blue. Average, sym. ND in red, pink, dark and medium blue, pistachio, dull gold, ivory. Good quality; good condition..................................
....Est. $7,000/9,000; sold for $8,050

Rug (last quarter 19th century, 5' × 6'7"). A gabled ivory-edged dark blue central medallion with floral vinery on a well-spaced floral-vinery-filled red field with palmette-decorated olive-tan spandrels, all within a dense, awkwardly resolved palmette and vine repeat on blue. Average, sym.; ND in dark, medium and light blue, blue-green, red, rose, gold, olive-tan, ivory. Very good quality; good condition. ....Est. $5,000/7,000; sold for $6,900

Rug (last quarter 19th century, 4'1" × 4'9") This unusually small Heriz has an angular polychrome serrated-leaf vinery on an ivory field within flower and vine meanders. Average, sym.; ND in red, rose, dark and light blue, gold, ivory. Good quality; good condition..Est. $3,500/5,000; sold for $4,025

Heriz Carpet, Northwest Persia, c. 1895, 9'10" × 12'2", $8,050. PHOTO COURTESY OF CHRISTIE'S

Carpet (1st quarter 20th century, 11′ × 12′6″). This almost square carpet displays a graceful version of the rectilinear Heriz format described above. A lobed, pale blue-edged and palmette-ornamented dark blue medallion on a red ground with floral vinery flanked by ivory and blue flower and leaf–filled spandrels. The dark blue main border has a pretty but poorly resolved flower and vine meander. Coarse, sym.; ND in dark, medium, and light blue, pink, gold, ochre, tan, ivory. Very good quality; good condition.....................................Est. $20,000/25,000; sold for $20,700

KURDISH, NORTHWEST PERSIA

Most of the village rugs made by Kurdish weavers are classified by the towns or areas where they were made. Some go begging for exact attributions either because not enough is known about the weaving in the area to allow accurate assignment, or because the person doing the classification lacks sufficient expertise. Whatever the reason, the following entries fall into this no-name limbo:

Corridor Carpet (c. 1850, 6′6″ × 17′6″). A variety of floral and classical motifs— Shah Abbas, Harshang, Afshan—in a gold vinery lattice on a dark blue ground. The red main border has a handsome repeat of stylized palmettes and flowers; the narrow guard borders have a reciprocal trefoil repeat in gold and blue. Average, prob. sym.; ND in dark and medium blue, blue-green, red, rose, green, gold, aubergine, ivory. Superior quality; good condition......................Est. $16,000/18,000; sold for $16,000

Long Rug (early 20th century, 3′8″ × 12′4″). A Serab-like format of large flower-ornamented ivory diamonds on a camel-grounded lattice composed of small geometric device–filled triangles, bordered by a stylized leaf and rosette repeat on ivory, a narrower reciprocal repeat, and a plain camel band. Average, prob. sym.; ND in dark and light blue, blue-green, red, gold, ivory, camel. Good quality; fair to good condition. ....Est. $2,500/3,000; sold for $2,990

Rug (early 20th century, 3′7″ × 7′8″). Six rows of three large rosette-encircled *boteh* on an abrashed dull red field within a stylized vine meander on ivory. Average, prob. sym.; ND in dark and light blue, blue-green, tannish red, gold, soft brown. Good quality; good condition...................Est. $1,000/1,200; sold for $1,035

Sampler (Wagireh), (early 20 century, 3′3″ × 5′3″). Densely packed stylized plant forms on a crimson field flanked by bands of geometric motifs, all within three borders, two of them Turkoman-style curled leaves. Average, prob sym.; ND in blue, blue-green, red, ivory, and possibly a synthetic crimson. Good quality; fair condition. ....Est. $700/900; sold for $1,495

Rug (c. 1850, 4′10″ × 5′10″). A triumph of balanced design, this small masterpiece has gold palmettes and ivory florettes within a bold arabesque composed of red-edged, medium-blue curved leaves on a dark blue ground. The stylized well-resolved border is a graceful leaf and palmette meander on medium blue, guarded by blue and ivory flower-meanders on red. Fine symmetrical knotting on a silk foundation; ND in dark and medium blue, red, muted gold, yellow, green, ivory. Superior quality; fair condition......................Est. $25,000/35,000; sold for $27,600

SENNEH, NORTHWEST PERSIA

The finely woven, delicately patterned, and closely clipped Senneh rug is entirely unlike the sturdy fabrics produced by other Kurdish weavers, with

*Kurdish Corridor Carpet, Northwest Persia, c. 1850, 6'6" × 17'6",
$16,000.* PHOTO COURTESY OF SKINNER, INC.

floral and *boteh* motifs favored. Unlike most old village rugs, the foundation is cotton, with silk used for the warps of the finest pieces. Ever popular
with collectors, its peculiar structure lends the back a distinctive gritty texture even the rankest amateur can readily identify. Sennehs are almost
always seen in area rug sizes.

Rug (last quarter 19th century, 4'6" × 6'2"). Thirteen rows of thirteen closely spaced finely drawn *boteh* on ivory within a narrow warm brown border with a leafy flowering vine meander. Fine, sym.; ND in dark blue, rose, green, pale yellow, ivory, cinnamon. Very good quality; good condition. ....
....Est. $4,000/6,000; sold for $4,025

SERAB, NORTHWEST PERSIA

Sturdy camel-color grounded runners were woven in the Heriz district in a group of market towns in the Serab vicinity. Typically, these rugs display pole-connected floral medallions in rose, gold, ivory, and two or three shades of blue.

Runner (last quarter 19th century, 3'4" × 17'). Six flower-ornamented and pendanted dark blue triangular medallions and symmetrically placed flower clusters on a dark camel ground enclosed by two narrow stylized floral borders, one dark blue, the other ivory. Average, sym.; ND in dark and medium blue, blue-green, red, rose, green, gold, ivory. Superior quality; fair condition..
....Est. $5,000/7,000; sold for $5,750

SOUTHWEST PERSIA

Some of the rugs made by the settled tribal groups of southwest Persia have been included with the tribal weavings, a few with the commercial rugs. The rugs listed below were made on rustic looms with an eye for profit but without compromising their tribal vitality. Their lively and distinctive patterning, soft lustrous wool, and vivid vegetable dyes are prized by collectors.

Qashqai Carpet (late 19th century, 7' × 9'6"). Diagonal rows of polychrome filigreed *boteh* crowd the dark field bordered with a cypress tree and "mother and child" *boteh* repeat on dark blue. Fine, asym.; ND in dark and medium blue, blue-green, dark red, rose, gold, ivory. Good quality; good condition. ....
....Est. $2,000/3,000; sold for $3,100

Qashqai Carpet (late 19th century, 5'8" × 12'8"). Two pendanted floral-ornamented stepped ivory medallions on a red ground with a variety of *boteh* and rosettes on a finely drawn vinery with latticed blue spandrels. The dark blue border has a polychrome flower, palmette, and leaf meander within ivory flower and vine guards. Fine, asym.; ND in dark and medium blue, red, green, gold, ivory. Very good quality; fair condition. ....Est. $4,000/6,000; sold for $4,025

Qashqai Rug (c. 1870, 3'10" × 4'5"). Narrow lustrous polychrome floral stripes in a chevron design with boxed *boteh* spandrels within an ivory border with a finely drawn latchhooked repeat of polychrome hexagons, and with decorative flat-woven skirts. Fine, asym., with silk and wool wefts; ND in dark, medium, and light blue, blue-green, red, dark and light greens, yellow, brown, brownish-black. Superior quality; good condition, but unlikely to lie or hang flat because of unequal foundation tension. ....Est. $15,000/20,000; sold for $17,250

Qashqai Gabbeh Rug (early 20th century, 4'7" × 7'8"). Large-scale zigzags composed of seven stripes in contrasting colors enclose a royal blue central column ornamented with quartered polychrome diamond-shaped motifs on a similarly ornamented golden yellow field. A plain black band and two reciprocal sawtooth

Qashqai Gabbeh Rug, Southwest Persia, c. 1920, 4′7″ × 7′8″, $5,462. AUTHOR'S PHOTO

borders—one black on ivory, the other red on abrashed green—provide a simple but effective frame. Average, asym.; ND in dark and medium blue, green, red, gold, ivory. Very good quality; good condition. ....Est. $3,500/4,500; sold for $5,462

TURKESTAN

Most of the Turkoman rugs will be found in the tribal weavings listing; however, noted rug scholar Jon Thompson has made a good case for classifying the Ersari rugs known as Beshir, which were "woven within the . . . cultural sphere of Bukhara," as a commercial village product. He cites their typically large sizes and use of nontribal motifs in formats that have more in common with classical Turkish weaving than tribal traditions.

Beshir Corridor Carpet (last quarter 19th century, 5′8″ × 10′10″). Although the design elements of this beautiful lustrous rug are often seen in Beshir weaving, the drawing and subtle variations found in this one are not. The narrow dark blue field has two columns of ivory-headed curled red "snake" figures (possibly a cloud-band variation); narrow gold floral meanders guard the dark blue border ornamented with detached palmettes, blossoms, and curved leaves interspersed with small geometric fillers. Average, asym.; ND in red, dark and medium blue, gold, ivory. Superior quality; fine condition. (See color section.)..................................Dealer rug, $24,000

Central Asian (?) Carpet (early 19th century, 4′6″ × 9′9″). Eleven rows of three gul-like large blossoms in red, gold, blue, and ivory interspersed with a variety of geometric fillers on a purple-brown field, within a bold, unevenly rendered reciprocal trefoil border on red. Coarse, asym.; ND in red, medium blue, blue-green, gold, ivory, purple-brown. Superior quality; fair to good condition..........................
....Est. $8,000/12,000; sold for $12,650

Tekke Main Carpet (last quarter 19th century, 7′ × 10′4″). Twelve rows of five Tekke main and minor guls on a mahogany field bordered by latchhooked octagons of a style associated with late Tekke rugs. Stylized plant repeats ornament the wide pile skirts. Fine, asym.; ND in dark blue, blue-green, brownish red, cochineal-dyed pink, apricot, ivory. Good quality; fair to good condition. ....
....Est. $3,500/4,000; sold for $3,737

Ersari Main Carpet, Turkestan, c. 1885, 6′2″ × 9′4″, $1,725. PHOTO COURTESY OF SKINNER, INC.

Ersari Main Carpet (last quarter 19th century, 6′2″ × 9′4″). Seven rows of three characteristically large octagons with dyrnak guls used as minor guls on a rust-red field within a mechanical, poorly resolved diamond and stylized hooked-vine meander. Average, asym; ND in red, rust-red, apricot, blue, ivory. Good quality; good condition. ....Est. $1,500/2,000; sold for $1,725

EAST TURKESTAN

The oasis-woven rugs of East Turkestan, which sprawls across the trade corridor linking China with western Asia and India, draw from both Far Eastern and Western design pools. The most commonly seen formats include symmetrically placed roundish medallions containing cloud-band floral figures, repeats of stylized floral and pomegranate figures, and tile-like repeats of latchhooked gul-like figures. Favored border motifs were fret repeats, cloud-band stylizations, rosettes, reciprocal trefoils—often on a gigantic scale—and stylized flower-and-vine meanders with a distinctly Persian look. The vegetable-dyed colors are intense and tend to be warmly toned; rugs with synthetic dyes often have fields faded almost to gray from the original mauve-magenta, an early and notorious fugitive dye.

Although sumptuous silk carpets were made, the examples of interest to most collectors have cotton warps, and the wefts may be cotton or wool, sometimes both in the same rug. The edges were rather insecurely finished with a single cord bundle overcasting, which may be why so few old rugs retain their original edges. The ends may have a plain-weave band.

Khotan Corridor Carpet (mid 19th century, 6′ × 11′2″). Three stylized flower-ornamented pale blue roundels on a rose and dark blue mazework ground. The stylized polychrome wave and cloud-band border is guarded by a flower meander and fretwork minor borders. Coarse, asym.; ND in rose, salmon, dark, medium, and light blue, gold, mustard, green, corroded black. Superior quality; good condition. (See color section.) ....Est. $6,000/8,0000; sold for $19,500

Khotan Rug (early 19th century, 5′7″ × 9′1″). A bright stylized all-over blossom and flowering branch design in vivid blue and gold on rusty coral, bordered with a flower-repeat on blue and a stylized polychrome wave and cloud-band outer border. Coarse, asym.; ND in sky and royal blue, pale lavender, gold, rose, ivory. Very good quality; good condition...............................Est. $8,000/12,000; sold for $8,625

TIBETAN RUGS

Until about ten years ago most collectors were both uninterested in and unknowing about the plushy, lustrous, gaily colored small rugs and saddle blankets woven by Tibetan weavers. The designs are for the most part quite similar to those seen on Chinese rugs but are more exuberantly expressed in a looser, larger scale with brighter colors. One indigenous design seen in many variations incorporates a flayed tiger skin symbolizing Buddhist efforts to control man's ego-centered mind, but to Western eyes the expression knotted on the tiger's face is usually more smile-provoking than sobering.

Weaving is a craft of comparatively recent vintage in Tibet, probably done on a primitive level in scattered locations before 1800 but not on a scale large enough to be documented before that time. The oldest rugs have all-wool foundations; cotton began to be used for warps around 1900, often in combination with wool wefts. Although synthetic dyes became available in the 1870s, vegetable dyes continued to be used as well.

Old Tibetan rugs were coarsely knotted, with a distinctive looping technique, and when finished, supplied with a border of stout red cloth on all four sides. The weaver, knowing the rug would be bound in this manner, left the edges and ends rather insecurely finished.

Rug (late 19th century, 4'7″ × 8'5″). A reddish gold and lavender peony trellis on an abrashed blue field is bordered with gold mazework. Coarsely knotted with so-called Senneh loop; ND in medium blue, reddish gold, and a possibly synthetic lavender. Good quality; good condition. ....Est. $3,500/4,500; sold for $3,737

CHINESE RUGS

Weaving in China is an ancient, well-documented craft. Old Chinese rugs are asymmetrically knotted, averaging 50 knots per square inch, and their warps lie in a single plane, which results in a rather loose-textured, flat-backed rug. The lanolin-rich pile of the best of the early examples has an incomparably lush handle.

Unlike most other rustic rugs, those made in China have cotton foundations: hand-spun in early examples, machine-spun after about 1850. The edges and ends, which were not as a rule very securely finished, were easily damaged, resulting in the frequent loss of adjacent pile knots. The palette of vegetable dyes was limited: indigo blues, yellow, ivory, blacks, and browns; although madder red was used, it was never to the degree seen elsewhere. Village rug designs tend to be simple blends of floral and symbolic motifs used together with medallions and tile-pattern repeats. Both floral and fret motifs are seen in borders.

Twenty years ago superb antique Chinese rugs could be bought here for comparatively little because they were little known and unappreciated, even by the trade. Today, except for the occasional unrecognized treasure spotted at a country auction or antique shop, this is no longer the case.

Carpet (early 19th century, 6'9″ × 13'11″). A dark blue floral roundel on an ivory field ornamented with a well-balanced dark blue peony and leafy vinery cornered by dark blue arabesques. An inner border of blue fretwork on gold is enclosed by an ivory and blue peony and vine repeat on coral. Coarse, asym.; ND in dark and medium blue, coral, gold, ivory. Superior quality; good condition. (See color section.) ....Est. $10,000/15,000; sold for $17,250

Chinese Banner Rug, c. 1875, 4'6" × 7'10", $2,875. PHOTO COURTESY OF CHRISTIE'S

Chinese Throne Cover, c. 1875, 2′3″ × 2′3″, $488.75. PHOTO COURTESY
OF SKINNER, INC.

Banner Rug (2nd half 19th century, 4′6″ × 7′10″). A polychrome Chinese "angel"
beneath an elaborate hanging lamp on a warm brown field further ornamented with
stylized clouds and flowering vinery, within cloud and geometric repeat borders.
Coarse, asym.; ND in dark and medium blue, rose, gold, cinnamon. Very good
quality; good condition. ....Est. $2,500/3,500; sold for $2,875

Rug (2nd half 19th century, 6′3″ × 8′10″). A dark blue roundel formed by sinuous
dragons centered on a spacious peony and leafy vinery on ivory and flanked by stylized dragon spandrels. The pale gold and blue inner fretwork border is enclosed by
a palmette and "butterfly" leafy meander in pale pink and buff on dark blue. Coarse,
asym.; ND in dark blue, pink, yellow, buff, ivory. Superior quality; some staining
but otherwise good condition. ....Est. $6,000/8,000; sold for $17,250

Ningshia Pillar Carpet (mid 19th century, 5′7″ × 10′3″). A centered large sinuous
dark blue dragon, stylized clouds, and a flaming pearl on a yellow field with a polychrome wave and cloud-band lower border. Coarse, asym.; ND in dark and light
blue, peach, yellow, buff, ivory. Very good quality; good condition. ....
....Est. $5,000/7,000; sold for $5,175

Throne Cover (2nd half 19th century, 2′3″ × 2′3″). A centered frontal view of a

hissing clawed dragon flanked by coiled clawed dragons on a rich gold field within a border of highly stylized mountain, rain, and cloud motifs. Coarse, asym.; ND in dark and light blue, gold, tan, ivory. Good quality; fair condition..............................
....Est. $600/800; sold for $488.75

FLATWEAVES, 1800–1925

Rug collectors attuned to the resonance of tradition are apt to be particularly attracted to flatweaves. In fact, a mystique—and ongoing controversy—has developed concerning the claimed neolithic origins of motifs seen on some very old Anatolian kilims. Neolithic or not, their slow evolution over the centuries provides the collector of these beautiful weavings a satisfying source of never-ending speculation.

Bales of rugs used to be shipped from the east wrapped in old kilims, which until recently were considered too humble to be collectible—assuming they were considered at all. Today those sadly undervalued wrappings would be reverentially hung where their exquisite colors and bold patterning could be seen to the best advantage.

Soumak rugs, whose structure is more technically demanding than that of kilims, were made in workshops in the Caucasus early on and produced there in quantity for commercial sale during the revival period. Although they lack the mythic quality of very old rustic kilims, they too are sought by collectors, who find their textured counterweave more appealing than what one aficionado, writing in *Oriental Rug Review*, referred to as "the harder, flatter kilim weaves or burr-cut stumps of yarn that constitute pile weaving." Tribal-woven soumak-faced bags—in fact, flat-woven bags of all types—remain a stunning and affordable alternative to abstract paintings despite their recent run-up in price.

Because flatweaves are not in the mainstream of oriental rug collecting, a representative selection of good off-beat examples is usually lacking among auction offerings. In the last year no noteworthy Turkoman and very few Central Asian—i.e. Uzbek, Kerghiz, Karakalpak, Kazakh—examples were offered, and only a limited number of Turkish flatweaves aside from kilims. Specialty dealers (see the Resource Guide) are still the best source.

KILIMS

TURKISH

Central Anatolian (mid 19th century, 5'7" × 11'3"). Horizontal bands of bold latchhooked polychrome medallions in two mismatched panels bordered at each end in ivory. ND in reds, blues, and greens. Very good quality; dirty but in fair condition. ....Est. $1,000/1,500; sold for $1,380

Kuba Kilim Rug, Northeast Caucasus, dated 1893, 6'3" × 10'9", $1,955. PHOTO COURTESY OF SKINNER, INC.

Shirvan Kilim Rug, East Caucasus, c. 1885, 7' × 11'4", $1,150. PHOTO COURTESY OF SKINNER, INC.

Anatolian Rug (early 20th century, 3'8" × 5'). An "eye dazzler" design of interlocking stepped checkerboard diamonds centered by a small geometric device. ND in red, medium blue, light blue-green, gold, ivory, reddish brown. End border stripe missing. Good quality; fair to good condition......Est. $1,000/1,200; sold for $1,150

CAUCASIAN

Kuba Rug, Northeast Caucasus (dated 1893, 6'3" × 10'9"). Bands of four to five staggered diamond-shaped medallions on a dark blue field bordered with large geometric devices on red. ND in red, rose, dark and medium blue, blue-green, gold, ivory. Good quality; good condition.....................Est. $1,500/2,500; sold for $1,955

Shirvan Rug, East Caucasus (last quarter 19th century, 5'6" × 7'9"). Bands of ivory-edged stepped polychrome hexagons alternate with narrow bands in plain red and blue and diamond-ornamented ivory. ND in dark and medium blue, blue-green, red, gold, tan, ivory, reddish brown. Good quality; good condition. ....
....Est. $800/1,200; sold for $920

Shirvan Rug, East Caucasus (last quarter 19th century, 5'10" × 8'2"). Wide bands in red and sky blue ornamented with bold double-ended ram's horn motifs alternate with narrow ivory bands with a large scale simple meander. ND in blue, light blue-green, red, green, gold, ivory. Good quality; fair condition......................................
....Est. $700/900; sold for $920

Shirvan Rug, East Caucasus (c. 1900, 5'4" × 10'5"). Narrow flat-woven bands with simple embroidered geometric repeats. ND in dark and medium blue, blue-green, red, gold, apricot. Very good quality; good condition. ....
....Est. $3,000/4,000; sold for $2,300

Shirvan Rug, East Caucasus (last quarter 19th century, 7' × 11'4"). Wide bands of bold latchhooked polychrome hexagons separated by narrow ivory bands with a precisely woven "running dog" meander within an ivory and brown reciprocal trefoil border. ND in dark and medium blue, blue-green, red, gold, ivory. Very good quality; fair to good condition. ....Est. $1,500/2,000; sold for $1,150

PERSIAN

Qashqai Rug, Southwest Persia (c. 1880, 4'7" × 7'9"). Distinguished by its lustrous wool and saturated colors, this kilim has two large polychrome diamonds, each with small centered geometric devices on ivory, within a dark blue and ivory reciprocal trefoil border, two narrow borders, zigzag borders in red and blue, and with narrow brocaded strips at each end. ND in dark and medium blue, blue-green, green, red, yellow, ivory. Superior quality; good condition. ....
....Est. $5,000/7,000; sold for $5,750

Senneh Rug, Northwest Persia (late 19th century, 3'2" × 4'6"). Staggered rows of generously proportioned, well-spaced *boteh* on a black ground within three narrow borders with geometric repeats. ND in sky blue, light blue-green, rose, red, gold, and corroded charcoal black. Superior quality; fair condition. ....
....Est. $1,200/1,500; sold for $1,495

Bags, Northwest Persian (early 20th century, 2'2" × 4'8"). Horizontal bands containing red and blue columns with ivory sawtoothed edging separated by narrow bands ornamented with stepped diamonds. ND in red, blue, blue-green, gold, ivory, dark brown. Good quality; fair condition. ....Est. $800/1,200; sold for $517.50

*Senneh Kilim
Rug, Northwest
Persia, c. 1890,
3'2" × 4'6",
$1,495.* PHOTO
COURTESY OF
SKINNER, INC.

SOUMAK (SOUMAC)

CAUCASIAN

Caucasian soumaks are generally attributed in the literature to either Kuba or Shirvan.

Rug (c. 1880, 6'7" × 9'7"). An unusual soumak design of six rows of four large stylized palmette medallions on a red ground with numerous geometric fillers within a gold main border with a stepped hexagon repeat, two geometric-repeat guards, and an outer "running dog" meander. ND in red, dark and medium blue, blue-green, gold, ivory. Superior quality; good condition. ....Est. $5,000/7,000; sold for $8,050

Long Rug (last quarter 19th century, 5'1" × 10'). Refined hexagonal lattice with palmette motifs on a yellow field within an ivory border with stepped hexagons and hourglass repeats guarded by narrow blue borders with rosette repeats. ND in dark and light red, dark and royal blue, blue-green, gold, yellow, ivory, Superior quality; good condition. ....Est. $6,000/8,000; sold for $6,325

Caucasian Soumak Rug, c. 1890, 5'6" × 7'8", $9,200. PHOTO COURTESY OF SKINNER, INC.

Rug (late 19th century, 5'6" × 7'8"). Highly stylized polychrome dragon motif on dark blue bordered with stylized palmette, blossom, and leaf figures on bright ochre, all within the elaborate blue and ivory "running dog" motif associated with Seichour weavings. ND in dark and royal blue, red, pink, green, ochre, ivory. Very good quality; good condition..............................Est. $7,000/9,000; sold for $9,200

Rug (late 19th century, 2'10" × 5'3"). A column of four complete and one partial Lesghi stars, each separated by three stepped diamonds, on a brick red ground with a reciprocal trefoil inner border and a main border with a polychrome repeat of "S"

Shahsevan Soumak Bags, North Central Persia, c. 1885, 1'9" × 1'10", $920. PHOTO COURTESY OF SKINNER, INC.

Shahsevan Soumak Bag, North Central Persia, c. 1920, 2' × 2', $632.50. PHOTO COURTESY OF SKINNER, INC.

Shahsevan Bag Face, North Central Persia, c. 1900, 1'5" × 1'7", $345. PHOTO COURTESY OF SKINNER, INC.

diagonals. ND in dark and medium blue, brick and cinnamon red, green, gold, ivory, light brown. Very good quality; fine condition...
....Est. $5,000/7,000; sold for $6,900

PERSIAN

The Shahsevan (Shahsavan) bags in the following list originated in a wide area from Teheran in Central Persia northward to Azerbaijan. Shahsevan weavers specialize in fine flat-woven articles.

Shahsevan Bags, North Central Persia (last quarter 19th century, 1'9" × 1'10"). Staggered rows of bold hooked squares on dark blue bordered with polychrome geometric repeats on ivory within reciprocal trefoil repeats. ND in red, dark and medium blue, light blue-green, ivory, reddish brown. Very good quality; fair condition. ....Est. $300/500; sold for $920

Shahsevan Bags, North Central Persia (c. 1875, each 1'9" × 1'10"). A format popular with collectors consisting of precisely woven arrow-headed, blossom-centered cruciform medallions on ivory, flanked by blossom-centered spandrels. The elegant border of polychrome interlocking triangles on dark blue has delicate reciprocal trefoil guards. ND in brick and dark red, dark, medium, and light blue, light blue-green, gold, tan, ivory. Superior quality; good condition. ....
....Est. $7,000/10,000; sold for $8,050

Shahsevan Bag, North Central Persia (early 20th century, 2' × 2'). Four rows of stylized plant motifs on an apricot field within polychrome "pinwheels" and diamonds on the ivory main border guarded with rosette repeats. ND in red, apricot, dark, medium, and light blue, ivory. Very good quality; fine condition, but lacks the age collectors prize. ....Est. $600/800; sold for $632.50

Shahsevan Bag Face, Central-North Persia (c. 1900, 1'5" × 1'7"). Uncommon design consisting of a red stepped polygon on a sky blue field flanked by bold

Left: *Baluch* Sofre, *Northeast Persia, c. 1890, 2'10" × 9', $517.50.* PHOTO
COURTESY OF SKINNER, INC. Right: *Northwest Persian* Jajim, *c. 1900,
4'10" × 6'4", $920.* PHOTO COURTESY OF SKINNER, INC.

highly stylized *Afshan* flower motifs knotted in white cotton. The narrow border
consists of diagonal stripes. ND in blue, red, ivory. Good quality; fair but dirty
condition. ....Est. $300/500; sold for $345

Shahsevan Cargo Bag, Central-North Persia (late 19th century, 3'6" × 1'8" ×
1'4"). Four bold hooked concentric hexagons on red, with serrated triangle borders.
ND in blue, blue-green, gold, red, ivory. Very good quality; fair to good condition.
....Est. $800/1,200; sold for $920

OTHER FLATWEAVES

Uzbek Bags, Central Asia (late 19th century, 2'8" × 5'2"). Hooked geometric
motifs within a diamond lattice on a red field. The interlocking-triangle border
has zigzag guards. ND in dark blue, red, gold, green, ivory. Good quality; good
condition. ....Est. $700/900; sold for $603.75

Baluch Meal Cloth *(Sofre)*, Northeast Persia (late 19th century, 2'10" × 9').
Narrow stripes with small geometric motifs on a finely woven ivory field with a

zigzag border in red and dark blue. ND in red, dark blue, aubergine. Very good quality; good condition..Est. $600/800; sold for $517.50.

Baluch Long Rug, Northeast Persia (c. 1875, 5'7" × 9'10"). Narrow bands of traditional Baluch tribal motifs woven in mixed techniques within a diamond repeat border guarded by a narrow ivory "running dog" repeat. ND in dark and medium blue, aubergine, ivory. Superior quality; poor condition. ....
....Est. $1,000/1,500; sold for $2,990

Bags, Central Caucasus (c. 1900, 1'9" × 4'4"). An all-over hooked diamond lattice bordered by a hexagon repeat in a balanced plain-weave technique known as *zili*, but often labeled inaccurately in the trade as *verneh*. ND in medium blue, blue-green, red, gold, ivory, black. Good quality; good condition. ....
....Est. $700/900; sold for $747.50

Jajim (Jejim) Northwest Persia (c. 1900, 4'10" × 6'4"). Elegant motifs and coloration distinguish this flatweave, which has finely detailed star motifs on ivory stripes alternating with stripes in plain blue and blue-green. ND in dark and medium blue, blue-green, gold, cochineal-dyed crimson, ivory. Very good quality; fair to good condition. ....Est. $700/900; sold for $920

Horse Cover, Central Caucasus (late 19th century, 5'7" × 9'3"). Appealing folky piece depicting in a horizontal format a hunting party with stylized but easily recognizable camels, dogs, and horses with riders carrying hawks perched on their wrists. The charcoal black field has a narrow, very simple geometric repeat. ND in medium and royal blue, blue-green, red, gold, ivory. Superior quality; good condition. ....
....Est. $10,000/15,000; sold for $14,900

Verni (Verneh) Karabagh District (late 19th century, 6'9" × 9'8"). A flatweave design popular with collectors, it features highly stylized dragons in large squared "S" shaped figures, typically four rows of four. The variegated red field also contains a variety of animal figures and geometric fillers and animal figures. ND in madder and cochineal reds, dark and royal blue, blue-green, gold, ivory. Good quality; good condition..Est. $2,000/2,500; sold for $4,025

Caucasian "Dragon" Verni, Karabagh District, c. 1890, 6'9" × 9'8", $4,025. PHOTO COURTESY OF SKINNER, INC.

COMMERCIAL CARPETS, 1875–1930

Upon hearing the phrase "oriental carpet," the average person pictures a room-size rug made in Persia and richly ornamented with swirling floral patterns. The rug that fits this mental image has a balanced design developed by an artist and woven with dyed-to-order wool supplied to skilled weavers working in an urban workshop under contract. Even the finishing stages of clipping and washing are carried out by specialists. The fact of its being a commercial product reproduced in quantity, perhaps in a variety of popular sizes, matters little to someone wishing a handsome floor covering, and indeed, why should it? If one is not a collector, a good commercial rug will provide not only many years of decoration and service, but assuming one chooses wisely, eventual price appreciation too.

Most of the rugs categorized as commercial *were* in fact made in Persia—known as Iran only since 1935—but workshops in Turkey and India and later in China were also active during this period. Many of these rugs, distinguished by the attention given to design details and the technical skill of their weaving, are justly highly valued. The majority were intended as floor coverings; the much smaller production of modestly sized, extremely finely knotted silks are best reserved for display as wall hangings or table covers.

The court carpets of the 15th–17th centuries were workshop extravaganzas made for a wealthy and aristocratic clientele; today rug workshops thrive in a dozen or more countries, producing rugs to suit every taste and pocketbook. Here we will be looking at rugs made between roughly 1875—when, if you will remember, entrepreneurs began organizing weavers to supply the needs of a growing and prosperous market in the West—and 1930, when Eastern traditions began being supplanted by transient Western color and design fashions. (An extreme example are the Chinese Art Deco rugs, long consigned to attics, which are now making a comeback.)

One way to distinguish a workshop rug made with an artist-designed cartoon from a freehand village rug is the regularity of the workshop product's layout and spacing of motifs. Although many well-made village rugs may appear to be unexceptional in these regards, a second look almost invariably reveals numerous variations and small irregularities that, despite their appeal to present-day collectors, are frowned upon in workshop products.

As you read through the list of carpets below, bear in mind that, according to the trade magazine *Decorative Rug*, "the word quality is used in the oriental rug industry to grade a rug's weave as to degrees of fineness. It is a descriptive rather than a judgmental term." In other words, given a selection of rugs all made with equally good materials, the more coarsely woven examples, no matter how attractive or serviceable they may be, are automatically considered of lower quality than more finely knotted pieces which may, in fact, not wear as well.

Note: Decorative commercial carpets offered at auction are more likely to have been "fiddled" than smaller collectible rustic and tribal rugs. Consult the auction house experts concerning any tinting, painting, or reduction in size that may have been done to carpets that interest you. Obviously, you shouldn't pay as much for an altered or painted carpet as you would for a similar unaltered example, but temper your decision with common sense: a rug destined for placement under a dining room table can afford to have areas of central wear, as these will hardly be seen; missing borders, which would be obvious in a dining room, might be unnoticeable in a living room in which edges are largely hidden by couches, chairs, and side tables.

TURKEY

Throughout the 19th century, a cottage industry producing great numbers of traditionally patterned rugs prevailed in Turkey and, for the most part, still does. Finely knotted commercial carpets, woven in response to the revival of interest in oriental rugs, were made in only a few urban workshops, the output both in design and palette bearing little resemblance to the colorful, sturdy rustic rugs now commanding very respectable prices from collectors.

HEREKE

The workshop rugs made in Hereke, 40 miles from Istanbul, were originally produced in a court manufactory established there in the mid-19th century. Designs borrowed from Ottoman and Persian Sefavid court rugs have been woven as finely as 800 knots per square inch. Ghiordes prayer rug designs have also been copied. Unlike other Turkish rugs, the knots are often asymmetrical; the materials range from all wool to all silk; the dyes and workmanship are impeccable. The best Herekes are very expensive, but the examples sold at auction during the past two years were not of this quality.

Hereke Carpet, West Turkey (last quarter 19th century, 15′ × 18′). Polychrome bouquets in muted hues within a blue curvilinear trellis on a cream field enclosed by a rose border with a stylized flowering vine meander. Fine, sym.; ND in medium blue, red, rose, pale olive green, dull gold, cream. Good quality; good condition. ....
....Est. $8,000/12,000; sold for $9,200

OUSHAK (USHAK)

The venerable Oushak name is unfortunately also attached to a large output of "rug revival" carpets, typically very coarsely woven in large sizes, originally in harshly bright synthetic colors and later in pastels that paled further in use. The symmetrical knots, ranging from 16 to 40 per sq. in., are tied on a wool foundation. Only occasionally does one recommend itself from an otherwise forgettable crowd and then more for its decorative than collectible potential.

Oushak Carpet, West Turkey (late 19th century, 8'11" × 10'2"). Often chosen by those seeking a rug with an undemanding palette for an existing interior color scheme, this typically washed-out looking example sold for a respectable price. The pale, grayed blue-green field has an open lattice vinery with dull gold palmettes and a scattering of dark olive leaves within a pale salmon main border with a crudely drawn palmette and blossom motif, enclosed by narrow dull gold guards with a flower and vine repeat. Coarse, sym.; ND and SD in pale salmon, dull steel blue, dull gold, dark olive, charcoal, ivory. Good quality for type, good condition............ ....Est. $7,000/9,000; sold for $8,050

CAUCASUS

Kuba Rug, Northwest Caucasus (late 19th century, 4'6" × 5'10"). Woven for the St. Petersburg and European markets, this rug features a rose medallion ornamented with stylized red and cream cabbage roses on a dark blue field with gold vinery and realistic cabbage rose spandrels within an exuberantly floral dark blue border guarded by narrow rose stripes. Fine, sym.; ND in midnight and medium blue, red, rose, pistachio, dull gold. Good quality; good condition. ....Est. $3,500/4,500; sold for $4,025

KARABAGH (QARABAGH), SOUTH CAUCASUS

Of finer weave than village Karabaghs, the workshop variety can often be identified by their larger size and a penchant for pinky-purple shades of red characteristic of cochineal-derived dyes. Old rugs have a wool foundation with each row of symmetrical knots separated from the succeeding row by two wefts.

Corridor Carpet (c. 1875, 7'3" × 22'4"). Centered upon the gold, blossom-ornamented symmetrical lattice on the dark blue ground is a red, pendanted and flower-filled diamond medallion. The red main border has a pretty *Mina Khani*–like floral repeat. Average, sym.; ND in dark and medium blue, blue-green, red rose, gold, ivory. Very good quality; good condition..............Est. $8,000/12,000; sold for $13,800

PERSIA/IRAN

The carpets included here are considered the most collectible of the commercial class of carpets made, roughly, between 1875 and 1930. Although some of the rugs may have been woven on village looms, non-traditional designs were either supplied or strongly influenced by commercial contractors.

Carpets were woven in so many locations in Persia that an across-the-board survey is not feasible in a book of this length. (Readers wishing a more encyclopedic treatment should consult the annotated book list in the Resource Guide.) The finely knotted rugs from Qum and Nain were not included because weaving did not begin in those cities until the late 1930s, and in any event, their sterile, mechanical look argues against their being considered collectible.

AFSHAR, SOUTH PERSIA

Afshari rugs and carpets with European-style floral patterns were probably made in workshops in the Kerman area, and influenced by Kerman designs. Unlike Afshar tribal rugs, this commercial production is apt to be asymmetrically knotted on a cotton foundation.

Rug (last quarter 19th century, 4'8" × 7'6"). This dressy rug woven for the European carpet features clusters of cream and crimson roses on a dark blue ground flanked by spandrels ornamented with filigreed *boteh* on dark blue. Roses are repeated on two cream and blue-grounded borders enclosed by reciprocal trefoil guards. Fine, prob. asym.; ND in dark blue, crimson, pale gold, pale green, cream, tan. Very good quality; good condition..............Est. $8,000/10,000; sold for $8,050

BAHKTIARI (BAKTIARI; CHAHAR MAHAL), CENTRAL PERSIA

Authorities doubt that Bahktiaris, a large tribal group inhabiting the territory between Isfahan and the Zagros Mountains, wove the pile rugs to which their name has been attached. Chahar Mahal, a district within the Baktiari-dominated region where weavers of Turkish and Kurdish descent live, is probably a more accurate label for the commercial weaving done in this region. The wool is of good quality; but in later examples of the commonly seen pattern described here, the colors are apt to be glaringly bright.

Carpet (late 19th century, 8'5" × 12'1"). Boldly patterned with polychrome trees within a vinery on a dark blue ground. Stylized blossom heads and clusters ornament a wide ivory main border that complements the scale of the field design. Average, sym.; ND in dark and medium blue, rose, red, gold, dark green, ivory. Good quality; good condition...........................Est. $10,000/15,000; sold for $9,200

Carpet (1st quarter 20th century, 11'7" × 19'5"). A stiff but decorative version of the *Bid Majnun* pattern on an ivory field, bordered by polychrome roundels and ivory pendanted medallions on dark blue within numerous narrow borders. Average, sym.; ND in dark and medium blue, red, rose, gold, dark green, ivory. Good quality; good condition...........................Est. $10,000/15,000; sold for $9,200

Carpet (c. 1900, 12' × 12'8"). Twelve rows of the polychrome boxed-trees-and-flowers format typical of 20th-century Baktiari weaving, which in later, synthetically dyed examples is apt to be glaringly bright. The red main border has a rather

awkward flower and serrated leaf repeat within ivory guards with stylized palmette and leaf meanders. Average, sym.; ND in dark and medium blue, blue-green, red, pink, green, gold, aubergine. Very good quality; good condition...............................
....Est. $12,000/15,000; sold for $18,400

BIDJAR (BIJAR), NORTHWEST PERSIA

The sturdy, coarsely woven scatter-size rugs with the "salt-and-pepper" back seen in millions of Western homes were woven in Hamadan, a famously productive weaving area northwest of Kashan. Although often appealing and "affordable," few of these rugs are as collectible as those made in the Kurdish weaving towns to the north and west of Hamadan, one of which is Bidjar.

The classic Bidjar rug has vegetable-dyed wool symmetrically knotted on a wool foundation. The thick warps—cotton in more recent examples— are alternately depressed to the degree that one of each knot's nodes is entirely hidden. Given the springy quality of wool, the high average knot count of old Bidjars—144 per sq. in.—required the two wefts between each row to be beaten in with unusual force, thus producing a tightly packed structure of unequaled density. Examples of these very hard-wearing old rugs are also included in the section on rustic rugs.

Carpet (last quarter 19th century, 13'3" × 22'). On a dark blue ground, a rather angular but lushly piled polychrome variation of the popular *Gerus* tree and blossom design within an apricot vinery trellis, bordered by a graceful palmette, blossom, and leaf repeat on ivory. Average, sym., knotted on a wool warp; ND in dark, medium and light blue, light blue-green, red, apricot, yellow, ivory. Very good quality; good condition..........................Est. $35,000/45,000; sold for $34,500

Rug (early 20th century, 3'7" × 5'5"). A gabled and pendanted medallion in rose and sky blue on a dark blue field with an allover *Herati* pattern within a palmette and serrated leaf meander on rose. Average, sym.; ND in dark and medium blue, blue-green, red, rose, gold, ivory. Good quality; good condition. ....
....Est. $2,000/3,000; sold for $2,875

Carpet (last quarter 19th century, 9' × 13'4"). An exceptional example of the *Gerus* tree and blossom design with ivory-edged rose arabesques on a lustrous dark blue ground. The tomato red border has a pretty palmette, blossom, and flowering vine meander; flowers and curved leaves ornament the ivory guards. Average, sym.; ND in dark, medium, and light blue, blue-green, red, rose, pink, saffron, gold, spring green, ivory. Superior quality; good condition. ....Est. $15,000/20,000; sold for $23,000

Sampler (*wagireh*) (last quarter 19th century, 5'9" × 9'1"). This prime collectible piece features a large-scale portion of the *Gerus* design in rich, saturated colors on an evenly worn dark blue ground bordered by a narrow, refined flower and leaf meander on ivory. Average, sym.; ND in dark, medium and light blue, red, rose, gold, spring green, ivory. Superior quality; fair condition.........Est. $5,000/7,000; sold for $12,650

FERAHAN, NORTH PERSIA

The trade has applied this name to a class of distinguished old rugs woven in the Arak district, mostly in traditional repeating designs, principally the Herati.

Bidjar Gerus Carpet, Northwest Persia, c. 1880, 13′3″ × 22′, $34,500.
AUTHOR'S PHOTO

Bidjar Rug, Northwest Persia, c. 1920, 3'7" × 5'5", $2,875. PHOTO COURTESY OF SKINNER, INC.

Ferahans are asymmetrically knotted, over 100 per sq. in., on a cotton foundation with wefts dyed pink or blue. Their excellent vegetable dyes commend antique examples to collectors. (See also Ferahan Sarouk under Sarouk.)

"Palace" Carpet (c. 1900, 16'10" × 27'). A dense pattern of polychrome Shah Abbas palmettes on a lustrous dark blue ground enclosed by a red main border with a stylized palmette, blossom, and vine meander. Fine; asym.; ND in dark and royal blue, red, rose, green, yellow, gold, tan, ivory. Very good quality; good condition... ....Est. $60,000/80,000; sold for $65,000

Silk Carpet (c. 1900, 6'2" × 9'10"). Flowering plants, stylized blossoms, and an open vinery on a honey ground. The ruby red main border has a stiff but well-resolved palmette and serrated leaf repeat enclosed by four pairs of very narrow guards. Fine, asym.; ND in medium and light blue, ruby red, rose, peach, green, gold, honey, pale aubergine. Very good quality; good condition. ....Est. $7,000/10,000; sold for $17,250

HERIZ, NORTHWEST PERSIA

The province of Azerbaijan in northwest Iran is home to the robustly patterned rectilinear medallion rugs known generically as Heriz. Also woven here are the similar but more finely woven type labeled in the trade as Serapi, and the distinctive, often spectacular, rustic-looking Bakshaish carpets. Although these rugs are for the most part a cottage industry, some of the designs, like those of the Bidjars mentioned above, have more to do with Western fashion than tradition. Symmetrically knotted and woven with varying degrees of fineness on a cotton foundation, very coarse examples are more appropriately labeled Gorevan.

A very beautiful, finely knotted class of silk rugs is also said to have been woven by Heriz weavers, an attribution denounced by at least one scholar who claims these rugs are Tabriz products which, in recent years, have been labeled as Heriz because of the drawing power of the name with contemporary buyers. But as long as they continue to be tagged by dealers and auction houses as Heriz silks, collectors seeking these lovely rugs are advised to inquire after them by that name, whatever their true origin may be.

Carpet (late 19th century, 8′10″ × 12′1″). A blue-bordered, floral vine-filled ivory medallion on a floral vine-patterned red field flanked by dark blue spandrels, each with a large Shah Abbas palmette and flowering vinery. The tannish gold border has a palmette, blossom, and vine motif. Average, sym.; ND in dark, medium, and light blue, blue-green, brick red, rose, dull gold, tan, ivory. Very good quality; fair condition, but with some tinting......................Est. $15,000/20,000; sold for $23,000

Carpet (1st quarter 20th century, 11″ × 12′6″). A lobed and pendanted dark blue medallion with rose palmettes on a red field with a leaf and flower vinery flanked by ivory and blue floral spandrels. The main border has a graceful gold vinery with a pretty assortment of polychrome flowers. Average, sym.; ND in midnight, medium and light blue, red, rose, pink, gold, dull yellow, ivory. Very good quality; fair to good condition. ....Est. $20,000/25,000; sold for $20,700

Carpet (last quarter 19th century, 10′1″ × 13′4″). An eye-catching but atypical format featuring a squarish blue-red and ivory medallion with long tendrils on an abrashed plain coral pink ground, with similarly ornamented yellow-lobed spandrels enclosed by a red main border with a polychrome palmette and blossoming vine meander, and ivory guards with floral repeats. Average, sym.; ND in red, coral pink, dark and medium blue, pale pistachio, yellow, ivory. Very good quality; fair condition. ....Est. $20,000/30,000; sold for $25,300

Bakshaish Rug (late 19th century, 5′8″ × 6′2″). A pleasing format consisting of realistic weeping willows and flowering trees within a rectilinear lattice on an ivory field enclosed by a flower and vine meander on royal blue and a plain red outer border. Average, sym.; ND in dark and royal blue, red, rose, apricot, green, yellow, ivory. Superior quality; good condition..............Est. $5,000/7,000; sold for $13,800

Serapi Carpet (c. 1880, 11′ × 15′). Serapi is the trade name applied to the finest production of the Heriz area, of which this beautiful rug is a prime example. Centered on the ivory field's polychrome palmette and blossom vinery is a floral vinery-ornamented and pendanted midnight blue medallion within which is a gabled rose medallion and a small gold square with polychrome geometric motifs. The midnight blue spandrels display a well-drawn palmette, blossom, and vine meander design typical of the region, guarded by floral meanders on ivory. Fine, sym.; ND in dark and medium blue, blue-green, red, rose, gold, warm brown, ivory. Superior quality; good condition. (See color section.)................Dealer rug, $65,000

ISFAHAN, CENTRAL PERSIA

Isfahan is a beautiful city in central Iran where carpets were made for the Sefavid dynasty. Two centuries later, finely woven carpets—200–400 asymmetrical knots per sq. in. on a cotton foundation—again began to be woven here, but the materials used in Isfahan rugs made after World War II—a period not discussed here—are considered better than those used at the beginning of the weaving revival.

Carpet (early 20th century, 8'9" × 11'10"). Symmetrically placed polychrome palmette and flower roundels on an ivory field within a dense vinery lattice. The wide rose palmette and flowering vine border is guarded by two pairs of floral repeats. Fine, asym.; ND and SD in dark, medium and light blue, red, rose, gold. Good quality; fine condition. ....Est. $10,000/15,000; sold for $16,100

KASHAN, CENTRAL PERSIA

About 100 miles south of Isfahan lies Kashan, which is also famed for the fine carpets and other textiles woven there during Sefavid times. Turn-of-the-century Kashans, tightly woven of wool or silk, sometimes in combination, are highly regarded in today's rug trade—particularly the wool-pile carpets distinguished as *Mohtashem*, a label variously interpreted to refer to a master weaver and a superior grade of wool. Although woven on cottage looms, the elaborate curvilinear designs were supplied by commercial contractors. The best Kashans boast velvety wool with tight asymmetrical knots, 300–400 per sq. in., on a cotton foundation. Alternate warps are deeply depressed; double wefts are typically blue. Kashan rugs are appropriate for formal, dressy interiors, with the silk-warped, silk-pile examples reserved for wall or table decoration.

Carpet, Manchester type (1st quarter 20th century, 11'11" × 18'). This large formal carpet, said to be woven from fine merino wool processed in Manchester, England, features detached floral sprays on a lustrous ruby red ground within a palmette, flower, and leafy vine meander on dark blue. Fine, asym.; ND in dark, medium, and light blue, ruby red, gold, ivory. Very good quality; good condition. ....Est. $20,000/30,000; sold for $21,850

Silk Rug (last quarter 19th century, 3'4" × 6'2"). An all-over loose pattern of flowering vinery, principally royal blue and red, on an ivory field within a royal blue border with a flower and vine meander. Fine, asym.; ND in red, dark and royal blue, gold, ivory. Good quality; fine condition. ....Est. $12,000/15,000; sold for $12,650

"Mohtashem" Carpet (last quarter 19th century, 11'11" × 19'1"). A large, handsome furnishing rug with a dense pattern of muted polychrome floral sprays covering a pale honey field bordered by a floral vinery on honey enclosed by three pairs of narrow *boteh* and flower repeat guards. Fine, asym.; ND in dark blue, pale red, rose, apricot, pale gold, honey. Good quality; good condition. ....
....Est. $25,000/35,000; sold for $59,700

"Mohtashem" Carpet (last quarter 19th century, 8'10" × 11'2"). Selling for almost twice the high estimate, this refined small carpet has a rose ground with an unusual pattern of 15 rows of 5 cartouches, each row alternately ivory and light blue-green; each cartouche filled with flower-ornamented Islamic calligraphy. Pale blue-green minor borders with a flowering vine meander enclose the calligraphy-filled cartouche repeat on the ivory main border. Fine, asym.; ND in dark and medium blue, light blue-green, rose, pink, pale gold. Very good quality; good condition. ....Est. $7,000/10,000; sold for $19,550

KERMAN, SOUTHEAST PERSIA

This formerly isolated provincial city was also a Sefavid weaving center, but it later gained fame for its shawl production, at one time rivaling that of Kashmir. The traditional Kerman rug of the revival period is short-piled and asymmetrically knotted on a cotton foundation with a density sometimes exceeding 400 knots per sq. in., rarely fewer than 140. Alternate warps are deeply depressed, and the Kerman uniquely has three wefts.

The designs used in the city workshops and surrounding villages were professionally conceived and are distinguished by their delicacy of both ornament and coloration. A lovely magenta shade of red obtained from cochineal is characteristic of many turn-of-the-century Kermans. Rugs particularly finely woven are known in the trade as Ravar—sometimes, wrongly, as Laver—Kermans, after a town supposed to be their source. These refined old rugs have nothing in common with the thick-piled, detached-floral and open-field pastel varieties designed in later years for the American market.

Prayer Rug (c. 1870, 4'6" × 5'8"). This charming antique rug features two golden tan, stylized cypress trees on a floral-swirled ivory *mihrab* beneath a dark blue palmette and vinery arch within a cartouche and blossom repeat on dark blue. Fine, asym.; ND in dark, medium, and light blue, red, rose, salmon, golden tan, ivory. Superior, fair to poor condition. (See color section.)...
....Est. $3,000/4,000; sold for $4,830

Ravar Kerman Carpet (c. 1875, 9'11" × 11'6"). An unusual oversized prayer rug format featuring three elaborate columns and loose floral vinery on an ivory *mihrab* beneath a dark blue flower-ornamented arch. The main border, a stylized palmette, blossom, and leaf repeat on ivory, is enclosed by three pairs of floral meanders on dark blue and ivory. Fine, asym.; ND in dark and medium blue, red, salmon, peach, pale yellow, ivory. Good quality; good condition. ....
....Est. $10,000/15,000; sold for $10,350

MALAYER

Lying south of Hamadan and west of Arak within a broad rug-producing area, Malayer produced rugs that, unlike their Hamadan cousins, were apt to be double-wefted. Seen mostly in scatter to area sizes with medallion-centered formats, they are as finely knotted and elegantly designed as Ferehan Sarouks, for which they are frequently mistaken. The foundation is typically cotton, and the pile is close-clipped.

Rug (c. 1885, 5'6" × 6'). A floral-ornamented and pendanted ivory medallion is centered on an abrashed dark blue ground ornamented with polychrome flowering

Malayer Rug, Northwest Persia, c. 1885, 5'6" × 6', $22,000. PHOTO 1990
SOTHEBY'S

vines and palmettes, and flanked by vine-decked honey-colored spandrels. The tan
primary border has a delicate flower and vine meander within ivory floral guards
and a bold reciprocal trefoil outer border. Fine, sym.; dark, medium, and light blue,
blue-green, red, rose, gold, honey, cream. Superior quality, good condition. In
1990, this exceptionally elegant rug sold for $22,000; it would probably bring a
similar price today.

NORTHWEST PERSIA, PRODUCTS OF
KURDISH WEAVERS

Corridor Carpet (last quarter 19th century, 6' × 16'6"). An ivory medallion with
a latticed polychrome Herati design is centered on a red pole extending the length
of a dark aubergine-brown ground and flanked by four pairs of diamond-shaped

fillers and Herati-ornamented medium-blue spandrels. The ivory main border has a blossom and vine meander and numerous narrow floral and geometric-repeat guards. Average, prob. sym.; ND in dark and medium blue, blue-green, red, rose-pink, gold, ivory, aubergine-brown. Very good quality; good condition....................
....Dealer rug, $10,000/$18,000

Rug (early 20th century, 4′7″ × 6′4″). A latticed polychrome *Mina Khani* design on a black field within a brown main border with a floral and leaf meander. Average, sym.; ND in royal and light blue, blue-green, dark red, rose, gold. Good quality; fair to good condition. ....Est. $1,000/1,200; sold for $1,035

QASHQAI

The weavers living in the Fars province bordering the Persian Gulf in the south of Iran are generally considered as belonging to tribal groups. Many weavers of the Qashqai group, however, can more accurately be described

Northwest Persian Corridor Carpet, c. 1885, 6′ × 16′6″, $10,000/$18,000.
PHOTO COURTESY OF PETER PAP ORI-
ENTAL RUGS, INC.

as workshop workers who, for 100 years or more, have lived largely settled lives. Fine old examples of these well-made, beautifully colored, and eminently collectible rugs are hotly competed for. Generally asymmetrically knotted on a wool foundation—occasionally silk-warped—the knot density averages 150 per sq. in.

Corridor Carpet (late 19th century, 7'3" × 13'5"). Justly selling for more than twice the high estimate, this lustrous carpet has 19 rows of filligreed polychrome *boteh* on a warm red field within a dark blue main border with a palmette and floral vinery, guarded by a graceful flower and serrated leaf meander on muted gold. Fine, asym.; ND in dark and light blue, blue-green, tomato red, salmon, rose, dull gold, green, brown, black. Superior quality; fine condition. (See color section.) ....
....Est. $6,000/8,000; sold for $20,700

SAROUK

The carpets bearing this name were woven in west central Iran, in and around the city of Arak, formerly Sultanabad, where workshop weaving was instituted in the second half of the 19th century. The best of these decorative rugs—known in the trade as Ferahan (Ferehan, Fereghan) Sarouk—were made mostly in floral-ornamented area sizes bearing elegantly drawn medallions. They are characterized by a short, tightly woven, velvety wool pile asymmetrically knotted, 100–200 per sq. in., on a cotton foundation with depressed alternate warps.

The modern Sarouk, a different kettle of fish altogether, has a longish, thick pile woven in detached floral spray designs developed for the American market after World War I. This generation of Sarouks has blue-dyed cotton wefts. Typically, the ground color varies from deep rose to maroon, achieved in early examples by bleaching a red considered too bright, repainting the pile with darker colors, and "restoring" the dulled pile to an artificial brilliance. Later rugs of this type were spared this torture, but if considering one, be wary.

Carpet (1st quarter 20th century, 10'6" × 13'8"). A refined version of the detached floral pattern on an unusual honey-cream ground within a wide blue-black border with a floral spray repeat, enclosed by medium blue floral-meander guards. Average, asym.; ND in dark and medium blue, light steel blue, brick red, pale honey, ivory. Average, asym. Good quality; good condition. ....
....Est. $15,000/20,000; sold for $13,800

Sarouk Rug (c. 1900, 4'4" × 6'6"). A floral-ornamented ivory medallion within a dark blue pendanted, stepped medallion on a terra-cotta red ground with an angular, all-over floral vinery flanked by wide floral ivory diagonals. The dark blue border has a palmette and vine meander. Average, asym.; ND in dark and light blue, blue-green, red, olive, ivory, reddish brown. A standard format of good quality in good condition. ....Est. $4,000/6,000; sold for $3,565

Sarouk-Ferahan Carpet (last quarter 19th century, 8' × 11'). This superb small carpet has a red star lattice with a symmetrically placed palmette and blossom vinery in a subdued palette within a wide midnight blue border with a polychrome

*Sarouk Rug,
West Central
Persia, c. 1900,
4′ 4″ × 6′ 6″,
$3,565.* PHOTO
COURTESY OF
SKINNER, INC.

floral spray and arabesque meander. Fine, asym.; ND in dark blue, medium and light steel blue, dark red, rose, dull gold, ivory. Superior quality; good condition.....
....Est. $12,000/15,000; sold for $16,100

Sarouk-Ferahan Rug (late 19th century, 4′ × 6′ 5″). Bidding rose well above the modest estimate on this elegant small rug featuring a bold blue polychrome floral-ornamented medallion on a cream field within a dark blue floral repeat border. Fine, asym.; ND in dark and medium blue, blue-green, red, rose, gold, ivory. Very good quality; fine condition..Est. $2,500/3,500; sold for $6,900

Sarouk-Ferahan Carpet (late 19th century, 4′ 4″ × 6′ 8″). A dark blue lobed, blossom-centered, pendanted medallion on an ivory field filled with polychrome flowering stems and flanked by vinery-ornamented, scalloped-edged, dark blue spandrels. The dark blue main border, which has a blossom, palmette, and vine meander, is enclosed by narrow floral-repeat guards. Fine, asym.; ND in dark and royal blue, blue-green, red, rose, gold, ivory. Good quality; good condition............
....Est. $1,800/2,200; sold for $2,645

*Sarouk Fer-
ahan Carpet,
West Central
Persia, c.
1885, 8' ×
11', $16,100.*
PHOTO COUR-
TESY OF
SKINNER, INC.

SERABEND, NORTH PERSIA

The field pattern of Serabend rugs, large and small, woven in the many villages that comprise this weaving district invariably consists of many rows of small *boteh*. The best of the older Serabends, of which the carpet listed here is an example, is the Mir.

Gallery Carpet (last quarter 19th century, 7'7" × 19'). Miniature polychrome *boteh* densely cover the abrashed red field of this Mir Serabend. A flower and vine meander on red is enclosed by cream borders with a stylized vinery meander usually associated with Ferahan rugs. Fine, asym.; ND in dark and medium blue, red, gold, ivory. Good quality; good condition. ....Est. $4,000/6,000; sold for $4,600

SULTANABAD, ARAK DISTRICT, CENTRAL PERSIA

Woven in the Arak district, best known for Sarouk rugs, Mahals and Sultanabads were largely a workshop production controlled by European firms

Sarouk-Ferahan Rug, West Central Persia, c. 1890, 4′4″ × 6′8″, $2,645.
PHOTO COURTESY OF SKINNER, INC.

like Ziegler. Both symmetrical and asymmetrical knots were used in these rugs, which, like the Sarouk, have a cotton foundation but are more coarsely woven and display a much less pronounced depression of the alternate warps. The designs tend to be sprawling versions of traditional floral motifs, but the best of them, thanks to good vegetable dyes, are admirably suited as decorative carpets for informal settings.

Mahal Carpet (late 19th century, 14′10″ × 17′4″). Bold palmettes, blossoms, and curvilinear serrated leaves are symmetrically arranged on a blue-black ground lacking all but one narrow flowering vine-meander border. Average, asym.; ND in dark and steel blue, red, apricot, peach, olive green. Good quality; fair condition.....
....Est. $15,000/20,000; sold for $14,950

Sultanabad Carpet (c. 1885, 9′9″ × 8′3″). The unornamented field is uncommon, but the floral vinery and width of the primary border is otherwise typical of the other workshop Sultanabad rugs described following. This rug sold at auction six years ago for $12,000, but considering the rise in popularity of Sultanabads as furnishing rugs—and the beautiful blue field of this one—it would bring more today. Average, sym; ND in dark and royal blue, blue-green, gold, red, green, cream. Very good quality, fair to good condition. ....Est. $15,000/$18,000; sold for $12,000

Sultanabad Carpet (last quarter 19th century, 11′9″ × 12′9″). A large-scale polychrome blossom and leaf vinery swirls gracefully across the abrashed spring green ground of this appealing decorative carpet, whose red wide main border has a palmette and leafy vine meander. Average, asym.; ND in dark and medium blue, brick red, gold, olive, ivory. Very good quality; good condition. ....
....Est. $20,000/25,000; sold for $27,500

Sultanabad Carpet (last quarter 19th century, 14′8″ × 17′). On a blue-black field whose visible wear failed to discourage bidders is a decorative, muted polychrome

Sultanabad Carpet, Central Persia, c. 1885, 9′9″ × 8′3″, $15,000/$18,000. PHOTO COURTESY OF SKINNER, INC.

palmette, blossom, and vinery lattice within a very wide warm brown main border with an angular blossom and vine meander. Average, asym.; ND in midnight and light blue, blue-green, red, rose, dull gold, olive green, tan, cinnamon brown. Very good quality; fair to poor condition.................Est. $10,000/15,000; sold for $27,600

TABRIZ

This well-known center of workshop weaving is situated in the far north-west corner of Iran. The rugs presented here have a symmetrically knotted wool pile, 200–250 per sq. in., on a cotton foundation, which is typically short and bristly. Silk Tabriz rugs are rather finer and occasionally knotted asymmetrically. Curvilinear and rectilinear medallion designs predominate on the wool carpets; the silks are often woven in a prayer format.

Carpet (late 19th century, 14'6" × 21'4"). A colorful version of the pendanted medallion design usually seen in muted earth tones in Tabriz rugs of this period. In this example, the peach-centered, stepped blue medallion is on an abrashed brick red field flanked by pale peach spandrels densely ornamented with polychrome floral motifs, all within a gold main border with a floral repeat. Fine, asym.; ND in brick red, midnight and medium blue, blue-green, pale peach, gold. Very good quality; good condition.................................Est. $15,000/20,000; sold for $24,150

Carpet (early 20th century, 10'6" × 17'1"). On a dark red ground, a variant of the classical Persian hunting design: lions, leopards, antelopes, and birds within a swirl of palmette and cloud-band ornamented vinery. A narrow border with calligraphy-ornamented gold cartouches separates the field from the dark green cloud band and flower repeat main border. Fine, asym.; ND in dark and medium blue, blue-green, dark red, rose, green, gold, ivory, tan, warm brown. Very good quality; fair to good condition. ....Est. $7,000/10,000; sold for $23,100

Carpet (late 19th century, 13'1" × 19'7"). This very dressy, lustrous carpet features three concentric, densely floral-ornamented medallions in red, pink, and blue on a similarly ornamented red field with blue floral vinery spandrels. Four pairs of narrow floral-repeat guards enclose the dark blue main border's palmette, flower, and vine meander. Fine, asym.; ND in red, pink, dark and medium blue, gold, tan, ivory. Very good quality; fine condition. ....Est. $40,000/60,000; sold for $71,250

Carpet (last quarter 19th century, 8'6" × 13'4"). This elegant small carpet has a midnight blue diamond-shaped medallion with floral vinery and cream and tan pendants on a cranberry rose ground swirled with floral vinery and flanked with dark blue floral spandrels, all within a tan main border with a palmette and vine repeat. Fine, asym.; ND in light cranberry, pink, dark and light steel blue, dull gold, tan, cream. Very good quality; good condition. ....Est. $15,000/20,000; sold for $14,950

TEHERAN

The present-day capital city of Iran was never an important weaving center, and its well-made workshop rugs are apt to be labeled as Isfahan. Asymmetrically knotted, about 200 per sq. in., on a cotton foundation, the double wefts may be pink or blue.

Carpet (c. 1900, 8'8" × 11'9"). A well-spaced, nicely drawn polychrome *Mina Khani* design on a royal blue field bordered by a palmette, blossom, and curled leaf repeat on red, within two pairs of floral-repeat guards. Fine, asym.; ND in midnight, royal and light blue, blue-green, red, rose, yellow, ivory. Very good quality; fine condition. ....Est. $6,000/8,000; sold for $9,430

INDIA

Except for the exceptionally accomplished and distinctive early weaving characteristic of the palace workshops, collectors have had little interest in Indian rugs. Although well woven of generally superior materials, the designs of later carpets are so derivative of foreign traditions they are routinely labeled Indo-Isfahan or -Kerman or -Tabriz—even Indo-Chinese.

The "jail carpets" from the venerable carpet-weaving center of Agra, where, in the mid-19th century, the British placed looms in the prisons, are often more interesting than other Indian carpets of this period. Like the cotton prison-made dhurries, native fauna were frequently incorporated into the designs, perhaps reflecting a yearning for the outside world. Of moderate density, they are asymmetrically knotted in wool on a cotton foundation.

Indo-Tabriz Carpet (1st quarter 20th century, 11'4" × 14'4"). A nicely spaced version of the classic Persian lattice design, in this case a red vinery on an ivory field, with polychrome palmettes, blossoms, and serrated leaves, including a flower-filled vase. The red main border has a palmette and arabesque meander within a pair of floral meander guards. Fine, asym.; ND in dark blue, medium steel blue, red, pale rose, yellow, ivory. Very good quality; good condition. ....
....Est. $18,000/22,000; sold for $20,700

Carpet (mid 19th century, 21'2" × 28'2"). A green and gold flower-filled lobed octagon on a cream ground swirled with a polychrome, bird-perched, floral vinery flanked by olive green floral spandrels and enclosed by a floral repeat on green. A curious feature of this rug is the miniature animal figures of the hunting-carpet variety used as fillers. Fine, asym.; ND in dark and brick red, dark, medium, and light blue, gold, dark and light olive green, spring green, peach, ivory. Very good quality; fair condition. ....Est. $40,000/60,000; sold for $46,000

Indo-Kashan Carpet (c. 1900, 10'4" × 19'4"). Within the curvilinear blue lattice, loose floral roundels on a cream field create a dressy pattern intended for the Russian and European market, which is also seen on many Bidjar carpets of the same period. The main border has a graceful flowering vine meander on red enclosed by floral meanders on dark blue. Fine, asym.; ND in dark, medium, and light blue, red, green, apricot. Good quality; good condition, but with some staining. ....
....Est. $25,000/30,000; sold for $26,450

Agra Carpet, Northwest India (last quarter 19th century, 16'4" × 20'6"). On a carmine red field, palmettes are centered within a lattice of criss-crossing bold serrated leaf figures in cream and olive green. The heavily abrashed olive border has a stylized palmette, flower, and serrated leaf repeat. Fine, asym.; the palette of carmine, rose, tan, and olive green is often seen in old Agra rugs, and although color runs indicate a synthetic red in this one, the bidding reached the ambitious low estimate. Good quality; fair condition. ....Est. $60,000/80,000; sold for $63,000

CHINA

The designs of commercial Chinese rugs made between 1875 and 1930 range all over the lot, from slightly stylized versions of traditional patterns to peacock-decorated Art Deco creations. Chinese rugs of this era were relatively coarsely and asymmetrically knotted—averaging 30–65 per sq. in.—on a cotton foundation. The wool used for the pile is lustrous, thick, and moderately long. Before the introduction of chrome dyes around World War I—earlier than in most rug-weaving areas—Chinese rugs were famed for the shimmering variations of their indigo blues. Aside from blue, the palette used in traditional rugs was limited to tans, yellows, ivories, peach, and occasionally a rather washed-out red.

Peking Rug (c. 1900, 5'5" × 7'9"). A roundel composed of a flowering leafy vine on a lustrous dark blue ground is flanked by trios of blossom clusters and flowering-vine spandrels, all within a flowering vine meander on a wide royal blue border. Coarse, asym.; ND in dark, royal, and light blue, pale blue-green, ivory. Very good quality; good condition..Est. $2,000/3,000; sold for $3,565

Carpet (c. 1925, 8'3" × 9'8"). The open lustrous camel field has spandrels composed of black Buddhist symbols and dark camel bat figures within a wide pale camel border with repeats of Buddhist symbols, bat figures, and stylized cloud forms, enclosed by a wide plain black outer border. Coarse, asym.; ND in dark, medium, and pale camel, rose, and a black which may be synthetic. Good quality; good condition. ....Est. $8,000/10,000; sold for $9,775

Peking Rug, China, c. 1900, 5'5" × 7'9", $3,565. PHOTO COURTESY OF SKINNER, INC.

CONTEMPORARY COLLECTIBLE RUGS

Like everything else collectible, oriental rugs have had their ups and downs in popularity. Many of the rugs being collected today were produced during the booming 19th-century revival fostered by a new appreciation of oriental rugs in the West, which was sparked by the paintings of a group of well-traveled artists known as the Orientalists.

By the turn of the century, dealers had begun a diligent search for old rugs to satisfy a more sophisticated market that developed during the 1880s, and the 1920s saw a tidal-wave surge in prices paid for classical carpets by highly competitive, well-heeled collectors.

The 1929 crash ushered in a long period of economic drought accompanied by wrenching changes in aesthetic as well as social attitudes, including a taste for clean, uncluttered lines and neutral colors promoted by a "less is more" mentality. Oriental rugs, seen as too busy and too bright, were banished to the attic in favor of calm expanses of carpeting. Rug collectors who maintained their interest through the 1940s and 1950s acquired rugs now considered world-class for sums that today would be insufficient to buy dinner for four at a top-rated restaurant and bought antique bags for less than the cost of a bottle of decent—not great—wine.

The era of the 1960s and 1970s witnessed, in addition to a bemusing variety of ways to prepare granola, a rebirth of interest in crafts and folk arts. Idealistic Americans returning from Peace Corps service in exotic places brought back with them a lively appreciation for the weaving arts they had seen practiced on a village and tribal level, and the new demand thus introduced was soon commercially supplied.

Many of the rugs produced for this folk art market are a mishmash of borrowed popular designs and cheap synthetic dyes debased further by bleaching and glossing. There are, however, some notable and shining exceptions, which, having already caught the rug world's attention, are worthy of yours. Collectors of antique traditional rugs often choose these honest new rugs for furnishing their floors; others find them worthy of collection regardless of any practical considerations.

Some of these enterprises are native cooperative ventures; some are promoter-driven; but whatever the engine that sparks them, in the case of the five I have chosen to present there is a sensitive appreciation of local history and craft as well as the possibilities and limitations of rug weaving as a viable cottage industry in the 1990s.

Retail outlets for these contemporary collectible rugs have increased enormously since the first edition of this guide was published. According to Ron O'Callaghan, editor of *Oriental Rug Review*, many dealers who formerly handled only antique rugs have been "searching for just the right rugs to provide the bridge from old to new," and the productions discussed below are prominent among those that have won their approval.

Collectors wishing to learn more about any of the rug projects described here should direct inquiries to the dealers profiled below. Details are provided at the end of this chapter.

DOBAG

The introduction of cheap, easily applied but stridently colored and unstable synthetic dyes during the 19th-century boom years led to a sad decline in quality—particularly in Turkey—and in the prices paid the weavers by wholesale buyers. The craft, however, continued to be practiced and taught, and this, together with the persistence of design traditions, encouraged a return to the use of natural dye methods and, when feasible in terms of supply, hand-spun, lanolin-rich local wool.

DOBAG, a Turkish acronym that stands for Natural Dye Research and Development Project, was the pioneer venture. All others were inspired by it and have benefited from the technical expertise DOBAG provided the two weaving cooperatives established with its guidance in 1981 in northwestern Turkey.

The vibrant vegetable dyes used for the rugs produced by the DOBAG villager-owned and -administered cooperatives are an outgrowth of the research and experimentation of a German chemist and rug scholar. Dr. Harold Böhmer, whose work was sponsored by Marmara University in Istanbul. The designs used for DOBAG rugs are traditional designs surviving in rugs given over many years to local mosques, but the choice and combination of motifs and colors in a particular rug are those of the woman or women who wove it.

DOBAG rugs have had no chemical or aging treatment of any kind. The low sheen of the hard-wearing long-staple wool is natural, and the rich, subtly shaded vegetable colors will mellow gradually over time. Each rug is registered with the cooperative: the number is recorded on an attached leather tag guaranteeing its quality and accompanied by a card bearing the rug's dimensions, knot count, and the names of the weaver and her village.

Gayle Garrett, a Washington-based photographer and educator, has been marketing DOBAG rugs since 1986 through her firm, The Rug Project. She has supported and publicized the Turkish cottage weaving industry through lectures and tours and, most notably, through the symposium she organized in 1987, *The Fabric of Daily Life*. It included a widely acclaimed exhibition of over 100 DOBAG rugs at the Washington headquarters of The World Bank.

DOBAG Rug, Yuntdag region, Turkey, 1987, 7'8″ × 4'8″, $1,700.
AUTHOR'S COLLECTION AND PHOTO

During the last decade Ms. Garrett has made numerous trips to the villages that contribute to the co-operatives, thereby gaining an intimate knowledge of the life and work of the weavers, whose weaving is done in the home as a natural part of the daily family routine.

While her stock on hand is small, and comprised mostly of scatter and area-size rugs she deems of particular merit, her unique knowledge of the Project enables her to have rugs woven for clients on a special order basis. Because the DOBAG co-ops yearly output is only about 2,000 rugs, special orders now account for most of the larger carpets, one of the largest of which was woven for the British Museum's Islamic Gallery.

Special orders, which require a nonrefundable deposit, may take from six to twelve months to accomplish: clients select from traditional designs and the DOBAG palette of natural colors, and skilled weavers work within these parameters to produce a one-of-a-kind woven expression of their art, which have a typical village-rug knot density of 56 to 63 knots per square inch.

As the co-ops approach their fifteenth year of operation, it has become clear that DOBAG rugs are collectible, not only on the basis of intrinsic merit but because weavers whose work is consistently distinctive deserve the same special regard as that accorded superior potters and silversmiths. Accordingly, the quality of each piece determines its price within The Rug Project's rather narrow retail range, and although prices have not increased dramatically in the last five years—they currently fall within a range of $55 to $70 a square foot with the variation roughly following that of carpet width—the system of special ordering has the advantage of locking in a price for a customer.

Return to Tradition, an attractive retail outlet that opened in San Francisco in 1989, is the only other DOBAG dealership in the United States. The retail price range is very similar to that of The Rug Project; the average cost is $60 per square foot. Specific information and a quarterly newsletter may be obtained upon request to Bill McDonnell, the store's personable manager.

WOVEN LEGENDS: THE AZERI PRODUCTION

Spurred by the appearance in 1982 of a few naturally dyed rugs in the Istanbul market, a young American dealer in old rugs, George Jevremovic, embarked on a career as a Turkish rug entrpreneur. His Philadelphia-based firm, Woven Legends, which is now the largest U.S. importer of Turkish rugs, is the umbrella under which his new rug enterprises cluster. Azeri, the name chosen for the production he organized in Eastern Turkey, produces room-size pile rugs in sizes 6' × 9' to 12' × 20' and runners. The knot count and handle is comparable to that of the DOBAG rugs. But although Jevremovic unhesitatingly credits DOBAG for the benefits its reintroduction of natural dyes brought to Turkish village weaving, he had ideas of his own concerning design.

Rugs made in the early days of the DOBAG cooperatives have been criticized for what some saw as a slavish adherence to the traditional design vocabulary; some other new village productions have been taken to task for their rote copies of designs foreign to the weavers. The Azeri rugs straddle the line, borrowing for one rug from popular southwest Persian designs, for another from Central Asian themes, with southwest Persian tribal and Caucasian and tried-and-true Turkish motifs thrown in for good measure. For the most part it works, perhaps because Azeri weavers are encouraged to adapt foreign motifs to their traditional taste; perhaps, too, because the exuberance of the palette and quality of the hand-spun wool remain wholly Turkish. This is not accomplished entirely without risk: at their best, Azeris are very, very good—see color section—occasionally, if the adaptions and spacing are clumsy and the colors ill-chosen, they can be downright horrid.

The *enormous* success the Azeri production is enjoying is unusual in a market whose acceptance of off-beat products is normally slow and reluctant. In this case, however, the quality of the materials—no chemical glossing here either—and the cheerful spontaneity of the designs have won plaudits from collectors and dealers alike, and the Woven Legends booths at the national wholesale markets are invariably sold out. Interestingly, Azeri rugs are generally stocked by dealers whose primary business is in antique rugs. The knot count, about 75 per square inch, is somewhat higher than DOBAG's; the retail cost is in the range of $90 a square foot. A knock-out 9' × 15' Azeri version of the willow-and-cypress Bid Majnun pattern I saw at a New York City dealership in early 1996 was tagged $12,495, which is appreciably less than an antique rug of similar size would be, and much more suitable for a heavily trafficked area.

A new line, Yatak, which is aimed at a lower price point, takes its name from the Turkish term for a long-piled, coarsely woven "bedding" rug. Patterned with bold, simplified versions of traditional Anatolian motifs, this series has a lower knot count than the Azeris and the foundation is wool rather than cotton. The names of dealers in your area offering both the Azeri and Yatak lines may be obtained from the Woven Legends headquarters.

GANGCHEN CARPETS OF TIBET

Tibetan rugs have been another success story, but until recently it was not, for the most part, due to adherence to tradition.

When Tibetans escaped to Nepal during the Chinese takeover of their homeland in 1959, a carpet production center was soon organized as a means of providing employment to the refugees while providing Nepal with needed hard currency. By the early 1980s the industry was well established, but although the wonderful long-staple Tibetan wool and sturdy, if coarse, structure of the rugs won favor with dealers everywhere, the demands of Western taste forced significant changes. Traditional designs and bright synthetic colors soon gave way to open-field designs and sophisticated Westernized floral motifs knotted in earth-toned, vegetable-dyed wool paled further with chemical washes. Decorators loved these tasteful, plush, durable, and reasonably priced small rugs; collectors sighed regretfully and chose the Turkish village rugs for their floor furnishings.

By the late 1980s a desire to return to the old weaving traditions had become manifest. To that end, an enterprise known as InnerAsia Trading was established for the purpose of "revitalizing Tibet's rug weaving heritage, developing a viable business and generating extra income for the Tibetan weavers and wool-producing nomads."

The moving spirit behind this revitalization of the Tibetan rug industry, once again able to flourish in its homeland, is Kesang Tashi, an American-educated member of a distinguished Tibetan entrepreneurial family. He switched to rug manufacturing in Lhasa from a career in banking in New York. "The time was ripe," he says, "and I took the plunge."

Tibet is economically backward even by third world standards, with endless frustrations and complications encountered in achieving the simplest aim. Fortunately, Tashi and his partner, George Doubleday, persevered, their hopes sustained by the excellence of the wool produced by the aboriginal sheep of the Tibetan plateau; the availability of skilled weavers, both male and female; and a reservoir of traditional rug motifs the other new productions had largely neglected.

Color choices and the selection and presentation of motifs are always critical factors in regard to market acceptance, but since oriental rugs now appeal to more than one kind of market, InnerAsia shrewdly decided to place its eggs in more than one basket.

Gangchen, the name chosen for the production, means "snowland." Gangchen rugs are made in Tibet with hand-spun, long-staple, lanolin-rich Tibetan wool richly colored with both natural and high-quality Swiss synthetic dyes. The knots are asymmetrical, and the density ranges from 40 to 80 per square inch, in keeping with the difference between loosely woven village rugs and those made in Gyantse and Lhasa workshops.

The rugs are woven in carefully reproduced traditional Tibetan designs, including dragons, tigers, geometrics, and florals. They retailed in 1995 for $50 to $60 a square foot in sizes ranging from 3' × 6' to 10' × 14'. Runners and oversize carpets can be made to order. I was particularly taken with one inspired by the "Khampas," Tibet's gallant warrior horsemen from the province of Kham.

A Gangchen folk art line inspired by the Turkish DOBAG experiment is in the process of organization. Assuming that all goes as planned, it will

Gangchen Rug, Tibet, 1995, 4' × 5', approx. $1,200. "Khampa Caravan," a reproduction from Inner Asia Trading Company. PHOTO BY JOHN BIGELOW TAYLOR, NYC

offer one-of-a-kind, vegetable-dyed pieces growing out of the weavers' experiences and reflecting their aesthetic sensibilities.

CULTURAL SURVIVAL RUG PROJECTS

The need for an Afghan rug project similar to DOBAG became apparent to rug dealer-scholar Chris Walter in the course of his work with Turkoman weavers among the Afghan refugees encamped in Pakistan. Rug weaving has always been an important part of Turkoman tribal life, and for the displaced refugees it became not only a crucial source of income but a means of maintaining cultural identity.

The aim of the project is to produce an authentic and beautiful rug through the reintroduction of vegetable dyes, hand-spun Afghan wool, and traditional designs not included in the sadly limited repertoire used by

Dudin Prayer Rug Reproduction, Afghan Turkoman Project, 1990, 3' 11"
× 5' 10", approx. $880. FROM THE COLLECTION OF WILLIAM MOR

Turkoman weavers for the commercial market. Start-up funds were granted in part by an organization called Cultural Survival, which, like Chris Walter himself, is based in Cambridge, Massachusetts. Essential assistance is provided in Pakistan by Jora Agha, a Turkoman from northern Afghanistan widely respected among his own people and knowledgeable about all local aspects of the rug business.

The Afghan Turkoman project, still in its infancy, turns out only 100 to 150 rugs a year in 3' × 5', 5' × 7', 6' × 9', and 8' × 11' sizes. Runners and room-size rugs are also available. Weaving, shearing, and washing—soap and water only—is done in the Haripur Refugee Camp in Pakistan; artificial aging and chemical glossing are not allowed. The retail price per square foot as of early 1991 was about $37.

In 1992, Cultural Survival initiated the Tibetan Rug Weaving Project in Kathmandu, Nepal. Only authentic regional patterns are used in these rugs, which are woven with hand-spun wool dyed with vegetable colors derived from indigenous Nepalese sources with the exception of indigo, which is obtained from India. All wholesale proceeds are directed either toward the

Gopcha, a reproduction by the Tibetan Rug Weaving Project, 1993, 3' 1" × 6' 6", approx. $725.

project's continued growth or the Tibetan refugee community and the children of Nepali weavers.

The retail price per square foot of the rugs produced by both the Afghan Turkoman and Tibetan projects remains at $37, the price given me in 1991 for the Turkoman Project rugs. Inquiries about the purchase of these handsome, well-made and authentic rugs should be addressed to Chris Walter at the address provided at the end of this chapter.

TURKISH KILIMS

In recent years, the American rug market has been flooded with small kilims, the majority of which are made in Turkey. Whether their acceptance stems from the enthusiastic reception accorded contemporary Indian dhurries, also flat-woven, whose peak of popularity seems to have passed, or a trickling down of the fervor for antique kilims shown by collectors, I hesitate to say. Whatever the reason may be, these widely available, loosely woven, inexpensive scatters, while satisfactory as furnishings accents, are in a different class altogether from the new kilims considered collectible.

Most dealers in collectible rugs (see the Resource Guide) stock at least a few of the new, good, largely vegetable-dyed kilims; some have small overseas productions of their own. One of the best of these was developed by Paul Ramsey of Shaver-Ramsey, a Denver dealership with a very large stock of flatweaves in addition to pile rugs, both old and new.

The family in Konya, Turkey, who handles the Shaver-Ramsey production has been making rugs for only 15 years, but it has been in the wool business for several generations, which no doubt accounts for the high quality of the wool in the finely woven pieces shown me on a recent visit to Denver. These superior kilims, which are available in sizes ranging from 3' × 5' to 9' × 12', retail for about $32 per square foot. Some special examples—one has a stunning design similar to the "Sunburst" or "Eagle" Karabagh Caucasian rugs—are priced by the piece.

(Note: Shaver-Ramsey also carries a limited selection of the pile rugs produced in Bergama by Toga Tollu, regarded in the inner circles of the Turkish rug world as a maker of outstanding carpets. His famously lustrous rugs—the pumice-combed wool has the shimmer of silk—are meticulously finished, and are either one-of-a-kind or one of a very small number of a particular design, usually with intentional variations distinguishing one from another. My favorite featured a stylized tree-of-life surrounded by judiciously spaced clusters of tiny yellow crosslike motifs which shone like stars on the subtly abrashed blue-green ground. This 4'5" × 5'2" rug was $1,800; the production generally retails for about $100 per square foot.)

Exceptional contemporary Turkish versions of the enchanting floral kilims of the traditional Romanian or Bessarabian type are occasionally available from Woven Legends. These finely woven pieces demand superior weaving skills, employing as they do both eccentric wefting and supplementary wefts for various of the design elements, and in both cases availability is quite limited. These lovely vegetable-dyed kilims average 4 × 6, and the prices range from about $900 to $1,200.

SOURCES FOR THE RUGS PROFILED ABOVE

DOBAG RUGS

The Rug Project
4814 MacArthur Boulevard, NW
Washington, D.C. 20007
(202) 965–2834
Note: Call for appointment.

Return to Tradition
3319 Sacramento Street
San Francisco, CA 94118
(415) 921–4180

AZERI AND YATAK RUGS

Woven Legends
4700 Wissahickon Avenue, #106
Philadelphia, PA 19144
Tel: (215) 849–8354
Fax: (215)–849–8354

Note: Many of the dealers listed in the Resource Guide now carry the Azeri line.

GANGCHEN RUGS

InnerAsia Trading Company
236 Fifth Avenue

New York, NY 10001
Tel: (212) 532–2600
Fax: (212)–532–5230

AFGHAN TURKOMAN AND TIBETAN RUG WEAVING PROJECTS

Yayla Tribal Rugs
283 Broadway
Cambridge, MA 02139
Tel: (619) 576–3249

TURKISH KILIMS

Shaver-Ramsey
2414 East 3rd Avenue
Denver, CO 80206
Tel: (303) 320–6363
Fax: (303)–320–1541

Note: Most of the dealers listed in the Resource Guide as specialists in flatweaves also stock contemporary kilims of superior quality.

OTHER SOURCES OF CONTEMPORARY COLLECTIBLE RUGS

The following dealers are direct importers of contemporary collectible rugs. Consult the Resource Guide lists for additional sources.

Turkish Village Rugs

Bergi Andonian
102 Madison Avenue
(at 29th Street)
New York, NY 10016
(212) 532–4688

Turkish Village Rugs and Kilims

Saul Barodofsky
Sun Bow Trading Company
108 Fourth Street
Charlottesville, VA 22901
(804) 293–8821

Note: Open seven days a week, the following home furnishings store in New York City carries a wide selection of Azeri, Yatak, and Gangchen rugs. Call for current information about hours:

ABC Carpet and Home
888 Broadway at East 19th Street
New York, NY 10003
Tel: (212) 674–1144

ORIENTAL RUG CARE

CLEANING YOUR ORIENTAL RUG

When I suggested to a woman visiting my rug booth at a Connecticut antiques show that her oriental scatter rugs could safely be washed in a solution of neutral detergent and water, she blinked in disbelief.

"Tea is what they use to clean rugs with," she corrected firmly.

"They," I assumed, referred to authentic rug merchants, the ranks of whom obviously could not include a female of Gaelic descent like myself. Nevertheless, I was amused by this latest addition to the list of rug-cleaning secrets of the Orient generously shared with me during the two-day show: new-fallen snow had been mentioned several times and vinegar twice, but I had been spared sauerkraut juice, an aromatic German recipe, and the romantic but risky instruction from Victorian England advising immersion of one's rugs in the clear, cold waters of a rushing mountain stream.

There seems to be something quirky in human nature that rejects simple solutions in favor of the complicated, the unlikely, and the arcane—a remnant of a primitive, mythic past, perhaps. The contemporary corollary is the insistence on applying to household furnishings museum standards that, although technically correct, are inappropriate to the situation. Some readers may object to this and succeeding chapters dealing with oriental rug care and repair on the grounds of their not being exacting enough in regard to materials and techniques. In my opinion, however, the average busy householder, who is perfectly able to differentiate between lukewarm and cool water when washing a rug, might very well abandon the whole business if exhorted to use water of, say, no more than 86° F, adjusted to a pH of 5.

The tested and conservative methods presented in this chapter are in fact *more* exacting than those employed by oriental rug cleaning firms, whose principal advantage is wide experience with all types of rugs and rug-cleaning problems and the ability to handle rugs of a size impossible to manage in the home environment. In the instructions and advice that follow, I have attempted to distill the best of current wisdom, tempered with my own strongly pragmatic turn of mind, but only you can decide what makes the most sense to you and for your particular circumstances.

THE IMPORTANCE OF PERIODIC CLEANING

The frequent inspection and cleaning of oriental rugs, whether used as floor furnishings or wall hangings, should be included in any household maintenance program. Grit trapped in carpet pile can quickly cause visible wear through abrasion, particularly on rugs piled with soft wool, like the Pakistani "Bokharas" or those with corrosive black or brown dyes, which are characteristic of many old Baluch tribal rugs.

Dirt allowed to settle and compact around the knots at the base of the pile restrict the ability of the foundations to adjust to the subtle tensions caused by changes in temperature and humidity and may eventually cause it to weaken and break. Rugs used as wall hangings will not, obviously, suffer abrasive wear, but dust and greasy cooking smoke, if allowed to accumulate over long periods, will dull the colors and luster.

VACUUM CLEANING

New or sturdy old rugs can be vacuumed once a week; antique and loosely knotted older orientals should be vacuumed only once or twice a month and in the direction of the pile only. A carpet sweeper may be used for the weekly once-over. There are several small, lightweight, and efficient models currently available that are handy for quick cleanups of all kinds. If a rug is very fine or fragile, purchase a square of plastic screening, tape the edges, and place it on top of the rug before vacuuming; this will protect delicate or loose pile fibers from the direct pull of powerful suction.

Small rugs can be shaken instead of vacuumed, but gently does it. If you snap them like a bullwhip, you could crack the ends and edges or cause the foundation to separate and tear. Periodically—at least once a year for large rugs—it is a good idea to vacuum the undersides of your rugs and inspect the foundation for mildew, insect eggs, and moth damage. This type of thorough cleaning is particularly necessary for rugs whose ends or edges are concealed under furniture, where drifts of lint, dust, and food crumbs are apt to accumulate. Failure to clean these areas is equivalent to hanging out a free-room-and-board sign for insect pests: not infrequently at auctions one sees an otherwise lovely rug with a sofa-length strip nibbled down to the foundation.

Moth damage is an even greater hazard on wall-hung rugs because of the easily accessible and protected egg-laying environment created by the space between the wall and the back of the rug, so remember to occasionally take down any hanging rugs for inspection and brushing or vacuuming.

SURFACE CLEANING

In the course of a year, your rugs may acquire a dulling film composed of dust and greasy smoke that resists removal by vacuuming. Assuming your maintenance program has been conscientiously observed, you should be able to revive the color and luster of your rugs with a simple surface cleansing of the pile with snow or detergent suds.

The only advantage snow has over suds, and only for the country dweller, is that it's more fun. The next time a winter storm hits your area, take your rugs out and place them pile-side down on a clean stretch of snow. Press them into the snow with the flat side of a broom, but try to avoid covering the back of the rug. When you pick up the rug and shake it out, you'll be amazed at the amount of dirt left behind on the snow. Before replacing the rug on your floor, towel-dry any residual moisture left by melting crystals trapped in the pile fibers.

To clean the pile surface of your rug with suds, add a neutral detergent to a bowl of lukewarm water and work up thick suds by repeated squeezings with a clean sponge. Apply *only* the suds to the pile with a strong wiping motion. Rinse the sponge in clean water after each application of suds to remove the dirt you have wiped up. After suds have been applied to the entire surface, go over the pile with a clean damp sponge to remove all traces of suds and loosened grime. Towel dry if necessary.

WASHING VERSUS DRY CLEANING

The wet or dry cleaning of a rug, especially a large one, is a stressful process and should not be part of your yearly maintenance program unless a combination of kids, pets, and heavy foot traffic produces an unusual amount of dirt and grit that cannot be removed satisfactorily by vacuuming and surface cleaning. There are, however, some situations that demand it as a matter of course:

1. Dirty and possibly moth-harboring rugs acquired at auction, from an antique shop, or through inheritance.

2. Rugs requiring repair—wool colors should not be matched to a dirty rug.

3. Rugs with small areas markedly cleaner than the rest of the rug, due to the removal of spots or stains.

When an oriental rug requires a thorough cleaning, wet washing is preferred to dry cleaning because the chemicals used in the dry cleaning process tend to remove the natural oils and patina from wool and give white wool a yellowish cast. But before you decide to slosh your scatter rugs and tribal trappings in the bathtub, there are a few facts about rug fibers in general and oriental rugs in particular, that should be kept in mind:

1. Vegetable fibers, like cotton and linen, become stronger when wet; animal fibers—wool and silk—weaken. This means that a heavy, wet wool rug can withstand less stress, less pulling and hauling, than the same rug can when dry.

2. Silk rugs, including wool rugs with significant amounts of silk in

design details, should be dry-cleaned by an experienced professional. *There are no safe exceptions to this rule.*

3. Bleeding dyes, generally reds and blues, are not necessarily a sign of poor-quality synthetics. Insufficiently rinsed naturally dyed wool may also bleed if water was in short supply for rinsing the wool after it was dyed. Always test dyes for fastness as later described. This test is not 100 percent reliable—the dyes may be fast in the test area but unreliable elsewhere—but it will pinpoint bad risks in the great majority of cases. If your rug fails the test, or if there are signs of past dye runs on the pile or staining on the fringes, you should have it cleaned by a commercial firm experienced in handling oriental rugs.

4. Any rug larger than about 3 × 6, regardless of the dye quality, will be difficult to wash properly in a bathtub. Unless it is quite thin, a rug folded in half or thirds will not only become unwieldy when wet but difficult to rinse entirely free of suds. If you have access to a clean, paved driveway and convenient hose outlet, a large rug can be washed with the aid of a squeegee mop to work the suds through pile and across the back and to squeeze out the suds while rinsing. However, unless you also have a satisfactory place to dry your rug and the assurance of two or three days of brisk, sunny, dry weather, you run the risk of mildew, or, in the case of a rug with a cotton foundation, dry rot.

5. Do not be tempted to use a carpet-washing machine of the type available for rent at hardware stores or to hire a firm that specializes in cleaning wall-to-wall carpeting. The treatment is too harsh for orientals, and it is very difficult to dry a large wool carpet *in situ.*

6. Finally, whether you wash your rugs at home or send them out to a professional firm, take the time to overcast and secure with stout button thread any damaged areas—holes, frayed ends and edges, and the like—so as to protect the pile knots from erosion during the cleaning process.

THE WASHING PROCESS

First, remove as much dirt as possible by turning the rug facedown and gently beating the back with the flat side of a broom to dislodge dirt that may have compacted around the pile knots. Follow by a thorough vacuuming of both sides, then test the dyes as follows:

1. Apply a few drops of the water and detergent solution you plan to use to each area of color. Allow it to sink in.

2. Blot firmly with a clean white cloth or paper towel.

3. If there is no evidence of color transfer, you may proceed with washing as described below.

Some authorities recommend routinely adding acetic acid in the form of white vinegar to the wash water to set the dyes, but this advice is sound only if one is sure the dyes are acid dyes. If one or more color is a basic dye, the acid may dissolve rather than set it; on the other hand, since the early basic dyes were for the most part fugitive, not enough color may remain from them to be worth worrying about.

Another factor affecting the stability of dyes during the washing process is the temperature of the water. Textile conservator James Rice, in his Textile Museum monograph on historic textile colorants, writes: "Some dyes are soluble at relatively low temperatures, while others will not dissolve until the water boils . . . this accounts for some cases of color change in cleaning when one of the components escapes before others in relatively cool water." This may also explain why rugs that have survived numerous washes may bleed during a succeeding one in which the water was warmer than before. Still another complication is the as yet undetermined role aging plays in the susceptibility of rug dyes to dissolution under varying and unpredictable conditions. In short, be prepared to remove your rug from the wash water immediately upon any sign of a color run, then thoroughly blot and dry on a flat surface to minimize the possibility of loosened dyestuffs staining adjacent color areas.

After testing, the next step is to fill your tub one-third to one-half with cool water and add 2–4 tablespoons of a mild hand-dishwashing detergent:

Although soap, a combination of fats and alkali, is probably more effective than detergents for removing dirt from heavily soiled textiles, it is not recommended for use on oriental rugs because dyed animal fibers can be harmed by alkaline solutions. Synthetic detergents are generally of two types: built and unbuilt. Built detergents contain varying amounts of alkaline chemicals to enhance cleaning action and sudsing, soften water, and brighten colors. Almost all powders and liquids formulated for laundry and dishwasher machine use are built detergents, as are those marketed for the hand-washing of woolen garments, and should not be used for your rugs.

Unbuilt detergents, among which are the hand-dishwashing liquids, may contain some brighteners but are near neutral in solution. The Textile Museum in Washington, D.C., recommends the neutral anionic detergent W. A. Orvus, a Proctor and Gamble product available through a conservators' supply house listed in the Resource Guide. An anionic detergent allows oil-attracting molecules to surround particles of dirt and pull them into the water. Unfortunately, Orvus is very difficult to rinse out, especially in a domestic milieu. David Walker, a highly skilled California-based restoration, conservation, and cleaning specialist who spoke at the third American Conference on Oriental Rugs, advised his audience that the liquid detergent formulations most likely to be free of harmful ingredients, readily soluble, and easily rinsed out in cold water are those stocked by health food stores. (Look for the EcoVer, Life Tree, Zout, Oasis, and Lifeline labels.)

There is, by the way, no "correct" amount of detergent one should use.

The quantity depends on the particular detergent, the softness of your water, and the amount of water needed to immerse the article you plan to wash. As a general rule, it is always better to use less and add more than to be overwhelmed with suds that will leave a dust-attracting film if not *thoroughly* rinsed out.

If your water is very hard, do not add to the wash or rinse water any softener containing the alkalies commonly known as sal soda, washing soda, or TSP (trisodium phosphate). Sodium hexametaphosphate, available under the brand name Calgon—do not mistake it for Calgon*ite*, a detergent formulated for dishwashing machines—is nearly alkali-neutral and may be used to discourage the scummy deposit characteristic of hardwater washing, but use it sparingly: excessive softening of the water may allow the detergent to remove the wool's natural lubricants along with the dirt. If your water is heavily chlorinated or commercially softened it may be alkaline enough to make it inadvisable for use with rugs colored with late-19th- and early-20th-century acid dyes. In these cases, your best bet is an experienced professional rug cleaning firm. You could, of course, collect rain water, but that is hardly practical for city dwellers and a bit much even for country folk, unless you happen to be a back-to-nature type with a rain barrel.

The washing process continues as follows:

1. Immerse the rug in the wash water and gently rub both the pile face and the back with a soft brush or sponge to loosen the dirt. If the water becomes dirty, drain and refill. Repeat the entire process until the water shows little discoloration.

Note: As your rug absorbs water it will become stiff and bumpy. Do not panic: it will resume its normal pliancy when dry.

2. Rinse the rug with cool water until the water running out of it is entirely free of suds. A hand-held shower spray or long swirl in a whirlpool bath will facilitate this process.

3. Sponge and drain as much water out of the rug as you can before removing it from the tub. Then, on a flat surface, blot or squeegee any remaining excess.

To dry, elevate the rug slightly. Do not hang or drape a rug unsupported between chairs or sawhorses. A wet rug, even a small wet rug, can be surprisingly heavy. The extra weight of the water can distort the foundation, creating wrinkles and sags; if the rug is old and brittle, the weight might cause it to tear. A clean window screen placed beneath it outdoors in a shady area with ample air circulation would be ideal; indoors, a fan, supplemented by a forced air heater in winter months, may be used. Drying may take one to three days depending on the size of the rug, its thickness, and the drying conditions.

Occasionally smooth the pile in its natural direction with a soft brush while drying.

Note: If the pile of your rug when dried seems a bit dull and lifeless, you may be tempted to treat it with lanolin, which is recommended by some authorities as a way of restoring a natural gloss to wool fibers. This can cause more problems than it might solve. Dead fibers are unable to absorb lanolin, and since it is fatty and sticky, even a thin and carefully dispersed solution will trap dust and dirt. It may also attract insects: a friend of mine who bought a lanolin-rich rug in Morocco found a large colony of plump maggots thriving on the oily wool when she unrolled it at home.

FURTHER CONSIDERATIONS CONCERNING HOME VERSUS PROFESSIONAL WASHING

At this point, some readers may be fretting about my admonition to leave the cleaning of silk rugs and rugs with unstable dyes to professionals, when this is precisely the kind of instruction they were hoping to find. Actually, the question in these cases is not whether you *could* do the cleaning but rather whether you *should*. Aged, dyed silk, in particular, is very tricky to work with, and all textile conservation bulletins approach the subject with the wariness of a high-strung horse on a wooden bridge.

The cleaning techniques professionals employ are not in themselves arcane, but the assessment of the problem presented by a given rug requires considerable hands-on experience. And if dry cleaning an entire rug is required, ask yourself whether you really want to undertake at home a process involving the use of flammable fluids on absorbent fibers, which will release while drying unpleasant and possibly dangerously noxious fumes over a period of several days.

What it comes down to, really, is the exercise of common sense. I have washed upward of 50 Baluch tribal weavings, and I now know just by looking at rugs of this type which ones may present cleaning problems. However, some years ago, when I acquired a rare, prison-made Indian pictorial dhurrie, I tested all of the dyes because they were unfamiliar to me. One of them, a dark brown, proved to be extremely unstable in water, so I entrusted the dhurrie to a textile conservation center, where it could be cleaned on a suction table—a device that pulls the cleaning solution and dissolved dirt out of the fabric, thereby depriving unstable dyes of a medium in which to spread.

Do not conclude from the foregoing that washing problems occur only with old rugs. According to the Rug Renovating Company in New York—founded in 1896 and the largest facility of its kind in the United States—new foreign, chemically washed oriental rugs, especially the lesser-quality Chinese, Indian, and Pakistani rugs, may suffer pile distortion and color changes when washed. Many cleaning companies refuse responsibility for such changes and warn customers accordingly. The most common complaint is the yellowing of ivory and white wools; but other colors sometimes become mottled, and when generally accepted methods of spot and stain removal are applied to these rugs, permanent alterations in color may result.

For More Information

Included in the Resource Guide in the back of this book are sources of washing compounds and the names and addresses of textile conservators and professional oriental rug cleaners (firms with equipment suitable for the washing and drying of large carpets) as well as individuals who will undertake the hand-washing of fine, small pieces. Consult oriental rug dealers in your area for additional recommendations.

SPOT AND STAIN REMOVAL

Should you ever contemplate buying a bargain-priced stained rug, think again: you must know what caused a stain before you can make an intelligent decision about how to remove it. Accepting stains of unknown composition, age, and previous treatment is asking for trouble and, in the end, no bargain.

If a guest spills wine on your cherished Kazak, spring into action. When it comes to removing soil from an oriental rug, immediate treatment is always your best and safest bet, for the longer soil or a stain remains on a rug the harder it will be to remove. If you can manage the cleanup with a lighthearted air, without making the offending guest feel like a boor, you may save yourself considerable postfestivity despair.

The removal of soil and its stains from a rug may require three separate procedures:

1. Immediate removal of the bulk of the soiling material by lifting or blotting it up before it has a chance to seep into the rug fibers.

2. Dissolving and washing out the residue with the aid of solvents.

3. Minimizing the effect of any residual stain by first rendering it colorless and then, if necessary, restoring the original color with dye or paint.

REMOVAL OF THE SOILING SUBSTANCE

The first step is the removal of as much of the soiling substance as possible by mechanical means. To accomplish this you will need:

1. A spatula or flexible dull-edged table knife.

2. A coarse-toothed comb.

3. Heavyweight paper towels or clean *cotton* rags, preferably white.

4. An absorbent powder like fuller's earth, available at drugstores.

Procedure

Thick, gooey stuff should be *lifted off* the rug with a spatula or similar flat-bladed tool. Jelly, paste, grease, ice cream, and animal feces and vomit fall into this category. Try not to press the offending matter into the pile. If the pile is long, what remains may be largely combed out with a coarse, blunt-toothed comb, but be careful not to loosen the pile knots.

Liquids should first be *blotted up*. This should be done gently with a patting and lifting motion to avoid either spreading the liquid outward or forcing it down into the pile. The object is the removal of as much liquid as possible before the fibers have a chance to absorb it; therefore, *do not rub*. Let the absorbency of the toweling do the work, and be generous with your use of it. Unless you are sure the cloth discards saved for household use are 100 percent cotton, use paper towels for blotting: cotton in combination with synthetics has very limited absorbency.

Another way to remove liquids is through the use of an absorbent material like fuller's earth. When applied to a wet spot, it draws up the soiling substance, which then can be brushed or vacuumed away when it has dried. Do not, however, use any of the commonly recommended substitutes on oriental rugs: talcum powder's fine particles tend to sift into rug fibers, making removal difficult, and cornstarch residues are an open invitation to hungry insects.

SPOT AND STAIN TREATMENTS

Once you have removed as much foreign matter as possible by mechanical means, a complete cleanup may require the use of solvents and bleaches. These can, if incorrectly chosen and applied, affect the dyes, the fibers, or both. Unfortunately, it is difficult to determine with complete accuracy the chemical composition of the dyes used in any given rug short of laboratory analysis. For centuries natural dyestuffs were the only source of color; but since the mid-19th century, synthetic dyes have been used extensively, often in combination with natural dyes. In addition, many late-19th- and 20th-century rugs have been chemically treated after manufacture to suit Western tastes, that is, bright colors bleached to fashionable pastels, with darker shades obligingly painted back in again if the result is *too* pale. Wool pile made limp and dull by all of this mucking about is then subjected to lusterizing processes that impart an attractive, if temporary, sheen to the pile. What this all adds up to in the context of spot and stain removal is that in the absence of certain knowledge of the dyes your rug contains and the chemical treatments it may have received, you should proceed very cautiously indeed.

To begin with, you should identify the fibers used in your rug because solvents and bleaches that are safe and effective on a vegetable fiber like cotton may prove harmful when applied to wool and silk. Rugs may be all wool, all silk, wool pile on a cotton foundation, wool and silk in various combinations, all wool with areas of white cotton in the pile, and so on. Sometimes, in cheap rugs, rayon or mercerized cotton is knotted into wool pile to impart a silklike luster. When in doubt as to what fiber or fibers you are dealing with, the following tests may be useful:

Wool burns slowly, with a sputter, and gives off the odor of burning hair. When the flame is removed, wool shortly ceases to burn. The residue is a brittle, blackish-brownish shiny coil that crushes easily into a powder. Wool yarns have a characteristic fuzziness, especially when new, which is clearly apparent under moderate magnification. The wool in antique rugs will be much less fuzzy as the result of decades of wear.

Silk also burns slowly, sizzling rather than sputtering, with the unpleasant odor of burning feathers. Its ash consists of small shiny beads, rather like wool but lighter and even more easily powdered. Pure silk pile and flatweaves have a distinctive cool, fluid feel or *handle*, an alive quality, peculiar to silk, that some people find vaguely repellent and others find decidedly sexy.

Cotton burns rapidly with a clear and even yellow flame. It produces smoke with the odor of burning leaves or paper and continues glowing long after the flame is extinguished. It leaves a fine, pale gray ash. Cotton fibers are smooth and obedient and have a softer, more pliant feel than most wools used in rugs, with the exception of camel and, rarely, mohair and cashmere. Cotton is found in the foundation structure of the finest antique Persian carpets and the majority of modern rugs.

Rayon melts when given the flame test and smells rather like burning rubber. Rayon made from cellulose acetate is the type most likely to have been used, so the cleaning instructions for cotton apply.

DISSOLVING SOIL RESIDUE AND REMOVING STAINS

The solvents and bleaching procedures recommended here are time-honored methods found in one form or another on every authoritative list. There are no space-age miracles. Some familiar methods may not be included if there is a possibility that harm to rug dyes or fibers may result; some common soils and stains may not be included if they require treatment best left to professionals.

Warning: Do not attempt to clean silk rugs with any home treatments. Old dyed silk fibers, long exposed to the light and dry heat conditions of the average home, are apt to become brittle and fragile. Prudence dictates avoiding placing a silk rug where it can be spilled upon. But if a spill occurs, immediate first aid of the sort previously discussed under mechanical soil removal should be applied so as to remove as much of the spillage as possible. Any residual staining should be referred to experienced professionals.

Soil Solvents

The terms "soil" and "stain" are not synonymous. Soil is a foreign substance that, although it may dirty a rug, may be lifted, brushed, blotted, or readily dissolved in water and washed out. Stains are caused by soil that has combined chemically with the fibers or dyes and therefore must be altered chemically to be removed or minimized. Obviously, it is very much to your advantage to avoid converting a simple spot of soil into a stubborn stain, either by delaying its removal or by hasty, ill-considered applications of familiar household solvents.

In the course of doing research for this chapter, I discovered that the removal of soil from textiles with water in combination with detergents is a surprisingly complex process, the understanding of which helped me realize why certain cleaning techniques are effective while others, seemingly as practical and sensible, are not.

Soil may be held by fibers in various ways: (1) mechanically, as when particles of foreign matter become lodged between the fibers, (2) by absorption, and (3) by chemical reaction, as in urine stains. By adding a detergent to water, the surface tension of the latter is lowered, making it "wetter." This wetting action of detergents allows water to permeate greasy surfaces more easily, and for this reason as much soil and spillage as possible should be removed *before* applying a detergent solution, which could have the undesirable effect of hastening the penetration of staining substances into the fibers. Dirt that has become embedded or absorbed into fibers can be washed out by a detergent solution, but stains created by a chemical reaction can only be neutralized or bleached.

Because of the practical impossibility of determining the composition of all the dyes in any given rug as well as any previous treatments it may have had, only a very limited number of solvents can be recommended safely. For all treatments you should have on hand the following:

Clean white cotton rags or paper towels.

Soft brush for smoothing pile.

Glycerine for pretreatment of some spots, available at drugstores.

Water, cool to lukewarm. Never use hot water as this may convert simple soil into a permanent stain or cause otherwise stable dyes to run. If your water supply is heavily chlorinated or commercially softened, keep a gallon of distilled water on hand to eliminate the possibility of an adverse alkaline reaction.

Neutral detergent. Soap and the majority of laundry detergents contain alkaline substances that may be harmful to some dyes, so it is important to use as near neutral a detergent as possible. Choose a type formulated for hand-dishwashing, as these contain few additives, or use the Orvus paste discussed in the preceding chapter if the size of your collection warrants the expense.

Trichloroethane and perchloroethane. This relatively safe, clear liquid oil solvent is widely available under the trade name Carbona. Carbona is also marketed in a spray can, which is more expensive and contains other, unknown, ingredients. Stick to the bottled liquid and use only in a space that can be well ventilated.

Note: There are some other commonly available solvents which should never be used on the absorbent pile of rugs because they are extremely flammable (naptha and benzine), have dangerously poisonous fumes (carbon tetrachloride), or may float away otherwise stable dyes (alcohol).

Procedure

Since rug dyes can be affected by solvents, always test them first in an inconspicuous place by rubbing the dyed wool with a white cloth moistened with the solvents, including water and detergent mixtures, that you plan to use. If an appreciable color transfer occurs, obtain the services of an experienced professional oriental rug cleaner; if only a trace of color is transferred, the advantage of prompt treatment may outweigh the possibility of a minor dye run. Only you can decide if the spotting or staining is serious enough to warrant some risk.

Pretreatment

If several hours have elapsed between the mechanical removal of the soil and treatment with a solvent, the residue may have hardened enough to make pretreatment with glycerine advisable, especially on rugs with dyes of dubious fastness. A little glycerine applied to the spot and left for about 30 minutes will soften and lubricate the soiling material so that it may be more easily dissolved by the appropriate solvent.

Treatment A—for nongreasy soil:

1. Test dyes as recommended above with a mixture of cool water and neutral detergent, $1/2$ teaspoon to 1 pint.
2. If there is no transfer of color, wet the spot with the water and detergent mixture.
3. Blot dry.
4. Continue wetting and blotting with dry sections of the rag or paper towel until no trace of soil is picked up.
5. Sponge with plain, cool water and blot as much moisture from the pile as possible.
6. Finish by gently brushing the cleaned area of pile fibers in the same direction as the pile in the rest of the rug. If possible, elevate the damp area so that air circulation under it will speed the drying process.

Note: Do not be alarmed by the stiffness of the damp area. This will regain its normal flexibility when dry.

Treatment B—for greasy soil:

1. Test dyes first with Carbona as well as with detergent and cool water, mixed $^1/_2$ teaspoon to 1 pint. Carbona will damage rubber products, so if the test allows you to proceed, either remove the rug from any rubber or rubberized pad or protect it with several layers of paper or cloth.

2. Apply Carbona generously and lift up both the solvent and the dissolved grease by blotting or wiping it *up*, not *in*, with a clean cotton rag or paper toweling. *Avoid inhaling the fumes and ventilate the room as much as possible.*

3. Once you have removed as much grease as possible with the oil solvent, sponge the cleaned area with detergent and lukewarm water, mixed $^1/_2$ teaspoon to 1 pint.

4. Sponge with plain cool water and blot as dry as possible.

5. Finish by brushing the pile and elevating the cleaned area, if possible, to speed the drying time.

Treatment C—for combination soil

1. Test dyes as above with both Carbona and the detergent and water mixture.

2. Sponge area with detergent and lukewarm water, $^1/_2$ teaspoon to 1 pint, to remove sugar and food coloring. Blot up the moisture before proceeding to next step.

3. Apply Carbona to dissolve grease or fats. Blot up—do not rub in—with a clean cloth or paper towel. Repeat if necessary.

4. Sponge area with detergent mixed with cool water, $^1/_2$ teaspoon to 1 pint. Blot dry.

5. Sponge with plain cool water and blot as dry as possible.

6. Finish by brushing the pile and elevating the cleaned area to speed drying time.

TREATMENT OF SPECIFIC SOILING SUBSTANCES

Acids See stain treatments, next section.

Alkalies See stain treatments, next section.

Animal soil Feces and urine should be removed as quickly as possible by mechanical means followed by Treatment A (for nongreasy soil). If several hours elapse between the accident and your discovery of it, staining may occur. See stain treatments in next section.

Blood Treatment A. If stain persists, see next section.

Butter, oils Treatment B (for greasy soil).

Candle wax Use Carbona-saturated cotton swabs to loosen; lift off with knife blade.

Chocolate Treatment C (for combination soil).

Coffee, tea With cream or milk, Treatment C; without, Treatment A. If stain persists, see next section.

Fruit juices Treatment A. See next section if stain persists.

Furniture polish Treatment B. If the polish contains color, use fuller's earth to absorb and contain the polish before applying the solvent. If staining occurs, see next section.

Glues Remove as much as you can mechanically, then call your local dry cleaner for advice, as formulas and treatments vary widely.

Gravies Treatment C.

Hand lotions Treatment C.

Ice cream Treatment C.

Ink If spilled, blot up as much as you can as carefully as possible to avoid spreading the damage; then consult your local dry cleaner about how best to deal with the specific ink involved. Treatments suitable for one kind of ink may set another.

Iron rust The tips of metal furniture legs may leave rust rings, especially in the course of a humid summer. See stain treatments in next section.

Liquor Treatment A. For red wine and punches, see also stain treatments.

Mayonnaise Treatment C.

Medicines Blot up as much as you can as quickly as possible. Medicines are tricky because of the difficulty of determining the composition of the base and coloring matter. In general, try Treatment C on oily medicines, Treatment B on syrupy compounds. If staining occurs, see next section.

Mildew See Special Problems below.

Milk Treatment C.

Paint See Special Problems below.

Sauces Treatment C.

Skunk odor See Special Problems below.

Soft drinks Treatment A.

Road oil, tar Scrape up as much as possible. If the material has begun to harden, soften with glycerine as directed in Pretreatment, above, and follow with Treatment B.

Table syrups Treatment A.

Urine See "Animal soil" above.

Vomit Remove as much as possible by mechanical means. Follow with Treatment A; then, because vomit contains powerful acids, see stain treatments in next section.

SPECIAL PROBLEMS

Mildew

Mildew is a whitish-grayish parasitic mold that flourishes in damp, warm, poorly ventilated, and dimly lighted areas. Its growth is characterized by an unpleasant musty odor and spotty discoloration. If mildew has invaded your rugs or you suspect its presence in a rug bought at auction, it is essential that the spore growth be stopped before it weakens rug fibers.

First, thoroughly vacuum the rug both front and back. Do this outdoors if possible to avoid scattering the mold spores in the house. Promptly seal and dispose of the cleaner dust bag.

Next, thoroughly air the rug on a dry, breezy day to eliminate dampness and mustiness and inhibit the growth of any remaining spores. If the mildew invasion was significant, the rug should be sponged or washed or, if the dyes are not fast, dry cleaned. Of course, the best way to deal with mildew is to discourage its onset. See the section on rug storage for a fuller discussion of treatment and deterrents.

Paint

Paint spills present a truly frustrating problem: the safest course is to leave its removal to a professional cleaner; but by the time one can get the rug to the cleaner, the paint will have hardened sufficiently to make a difficult problem worse. With this in mind, the most practical approach is the prompt removal of as much of the spill as possible by mechanical means. Then test the dyes as earlier described: if the paint is of a type that can be cleaned from brushes with water, use Treatment A. If it is an oil-based paint, sponge with turpentine and follow with Treatment B. If the paint has begun to set, pretreatment with glycerine may facilitate its further removal with a solvent; but don't use paint thinners or removers containing alcohol, as this may lift the dyes. If an unsightly residue remains, call your dry cleaner for advice. He will need to know what kind of paint was spilled and how you have treated it.

Skunk odor

This is not a common problem, but when it occurs it can create more alarms and excursions than a Laurel and Hardy comedy. The tried-and-true remedy for removing skunk odor from its unhappy canine recipient is a dousing of tomato juice. I've tried it and it truly works, but its use on rugs a frantic dog has rolled on may cause a stain that lingers longer than the odor of skunk. The safest course is to sponge sparingly with Carbona only where necessary, then blot dry. Follow with a sponging with plain cool water and blot as dry as possible. If the next day is dry and sunny—skunk spraying invariably happens at night—the rug would benefit from a good airing, but be prepared for the memory to haunt you on humid days for several weeks thereafter.

STAIN REMOVAL

Sometimes it just isn't possible to attend to soiling and spills immediately. Sometimes the problem may be undetected for hours or days, especially if the culprit was an unreliable pet or a child reluctant to confess. In short, stains can occur in even the most competently managed households, but with proper treatment they can often be reversed or at least minimized.

Stains may result from a deposit of color from a spill (blood, red wine, fruit juices, medicines, furniture polish, etc.) or from a chemical reaction left either untreated or improperly treated (iron rust, urine, vomit). A color-deposit stain will require bleaching; chemical stains must first be neutralized, then bleached if staining persists. But before you whip out your trusty bottle of Clorox, please bear in mind that many commonly available household cleaning agents can seriously damage and discolor rug fibers and dyes. Accordingly, never use any of the following on oriental rugs:

Chlorine bleaches (sodium hypochlorites).
Washing sodas, including sodium carbonate.
Trisodium phosphate, or TSP, a principal ingredient in many heavy-duty household cleaners.
Laundry liquids or powders containing alkaline builders.

Unfortunately, despite advertisements to the contrary, there is no such thing as a universal stain remover. Stains that persist after all of the soiling substance has been removed are the result of a chemical reaction. The nature of that reaction, acid or alkaline, would in ordinary circumstances determine what should be applied to neutralize it, but there may be other factors to consider.

Textiles stained with an acidic substance like vomit or fresh urine ordinarily require the application of a neutralizing alkaline solution; but if the textile dyes are acid, an alkaline solution may cause them to bleed. The same holds true for basic-dyed textiles stained with alakli: an acid solution applied to neutralize the stain may dissolve the dyes. For our purposes, then, one should choose the mildest agent in the most dilute form capable of doing the job.

Substances with acid or alkaline properties exhibit a wide range of activity: the typical mineral acid, such as sulfuric or hydrochloric, is violently reactive with many substances, including cotton, and strong alkalies like lye, (i.e., sodium hydroxide) can severely damage wool and silk fibers. But no matter how concentrated a solution of a mild alkali like sodium bicarbonate (baking soda) may be, it will never attain the degree of caustic activity of a dilute solution of lye; similarly, acetic acid is weakly active in comparison to hydrochloric acid.

Because the chemical makeup of the dyes in your stained rug may be unknown, you should initially apply the mildest available neutralizer in the hope that the color damaged by the stain can be restored without provoking the side effect of an undesirable color change in adjacent areas. If a mild solution of the neutralizer you have chosen is ineffective, you will have to decide whether the need to remove the stain outweighs any negative effect a stronger solution might have on unstained portions of the rug. If you decide that it does, test the stronger solution in an inconspicuous area colored with the same dyes as the stained section.

With the foregoing in mind, the following can be used with caution and should be included among your cleaning supplies:

Hydrogen peroxide in a 3 percent solution available at drugstores. It should be stored in a dark, cool place to maintain effective strength.

Sodium hydrosulfite, a color remover packaged as a powder and available under the Rit and Tintex labels.

Ammonia, household strength, for neutralizing acids.

White vinegar (acetic acid) for neutralizing alkalies.

Some useful accessories are:

White cotton rags or paper toweling.

2 or 3 watercolor brushes of varying fineness.

Medicine dropper.

Uncolored wooden toothpicks or similar narrow, blunt-ended tool.

Discarded toothbrushes.

Small-headed stiff brush of the type used to apply shoe polish.

Metal cuticle pusher, the type with blunt edge on one end and arrow-shaped point on the other.

Procedure

The usual admonition about testing dyes before applying any treatments applies; although in the case of stains complicated by dye runs, the dyes are obviously not entirely fast or they wouldn't have run in the first place. If the bleeding is extensive and pervasive, there is little or nothing you can do to correct it with home remedies. Never buy a rug in this condition, and if it happens to one you already own, consult an experienced oriental rug cleaner. If, however, the dye run is noticeable only in isolated areas of white pile, it may yield to Treatment 2 described below.

Treatment 1—hydrogen peroxide bleach. Apply peroxide directly to the stain with a medicine dropper. Work the liquid into the pile with a watercolor brush, being careful to stay within the stained area. Allow the peroxide to remain for several hours, but check frequently to be sure the rug dyes are not being adversely affected. After treatment, sponge the area well with plain cool water and blot dry.

Treatment 2—sodium hydrosulfite color remover. This should be used with caution—only if the peroxide treatment is ineffective and only on white or ivory areas of pile. Moisten the stain with warm—not hot—water, using a dropper to confine the moisture to the stained area. Apply the sodium hydrosulfite powder directly and carefully to the moistened area—the blunt, shovel-like end of the cuticle pusher is ideal for this purpose—and work it into the pile with a plain wooden toothpick or similar tool. This treatment works quite fast if it is going to work at all, so after about 10 minutes sponge the area carefully and thoroughly with cool water. Blot dry.

Treatment 3—for acid stains. Use household ammonia diluted $1/2$ strength with plain cool water. Moisten the stain with cool water, then, after first testing its action on the dyes in an inconspicuous spot, apply the dilute ammonia with a dropper and tamp with a brush to work it into the affected fibers. The tamping action can be compared to driving a thumbtack with a light hammer. Ammonia is alkaline, so do not allow it to remain on wool for more than about 15 minutes. Sponge the area with plain cool water, then carefully apply a solution of half white vinegar and half cool water to neutralize the ammonia and restore any color that may have been affected by it. Finish with a thorough sponging with plain cool water. Blot dry.

Treatment 4—for alkaline stains. Use white vinegar diluted $1/2$ strength with plain cool water. Moisten the stain with water, then, after testing its action on the dyes in an inconspicuous spot, apply the dilute vinegar with a dropper. Tamp gently with a brush to neutralize the alkaline stain and restore color affected by it. If the vinegar appears to affect the dye colors, sponge the area with cool water to which a few drops of ammonia have been added. Finish with a thorough sponging with plain cool water. Blot dry.

TREATMENT OF SPECIFIC STAINS

Animal Soil

Feces Once you have removed as much as possible as directed under "Removal of the Soiling Substance," apply Treatment 4. If a stain persists, follow with Treatment 1.

Urine Fresh urine stains are acid, but as they age, they become alkaline. On a fresh deposit, use Treatment 3 and apply Treatment 1 if some staining persists. If yellowing of white pile is still noticeable, try Treatment 2.

If Treatment 3 is ineffective because of the age of the deposit, try Treatment 4 followed by Treatment 1, and if necessary Treatment 2, to minimize yellowing.

Urine stains on indigo blues are very difficult to treat successfully for complicated reasons involving the chemical processes of dyeing with indigo. One textile conservation authority advises that if left alone and given enough time, the color may return to the original hue. This does not mean you can omit sponging the area with cool water after blotting up as much urine as possible; it means that further treatment may be ineffective. This is a case where painting to disguise an unsightly stain is a reasonable option.

If you catch a puppy in the act, blotting followed by an application of soda water, which combines a mildly alkaline substance with water in a single treatment, may be sufficient to counteract the fresh, relatively weak acid content. Unfortunately, the residual odor, even when too faint to be detected by humans, may continue to attract the offending pet, and anything strong enough to kill it presents risks. Try masking the odor with a carpet freshening powder, as animals tend to shun chemical fragrances.

Blood Treatment 3, followed if necessary by Treatment 1.

Coffee, tea Treatment 1. If stain persists on white or ivory pile, try Treatment 2.

Fruit juice Pretreat with glycerine to loosen the staining material and follow with Treatment 4. If necessary, apply Treatment 1 or, on white or ivory pile only, Treatment 2.

Polishes If a color stain remains on white or ivory areas after the spot removal treatment detailed in the preceding section, try Treatment 2. If the polish color has stained a dyed area, anything that will remove the polish dye will also affect the rug dyes. If the spot is not large, it could be bleached and painted; if extensive, the stained wool could be replaced, a job for a professional.

Iron rust First try applying a paste of table salt and white vinegar. Work the paste into the stain. After 30 minutes, thoroughly sponge it out with plain cool water. Repeat if necessary. If rust stains persist on white or ivory pile, try Treatment 2.

Vomit Vomit contains strong acids that should be neutralized as quickly as possible with Treatment 3. If the acids have begun to affect the dyes, this treatment may restore them, but if the process is well advanced, the area will probably have to be painted.

Wine, red Pretreat with glycerine as described in the preceding section on spot removal, then apply Treatment 4. If staining persists, try Treatment 1.

It should be noted that the treatment of any spot or stain, whether successful or not, may present you with a new problem: the creation of a small area of pile noticeably cleaner than the rest. You can, of course, wash the entire rug, but if the rug is relatively clean, you can drab the area by judiciously applying ashes or charcoal from a burned match rather than subject the rug to the stress of a largely unnecessary washing.

For More Information

If you are unable to remove a stain using the methods suggested here, consult an experienced oriental rug cleaning establishment recommended by a local rug dealer or included in the Resource Guide in the back of this book. For valuable rugs, an alternative is a textile conservation service, names of which will also be found in the Resource Guide. In either case, describe the situation and the methods you have employed and inquire what the approximate cost might be for whatever treatment is suggested. Do not expect a firm estimate until the rug can be seen and evaluated.

UNDERLAYMENTS

In the years before World War II, the sort of people who accumulated oriental rugs were likely to be wealthy enough to maintain servant-staffed houses with many amply dimensional rooms where rugs could be seen and enjoyed but rarely walked upon. In those well-ordered households, the children lived in the nursery, the dogs in a kennel, and both were suffered to join the family only for brief, well-mannered visits. Given such hothouse conditions, it was easy to maintain a fine, lustrous-piled rug in mint condition for fifty or more years.

Today wear caused by constant foot traffic and stains deposited by imperfectly trained pets is taking a drastic toll of old rugs, particularly the little tribal pieces too often used as door mats or to line old Bowser's basket. If you buy or inherit a small antique rug in good condition but have no sheltered floor space, consider displaying it on a wall, as described in the next chapter. If it is a fine old silk piece, you really have no reasonable alternative; unless treated as wall hangings they will wear rapidly and ruinously. But even a sturdy new or used rug bought to furnish your floors will probably require a protective pad beneath it, the type depending on the size and weight of the rug and the use to which it will be put.

A large rug bought for a living room, bedroom, or dining room should be equipped with a dense, firm pad to cushion the weight of furniture standing on it. This is particularly necessary for a dining room carpet subject to the repeated sliding of chairs and feet, and for that reason it will also benefit from a half-yearly reversal of its position to distribute the wear.

A light scatter rug or a large but thin carpet on a polished floor adds up to a potential accident in any room of the house. To protect your family and guests from needless injury you must provide a nonskid underlayment. Do not attempt to anchor lightweight rugs by tacking them directly to the floor, by applying latex, or by gluing nonskid strips to their backs.

Although oriental runners are not the best choice for stair coverings, they are undeniably attractive when used to accent a graceful stairway. It is essential, however, that the rug chosen for this purpose be free from holes, splits, and badly worn or weakened areas that could be caught and torn by high heels. Stair rugs may be fitted over flat carpeting or provided with a thin underlayment, but in either case they should be secured with wooden or metal stair rods (see Resource Guide), which will allow the rug to give a bit with the push and pull of stairway traffic. This movement is necessary: if the rug is tacked directly to the treads or sewn to an underlayment, it will tend to tear under stress rather than adjust to it. To further extend its years of safe use, a stair rug should be shifted slightly up or down once or twice a year to distribute wear.

A pad protects the foundation of a rug from both the abrasive action of grit trapped between it and the floor and the wear caused by repeated rubbing against uneven flooring. This latter problem can be a serious one in antique houses with wide handcrafted floor boards and in rooms and hallways surfaced with stone or tile. A pad will also cushion a rug against hardsoled and high-heeled shoes, and although it cannot eliminate the dents caused by the feet of heavy furniture, it can at least buffer the mortar and pestle effect of a vulnerable textile trapped between furniture and an unyielding floor.

TYPES OF RUG UNDERLAYMENTS

There are two schools of thought about the proper kind of rug cushion. Traditionalists, particularly old line rug dealers, are loyal to the hair and jute pad, the one that looks like a coarse and hairy brown felt. Newer versions have a rubberized bottom to guard against slippage. If cost is a significant consideration, jute is your best bet. However, jute pads are heavy and awkward to move; they have a tendency to shed clingy bits of hairy stuff; and if you intend to store your rugs, they make very bulky, mildew-prone rolls that will absorb moisture like a thirsty camel.

The preferred pad is a densely compacted rubber or synthetic cushion, $1/8$ inch to $1/4$ inch thick, available either in rug-size widths or narrow strips that can be joined by duct tape to make up the required width. Although expensive compared to jute, these paddings provide a firm, secure cushion that is also clean, lightweight, and durable. The synthetic variety is also mildewresistant, an important consideration if you intend taking your rugs up in summer. Pads of this type may be obtained from dealers who specialize in oriental and other fine area rugs. Some dealers provide free $1/16$-inch flexible sheeting with the purchase of a rug—the type I have seen most often is a rather nasty shade of mint green. But although these sheetings are reasonably good for anchoring a rug, they provide almost no cushioning.

There are other kinds of padding materials stocked by retailers of bulk carpeting that should be avoided unless there is no alternative easily available to you. These include bubble padding and expanded plastic foam padding.

Bubble padding is a thin layer of rubber or comparable synthetic material pressed into large puffy bubbles and backed with a mesh netting. The rubber layer is so thin it dries out in a comparatively short time, and the brittle edges then break down into a fine powder. Another drawback is that lightweight rugs tend to "copy" the bubble pattern, resulting in a curious effect rather like seersucker on a grand scale.

Expanded plastic foam padding is very lightweight and is manufactured in a variety of thicknesses for use under wall-to-wall carpet installations. Although mildew- and rot-resistant, it is too compressible to provide firm cushioning for oriental rugs, and because of its extreme lightness, it tends to shift under foot. A cosmetic objection is that since it is made only in very pale colors, the effect created by rugs sliding on this padding is that of a white petticoat dipping unevenly below the hemline of an otherwise smartly turned-out woman.

Carpeted rooms present the owners of oriental rugs with a unique difficulty. Until recently, scatter and area-size could be used satisfactorily only on very low-loop or flat-faced carpeting, because the tufts in cut-pile types will inch a small rug across its surface just like the legs of an upside-down caterpillar. I once purchased for my bedroom a luxuriously thick, cut-pile carpet in a soft camel-hair color as a background for a couple of antique Baluch prayer rugs. They looked wonderful when I first put them down, but within an hour the little rugs had scooted noticeably out of place, and by the end of the day they were creeping under the bed like a couple of naughty puppies anticipating a scolding. Now, thanks to products developed specifically to counteract this problem, orientals may be used in combination with wall-to-wall carpeting.

The following underlayment materials were on the market as of early 1996. Call the manufacturer or wholesaler for a retail supplier in your area. If the underlayment of choice is no longer available, or if your choices are very limited, I want to emphasize that any type is better than none. Its dimensions should be the same as the rug, minus 1 inch all the way around. Rug dimensions, by the way, ordinarily exclude the end finishes, with the exception of those with significant flat-woven skirts, like most old Turkoman and Baluch pieces, which should be protected to within 1 inch of the edge.

Underlayments for use between rugs and hard-surfaced floors:

Rug Anchor II, Jade Industries, Inc., 257 East Lancaster Avenue, Wynnewood, PA 19096; (610) 649–1600
    Rubber sheeting available in four thicknesses ($1/16''$, $3/32''$, $1/8''$, and $1/4''$) to suit every rug need. Excellent quality; neutral color.
Dura Hold: No-Muv Corporation, Inc., 5801 Phillips Highway, Jacksonville, FL 32216; (904) 739–3636, Fax: (904) 739–3093

Synthetic fiber compound-bounded to waffle-patterned rubber backing, at $^1/_4$ inch thick enough to provide good padding. Moisture- and mildew-resistant; lightweight yet sturdy; dark neutral color.

Lok-Lift: Optimum Technologies, Inc., 570 Joe Frank Harris Parkway, Cartersville, GA 30120; (770) 386–3470

This 6″ wide, easily removable sticky netting is applied in cut-to-measure strips to the floor and the rug pressed onto them once the plastic liner is removed. It is not a cushioning material, but useful for anchoring sturdy small rugs that persistently slip out of place. Available at Home Depot, Target, and similar outlets.

Underlayments designed to prevent the movement of rugs placed on carpeting:

Rug-To-Rug: Rug-Hold, 817 North Hamilton Street, Dalton, GA 30720; (706) 279–2733, 1–800–284–2537

A thin, lightweight, and odorless synthetic material treated with a specially formulated adhesive on both sides.

No-Muv: No-Muv Corporation, Inc., 5801 Phillips Highway, Jacksonville, FL 32216; (904) 739–3636, Fax: (904) 739–3093

This is a dense and rigid product whose toe-stubbing thickness (approx. $^1/_2$″) makes its use under scatters problematical, but the dealers I surveyed consider it effective in controlling the movement of area and room-size rugs.

WunderGrip: WunderGrip, Inc., 717-G Fellowship Road, Mount Laurel, NJ 08054; 1–800–NON SLIP (666–7547), Fax: (609) 439–9494

DISPLAYING YOUR COLLECTION

When all of your floors have been splendidly furnished and each chair and couch has accumulated its quota of artfully draped tribal trappings, the next step is the creation of a display area where your finest pieces can be hung properly lighted and viewed to their best advantage. Few of us have space enough to display more than one or two wall-hung rugs at a time, but that is all to the good: frequent changes of rug displays will discourage dust from settling and insects from setting up housekeeping.

Another benefit conferred by a vertical display area is that it allows one to buy with a clear conscience—and, one hopes, for less money—fine antique rugs too fragile to use as floor coverings. This can include fragments with exceptional color and design like the mid-19th-century 3 × 15-foot Turkish kilim panel I found in a rural New England antique shop. One end of this handsome piece had been damaged beyond repair, but it was long enough to allow me to cut off the top 6 feet for a dramatic wall-mounted display, turn the next 2 feet into a striking pillow, and bestow the remaining undamaged portion upon a grateful textile collector to whom I owed a favor. Most fruitful $50 I ever spent.

Most houses are unsuited to the hanging of very large rugs. Not only are the mechanical problems daunting, but once one has gone to the considerable effort of hanging a large carpet, it is all too easy to postpone taking it down again, to the eventual detriment of the rug. Wool fibers are subject to stretching if the moisture content of the wool or the atmospheric humidity is high, and under these conditions a large rug whose weight is unsupported except at the top can stretch considerably over time. If the fiber extension is moderate, it may eventually retract to its original dimension once taken down, but too great a percentage of stretch may distort a rug beyond recovery.

Since rug warps are stronger than the wefts, pieces chosen to hang for display, except for small mats and big faces, should always be suspended vertically. If the rug must be hung sideways because of the design or the limitations of the wall space available for this purpose, it would be prudent to limit the display period, especially if the rug is an old one with fibers less able to respond well to stress than a new and supple rug.

Few handmade rugs are dimensionally true—nomadic tribal pieces are often noticeably skewed—and it is harder to make them hang flat than to lie flat. A rug suspended with rings or clamps attached to wall hooks often presents a visually untidy effect unless one is willing to tinker at tedious length with the placement of the hooks. Even if a successful arrangement of hooks is finally achieved for one rug, it is unlikely to suit another's peculiarities, and suspension for long periods from rings or clamps subjects the warps to unequal stress that in time can cause waves or scallops to form between the suspension points.

THE VELCRO DISPLAY SYSTEM

The most satisfactory method for displaying rugs employs Velcro, a patented fastening material that consists of two strips of woven nylon: one is faced with tiny hooks and the other with fluffy fibers with which the hooks interlock in much the same fashion as a burdock fastens itself to the tails of hapless horses. Velcro is available at almost any notions counter in black, white, and beige—additional colors may be found at specialized stores—and in four widths: $5/8$ inch, $3/4$ inch, 1 inch, and, less commonly, 2 inches. The expense is not insignificant considering that once you have mounted a length of the hooked Velcro strip on the wall, half the cost of subsequent purchases is wasted, except in a special circumstance I will discuss later. Nevertheless, the ease of hanging and adjusting rugs using this method far outweighs the cost of materials.

1. Determine how high the wall-mounted Velcro strip must be to accommodate your longest rug, then see if your shortest rug can be hung from the

same point without having to crane your neck to view it properly. If you have any leeway, try to achieve a happy medium; if not, you may choose to attach mounting strips at two or more heights.

2. Cut a wooden batten to fit the width of the wall space selected. If you live in a house with conventional wood framing, secure it if possible into the framing studs, which are normally placed 16 inches apart; if your house or apartment is of brick or concrete construction, consult your local hardware store or the building superintendent about the most practical way to attach battens to the wall in question.

3. Paint or stain the battens the same color as the wall to reduce visual clutter.

4. Closely staple or tack to the mounted batten a hooked Velcro strip long enough to receive the widest rug you plan to display.

5. Attach the fluffy-faced Velcro strip along its top and bottom edges directly onto the back side of the top edge of the rug with moderately long stitches of stout button thread of a blending shade; or sew it first onto a cotton twill tape, which is then sewn to the rug. The latter extra step might be prudent if your rug is old and fragile or if you plan to hang a rug for long periods of time. If the weave is tight, you will need a strong, sharp needle, a thimble and possibly a small pliers with which to pull the needle through.

Note: To determine the top of a rug with an allover pattern, run your hand over the pile. The smooth feel runs towards the bottom of the rug, where the weaver began; the rough feel runs toward top, where the Velcro should be attached.

6. Attach the rug to the wall mount by firmly pressing the tapes together. If the rug hangs unevenly, and it probably will initially, the strips can be pulled apart here and there to make the necessary adjustments. For maximum positioning flexibility, use the 2-inch wide Velcro tape on the wall mount.

DISPLAYING FRAGMENTS, MATS, AND TRIBAL TRAPPINGS

Fragments of rugs suspended without a backing look rather forlorn; the same piece mounted on a neatly covered panel achieves instant respectability. Permanently mounted fragments of museum quality require, and deserve, fabric-covered stretchers and frames made to order for a particular piece. For display in the home, a fabric-covered, unframed panel of Homasote or plywood is an easy and inexpensive alternative more appropriate for the purpose than a frame, which is a bit fussy for a coarsely woven textile like a rug.

Homasote is a type of building panel suitable for both interior and exterior applications. It is made of 100 percent recycled processed paper and is available at very reasonable cost in $4' \times 8' \times 1/2''$ panels, known as 440 board, at building supply outlets. Its advantage over plywood is that $1/2$-inch

plywood is appreciably heavier and 20 percent higher in cost than Homasote, and thinner panels tend to torque and look flimsy when wall-mounted.
Homasote's disadvantage is that since it is a relatively soft material, ordinary staples used to attach the fabric covering may pull out. Be sure you
have a staple gun capable of driving staples with legs at least $5/16$ inch long.
If you can find the type of staple designed to mount ceiling panels—with
slightly offset legs and superior holding power—so much the better.

Although Homasote is easily sawed, a full-sized panel is a bit awkward
to transport. Determine what size you need beforehand and ask to have it
cut to order at what is usually a modest additional cost.

Your next step is to choose a fabric covering for the cut panel. Most
museums and galleries use linen or monk's cloth, but I chose a matte nylon
upholstery fabric with a surface texture just fuzzy enough to connect with
the otherwise discarded lengths of hooked Velcro tape, which I sewed to
the tops of pieces selected for panel display. To my pleased surprise, the
kilim fragment mentioned earlier clung to the textured nylon not only
along its top edge where the hooked tape had been sewn—which I had
expected—but throughout its length, almost as if glued. The attachment of
heavier-pile pieces, however, usually has to be augmented with T-shaped
upholstery pins unobtrusively added along the top and at the bottom corners. To be sure of achieving a similar result, take a test strip of the hooked
Velcro with you when shopping for your panel covering.

If you choose a neutral color for your panel cover, bear in mind that the
white and ivory portions of old rugs are usually quite a bit darker than one
realizes: placed against too pale a hue they will look drab and dirty instead
of pleasingly antique. If you doubt the accuracy of your visual memory,
don't haul your rugs around with you: instead, match the wool colors to the
sample paint strips available in a tremendous range of colors at all paint
stores. Fabric remnants are usually much less expensive than lengths cut to
order from a bolt, but be sure the piece you select is wide enough and long
enough to overlap the panel on all sides by about 3 inches.

You will need a second pair of hands to help you cover the panel with
the fabric you have chosen. One person cannot pull the fabric sufficiently
taut and simultaneously staple it into place. If the material has substantial
body or texture, it may be difficult to achieve neat corners without a bit of
snipping and sewing, but don't do any cutting until you have studied the
situation carefully. One mistake may force you to discard the entire piece.

After the panel has been covered, it should be mounted to the wall by
nailing or screwing through the fabric and panel and into the studding with
large-headed fasteners spaced about 1 foot apart in an area that will be concealed by the smallest of the pieces you plan to display. If the mounting is
to be temporary, investigate fixtures used to hang mirrors of comparable
size and weight. The object is to create a smoothly covered matte surface

held tight to the wall yet projecting sufficiently to convey the impression of a vertical stage set apart from it. The effect is a subtle one, but it will lend the pieces you display an air of specialness.

LININGS

If you plan to hang a rug for appreciable lengths of time, it is advisable to shield the back from dust and insect damage. Materials chosen for lining should be lighter in weight than the rug and preshrunk to eliminate any possibility of shrinkage should it become damp due to high humidity, as this would create uneven tensions.

Lining a rug can be a maddening process if the lining material is in the least slithery. A well-washed old bed sheet is an ideal choice for texture, weight, stability, and, for most wall-hung pieces, size. If you don't have one, any thrift shop should be able to oblige you.

Hem on all sides a lining piece just large enough to cover the entire rug minus the edges and ends. Tack the lining with linen or button thread at the top, just below the Velcro fastening strip, and all along the sides with moderately large, loose stitches, leaving the bottom end unfastened. Then hang the rug for a few days to see if any signs of uneven tension develop, such as puckering or pull. Once you have made any necessary adjustments, which may include tacking the lining here and there to forestall sagging, the bottom may be stitched into place.

DISPLAYING FRAGILE OR DAMAGED RUGS

A very worn or damaged antique rug may require a little something extra in the way of support to prevent the rug's own weight from pulling weakened warp threads to the point of separation. The easiest and least expensive way to accomplish this is to tack strips of the fuzzy-sided Velcro across the back of the rug at 1- to 2-foot intervals and then attach to the wall battens stapled with the hooked mating strips at the corresponding wall heights.

WALL RACKS FOR VISIBLE RUG STORAGE

Dedicated collectors may choose to combine the functions of storage and display by devoting an entire wall to this purpose. At the Textile Museum in Washington, D.C., the storage rug racks consist of wooden uprights placed along the walls at 4-foot intervals, although tighter spacing may be indicated if your collection consists largely of small pieces. From the uprights, arms 3 feet long extend horizontally at 1-foot intervals, but in a home situation you may have neither the space nor the need for arms that long. The upright members are mounted so that the top rests against the wall and the bottom is 1 inch away from it, which tilts the arms just enough to keep the rolled rugs placed across them from sliding off. With this system, a large rug may extend across several arms; a small rug, only two.

And unlike rugs piled on shelves, it is seldom necessary to move more than one or two to get at the piece you have chosen to display.

Museums use metal or acid-free tubes to roll rugs on, but a satisfactory substitute for home use are the cardboard tubes used for shipping and displaying upholstery and drapery fabrics. Ask a local fabric retailer to save discards for you. Whether or not you use tubes, rugs should be rolled in the direction of the pile and with the pile side in.

LIGHTING

Lighting wall-hung rugs with two to four instruments will enhance the natural luster of the pile and emphasize the charm and artistry of the design. In fact, this enhancement effect is so pronounced, one should never bid on rugs on impulse during an auction that has not been previewed: flaws, even quite pronounced ones, are remarkably minimized by theatrical lighting.

You can either have elegantly designed track lighting professionally installed or achieve satisfactory results at much less cost with mass-produced do-it-yourself track lights requiring only a screwdriver and a standard wall outlet. The only drawback to the latter is that unless your home is suited to the high-tech look of exposed electrical cords, it may take a bit of ingenuity to conceal or minimize their clutter.

Because of justifiable concern about the long-term effect of light upon textiles of unusual historic and aesthetic interest, conservators severely restrict both the wattage and type of lighting used for museum displays. Collectors with qualms about the illumination of home displays might consider installing dimmers and reserving the highest levels of light for special occasions.

RUG STORAGE

The proper storage of oriental rugs is not easy to manage in the average domestic environment. Hot dry attics and cool damp cellars can cause problems, and closets are apt to be too small or already overcrowded. That leaves only the storage facilities offered by your local dry cleaner or a second look at your home to see if satisfactory storage space can be found or created. But first, let's back up a bit and determine whether or not you will want to store your rugs at all.

Even if your interest in rugs begins and ends with the sensible desire to furnish your home with a few attractive pieces, there are two practical reasons for deciding to store your rugs on a seasonal basis. The first is that the rugs that look so warm and glowing in winter may make your home seem stuffy and overfurnished in summer. The second reason is threefold and has as much to do with your rugs' well-being as your own: rugs will last longer if exposed to family traffic only part of each year; the necessity for a periodic inspection for damage and a thorough cleaning becomes virtually automatic when rugs are taken up for summer storage; then, when they are put down again in the fall, you will fall in love with them all over again.

FINDING SPACE

Most houses have closets with an inconveniently high top shelf relegated to the domestic detritus known as it-may-come-in-handy-someday. This includes games bought for children who are now away at college, hats too dowdy even for funerals, and boxes of papers relating to community projects long since accomplished. Clean out those shelves, buy a sturdy, well-balanced step-stool, and alert the family that henceforth this area is for rug storage only. Since collectors are apt to accumulate smallish pieces—easier to handle and display—one or two such areas, approximately $1 \times 2 \times 6$ feet will hold a respectable number of rolled scatters and tribal trappings. Under-bed storage is suitable for larger rugs, provided that the rugs are well wrapped and mothproofed. Another possibility is to make rug storage part of the decor by building museum-style racks against the wall of a study or bedroom. If combined with a lighted display panel, the effect can be quite handsome.

ROLLING AND WRAPPING FOR STORAGE

Rugs to be stored over a season should first be vacuumed front and back for any insect-attracting spills: food spills principally, but animal urine residues are also very appealing to moths. These should be dealt with according to the instructions in the section on spot and stain removal before the rugs are rolled for storage.

1. Make note of how your rugs are placed on the floor so that you may reverse their position when you put them down again. This will distribute the wear more evenly over the years.

2. Roll the rugs with the pile inward and in the direction of the pile to prevent crushing and crimping of the fibers. This is particularly important in the case of large, thick rugs. To determine the pile direction, run your hand over the surface: the smooth feel is with the pile; the rough feel is against it.

3. Do not fold a rug in half or thirds before rolling, as this will create unsightly creases that will be difficult to remove and, if the rug is old and dry, may crack the foundation.

Dealers often fold and roll large rugs into squat cylinders, but this is done to make them easily accessible for frequent display to customers. Museums customarily store rugs by rolling them on tubes, which are then placed on racks or across long pegs projecting, slightly angled, from the wall. This system is useful for large and valuable collections as it prevents the rugs from compressing each other, as would be the case if they were stacked for long periods without support.

Museum standards for textile conversation include the use of acid-free papers, boxes, and tubes, but unless your collection includes fragments of classic rugs, this would be gilding the lily in the context of temporary home storage.

You should, however, assiduously avoid using plastic to wrap your rugs because most plastics seal in moisture, which in turn promotes the growth of mildew, especially in hot, dark, airless storage areas. Use instead large sheets of heavy brown wrapping paper. Most hardware and variety stores stock paper of this sort, and if handled with reasonable care, it may be used over and over again. After sprinkling or spraying with one of the insect repellents discussed later, the rug should be rolled, wrapped, and securely sealed with one of the many excellent tapes now available for home use.

STORAGE PROBLEMS

Rugs stored for as long as a season, especially summer, should be protected against the following: (1) insect damage, (2) rodents, (3) dry rot, (4) mildew, (5) excessively dry heat.

Insects

Clothes moths. The two most common clothes moths, the webbing moth (*Tineola bisselliella*) and the casemaking moth (*Tinea pellionella*) look very much alike. The adult moths are yellowish or buff in color and have a wingspan of about $1/2$ inch. They are not strong flyers and are not attracted to bright light; instead, they may be seen flitting erratically in dim corners. Female moths usually lay from 200 to 300 tiny pearly eggs upon a material the larvae can feed on, which includes all animal products and, as mentioned earlier, urine residues. The egg-hatching period is about four to eight days in summer, but may take longer in cooler weather.

The webbing moth spins a silky coverlet, usually concealed in a fold or crevice, under which the white-bodied, dark-headed larvae feed and then pupate at the conclusion of the feeding period. Its life cycle is variable, extending from three months to a year.

The casemaking moth larvae construct a small portable case of the woolen material it feeds upon. The case enlarges and is dragged about as the larva feeds. But after the feeding stage has concluded, the larva attaches the case, in which it will pupate, in a secluded place. The length of the life cycle is extremely variable: depending on the food supply, temperature, and humidity, it may require from two months to four years.

Carpet beetles. Four species of small, oval dermestid beetles, which may be either solid black or mottled with white, brown, yellow, or black. The larvae have gold, brown or black bristles terminating in a tuft of long hairs, and grow to be $1/4$ to $1/2$ inch long, depending on the species.

Although the adult beetles—commonly known as Buffalo moths or bugs—feed on pollen and vegetable matter, museum curators are constantly on the watch for their larvae, which can consume insect collections and the wool, hides, and fur of stuffed animals in a very short period of time.

According to the U.S. Department of Agriculture and the conservators at the Merrimack Textile Museum, carpet beetles are more abundant in many areas than clothes moths and are often the cause of damage attributed to moths. The adult beetles fly readily and can enter houses through cracks as well as open doors and windows. Their destructive larvae may be deposited either as eggs by the adult females or carried into homes on secondhand furnishings. Although it may be possible to prevent beetle larvae from damaging rugs through the use of products mentioned later in this chapter, a significant infestation may require fumigation by a professional exterminator.

Control of rug-damaging insects. To control clothes moths and carpet beetles, rugs being prepared for storage should be sprinkled with paradichlorobenzine flakes or crystals at the USDA-recommended rate of at least 1 pound per 100 cubic feet of space; then the rugs should be rolled and securely wrapped to retain the vapor. An alternative treatment may be provided by Chemtreat, a powder used to prepare a mothproofing solution. (See the end of this section for details.) Do not substitute the cheaper and somewhat more easily available napthalene "moth balls" for paradichlorobenzine. Napthalene is not as effective, and conservators suspect that long-term use may cause color changes in rug dyes.

Concern about insect damage should not be limited to stored rugs. Rugs kept in rooms with little traffic and portions of large carpets that extend under furniture are also subject to moth and beetle infestation and can suffer extensive damage in a surprisingly short time. A friend of mine, a resident faculty member of a New England preparatory school, returned from a three-week Christmas vacation to find a wool Tunisian wall hanging infested with casemaking moth larvae and riddled with holes. Additional larvae were discovered on and behind all of his other rugs, and the cracks in the wooden wall behind the badly damaged hanging were stuffed with pupating larvae. All of this occurred in a small two-room apartment which, though attractive and tidy, was thoroughly dusted and vacuumed about as often as could be expected of an overworked young bachelor.

In short, even actively used quarters can harbor hordes of destructive insects if their food source remains undisturbed, and their ranks can include cockroaches and crickets attracted to rugs sauced with neglected food spills and crumbs. If you discover larvae on your rugs, brush them off—outside if possible—and follow with vacuuming front and back. A small moth-infested weaving can be tightly packaged in polyethylene, placed in a chest freezer, and vacuumed free of frozen moths and larvae after a stay of no less than 48 hours.

During the warm weather months I routinely use insect foggers in clothes and rug storage areas to control destructive insect populations, but in view of the constantly evolving standards of acceptability regarding insect spray and fogger components, I am reluctant to recommend any commonly available brands. Either apply Chemtreat to your rugs (see end of chapter for details) or consult an exterminator concerning chemicals currently considered both safe and effective.

Cedar-lined closets and chests, although certainly useful as storage areas, should not be relied upon for complete protection from the ravages of destructive insects. A New York City dealer suggested wrapping rugs in newsprint because, he said, the inks would act as a repellent. But I have found no proof of their effectiveness, and the extremely high acid content of printing inks argues against their involvement with the long-term storage of textiles.

Worst of all is the recommendation to place saucers of feathers among stored rugs because moths supposedly vastly prefer a feather diet to all others. This balmy notion first appeared in 1922 in a respected handbook by Kendrick and Tattersall and was cheerfully repeated as gospel in an otherwise useful guide published in 1980. Not only is the premise unsubstantiated, but it ignores the question of what the larvae eat once they have consumed the favored feathers.

Rodents

Damage caused by mice, rats, and squirrels seeking nesting materials can sometimes be a concern, especially in old rural houses with dry wall foundations and less than airtight attics. If you have had rodent invasions in the past, your best bet is to store rugs in a commercial facility unless you can ensure a rodent-free storage area through the use of poison baits or traps or by preparing an enclosure of coarse metal screening.

Dry Rot

According to one of the auctioneers I consulted, dry rot is a significant cause of value-robbing damage to cotton-wefted or -warped rugs consigned to auction by private owners. The culprit is an airborne, microscopic plantlike fungus that feeds on cellulose fibers, principally wood but including cotton. Although its insidious growth can be arrested, its effect is irreversible. The alternate wetting and drying of fibers leads to the rapid growth and spread of dry rot. Although an infected rug may *look* perfectly normal, the affected fibers become brittle and will eventually crack and disintegrate when subjected to stress. That is why you will sometimes see dealers at auction previews lean close as they carefully bend particular rugs back and forth at various points, listening for the telltale "chut-chut" or cracking of a weakened cotton foundation.

Storing a rug in winter in a damp, cold place that becomes warm and moist in summer invites the growth of dry rot; therefore, cellars, garages, and leaky attics should be avoided as storage areas. If you have rugs where they occasionally become damp, such as an entry hall or bath area, they should be taken up and allowed to dry thoroughly, front and back, before being replaced. The practice of standing large potted plants on rugs is a common cause of severe damage. Even if you are scrupulous about emptying the overflow out of the saucers in which the pots stand, the airless moisture trap created beneath them can rot out a rug in an alarmingly short time. Either place the pots elsewhere or upon a rack that will allow air circulation beneath them.

Although the animal fibers, wool and silk, are not subject to dry rot—indeed, wool requires a certain degree of moisture to remain supple—the silk content of rugs made in the 19th and early 20th centuries may deteriorate if allowed to become damp because the dyeing processes employed during that period increased the natural tendency of silk fibers to become brittle and eventually shatter when exposed to high levels of either moisture and dryness.

Mildew

Mildew is a thin, often whitish fungal growth that also requires moisture in which to thrive. The spores are likely to develop in hot humid weather in poorly ventilated spaces on rugs that are soiled or stored in plastic bags or plastic-coated wrappings.

Unlike dry rot, mildews attack just about anything, with the exception of some synthetics; and as they grow, they become unsightly and can cause considerable damage. Mildew molds leave greenish gray or grayish black splotches that will eventually weaken rug fibers, and their strong musty odor is difficult to dispel.

Atmospheric humidity is beyond our control, but the problems attendant upon its pervasive dampness can be mitigated by the following:

1. Drying the air through the use of air conditioners or dehumidifiers. In closets, a continuously burning electric light bulb may provide sufficient heat to discourage the growth of mildew.

2. Moisture-absorbing chemicals such as silica gel or activated aluminum may be obtained at hardware and building supply stores under various trade names. To use, hang in a cloth bag or place in an open container in the storage area. Both of these chemicals can be recycled by drying out at 300 degrees in a vented oven for several hours, then cooling before reusing.

Mildew can be deterred by the vapors of paradichlorobenzine, which is also the only insect repellent recommended by the textile conservators I consulted. Use no less than 1 pound per 100 cubic feet, replenishing the supply periodically to ensure a sufficient supply of effective vapor.

In the eastern half of the United States, where high humidity is virtually synonymous with summer, rugs can develop mildew even on the floor, especially in small, airless rooms and hallways and under furniture. Brush or vacuum off any surface growth—if possible outdoors to prevent scattering of the spores inside the house—then seal and dispose of the vacuum cleaner bag.

Sun and air will stop mold growth, but if you discover it during a prolonged spell of hot, humid, overcast weather, dry the rug front and back with a forced-air heater or, if the rug is quite small, with a hand hair dryer. If you are using a jute rug pad, this too may require vacuuming and drying. Then, during the next spell of dry weather, expose rug and pad to the sun after sponging the affected areas with the suds of a neutral detergent—as described in the section on rug washing—followed by their removal with a water-dampened sponge. Unless city dwellers have the luxury of a large sunny window, they will have to settle for an electric heater and fan. In either case, the rug and pad should be completely dry before replacement.

Unfortunately, the mustiness characteristic of mildew is very persistent. Sponging and airing may help, but on dank days be prepared for a cryptlike smell well into the fall heating season. Avoid artificially perfumed, sweet, floral room deodorants: they can be nauseating in combination with the lingering odor of mildew. Instead, try pungent incense sticks like balsam fir or piñon pine.

Dryness

Excessively high heat can also be damaging, especially to rugs containing significant amounts of silk. Wall-hung rugs are apt to become dry in the upper third, where heat rises and concentrates; dulled pile and a brittle foundation may be the price your rug pays for being placed too near a source of heat, in front of a large unshaded window with a southern exposure, or stored in an unventilated attic where summer daytime temperatures can soar well above 100 degrees.

Additional Information About Chemtreat Mothproofing Treatment

This colorless, odorless, nonflammable treatment is virtually identical to Crispell's Mothproofing Solution—recommended in the first edition but no longer available—used by the rug trade for about 20 years on all types of rugs. Chemtreat is *not* an insecticide: it renders wool inedible, but will not kill moths or larvae already present that could migrate elsewhere. Before treatment, therefore, rugs and trappings should be thoroughly vacuumed and washed (see section on rug washing).

Chemtreat powder is available from the Chatalbash Rug Co. (see list under Cleaning and Repair Supplies in the Resource Guide). When mixed, a quart will mothproof a rug of about 50 square feet; one third for the back, two thirds for the pile. More may be needed for a very thickly piled rug, less for a worn rug and flatweaves. The liquid should be applied with a hand or power sprayer with a glass or plastic reservoir.

Rugs should be both clean and dry before treated. Place the rug face-down on a flat surface, which, if indoors, should be protected with a heavyweight paper or plastic sheeting. After applying the solution according to the directions on the container, drag an old-fashioned broom across the rug to break up any beading and allow the solution to penetrate the fibers. When the surface has dried—a fan will facilitate the process if weather conditions are unfavorable—turn the rug pile-side up and repeat the process. Do not fold or roll a treated rug for storage until completely dry. Rugs should be re-treated after washing.

REPAIR, RESTORATION, AND CONSERVATION

Compared to other works of art and fine craftsmanship, the treatment oriental rugs are expected to endure is really quite unreasonable. Would we cut down a painting by Canaletto to fit the space between the dining room windows? Do we feed the family pet from an antique Meissen bowl? Yet splendid old runners are blithely butchered to suit the dimensions of apartment hallways, and we literally wipe our feet on finely woven 19th-century Sarouk mats.

I'm not suggesting that all rugs be taken out of domestic service and hung reverently on artfully lit walls; but unless aesthetic and monetary value and ongoing usefulness are of no interest, every rug owner has very practical reasons for learning how to distinguish use from abuse. Once a rug's edges and ends break down to the point where the pile knots are no longer secure, or when a weak spot in the foundation abrades into a hole, the situation has already deteriorated beyond the point where the average rug owner has the time, materials, skill, and knowledge to make acceptable repairs. Rebecca Venable, who writes on restoration for the trade journal *Rug News*, summed it all up back in 1981 in one sternly succinct phrase: rugs are not ruined in a day or restored overnight.

One of the purposes of this section will be to acquaint owners of rugs in good condition with techniques that will help keep them in their present fine state of repair. These maintenance measures can be done at home with basic needle-and-thread skills and easily obtainable materials; yet because they are time-consuming, they can be expensive to have done professionally.

But what about the rug that was worn or damaged before you acquired it? The rug you inherited or picked up for peanuts at a house sale or an exceptional example affordable because of its problems? In cases like these, the most important part of the repair is the assessment of the rug as an entity. Once that has been dealt with, the type and quality of repair best suited to it will be much easier to decide.

First of all, is more of the rug in reasonably good condition than in need of repair? If not, but the rug has outstanding color and design, then mount or hang it as you would a fragment. If only small and scattered areas of the original glory remain, you could incorporate them into pillows, vests, or pocketbooks.

Next, the *quality* of the rug should be determined in regard to its age, rarity, design execution, historical significance, and quality of the fibers and dyes. You may wish to seek advice from a knowledgeable collector— another good reason for joining a rug society—or museum curator. A dealer or a rug specialist at one of the major auction houses can also provide information, but you may have to pay an appraisal fee to get it.

The *structure* of a rug can affect both the solution of a repair problem and its cost, which is often the explanation for the seemingly inexplicable variation in prices dealers are willing to pay for damaged rugs at auction. For example, the edges of old Baluch rugs are wrapped with goat hair of a type rarely available in this country; if the original edges are missing, a dealer knows that the cost and extra work involved in adhering to authenticity will outweigh the price he can get for all but the finest Baluch work.

Caucasian and village Turkish rugs, on the other hand, are not only highly popular with collectors but are among the easiest to repair. They are relatively coarsely Turkish-knotted, and the colors and wool are fairly easy to match, which allows reknotted areas to blend readily into the original.

Finely woven Persian rugs can be very difficult to reweave, especially if the warps lie on two levels as they do in densely structured types like old Bijars and Kermans, which is why it may cost appreciably more to repair a hole in a worn, mediocre old Bijar than in an antique Kazak worth thousands more.

Chinese rugs present the greatest repair challenge because of the problems encountered in matching Chinese wools. I am told that a reknotted repair that blends perfectly at one angle of light will most likely be very apparent in another light, no matter how skillfully the repair itself has been done.

The rug's *primary purpose* should be defined: do you consider it as a floor furnishing only or as part of your collection? If the latter, did the expectation of eventual profitable resale affect your decision to buy it? If no longer serviceable as a floor covering, is it small and handsome enough to be used without repair as a wall hanging?

Finally, there is that intangible element best defined as *point of view*. An example of this is the friend who referred apologetically to an antique Heriz in his Federal Connecticut home as a "beat-up old thing we really must replace." This lovely old carpet has obviously seen better days, but it suited its 19th-century setting much better than would a newer rug in mint condition. And since the market value of this worn rug had been further reduced by the removal of a substantial portion of one corner, it was a prime example of a severely damaged rug not worth expensive repairs that could have been markedly improved with a little paint and the overcasting of frayed edges.

Once the condition, quality, and proposed use of a damaged rug have been defined, the appropriate level of repair can be considered. If professional repairs are not required or must be delayed, some basic preventive measures not only can but should be undertaken at home to prevent further damage and additional expense. These include overcasting ends to arrest the unraveling of wefts; stabilizing edges that have loose or missing sections of the original overwrapping material, and securing and backing holes and tears. Techniques and materials will be discussed in the following section. Rug painting, the method of last resort, will be treated separately.

Treatments beyond the competence of most collectors fall into three broad categories: functional, restoration, and conservation:

FUNCTIONAL REPAIRS

The aim of functional repairs is to return a damaged rug to useful service in the home. At its best, this type of repair approaches true restoration: fiber type, weight, ply, and color are closely matched to the original warp, weft, and pile fibers; and the workmanship is such that the repaired area can be detected only upon close examination. Work of this quality is expensive, so it is important to resolve the following questions before embarking upon a costly program of professional repair:

1. Will the market value of the repaired rug compensate for the cost of repairs?

2. Does the decorative or sentimental value of the rug outweigh monetary considerations?

Unless you are familiar with the rug market, the only way the first question can be answered is by having the rug appraised and its repaired value estimated by an experienced dealer. Consider the fee as part of the cost of repairs.

An auction bargain can become very expensive once repair costs are added, so if you have your eye on a fine but damaged rug being offered at auction, it would be worth paying a fee to a freelance rug repairer to attend the auction preview and provide you with an estimate.

Established dealers usually have competent craftspersons on the premises who do custom repair work in addition to readying old rugs for sale. Since repair work is a necessary adjunct to a successful dealership in old rugs, the cost, although always high, will be competitive. Some dealers include the price of repairs in the old rugs they sell, so if you are considering buying a rug with problems, be sure you know what its price includes and that both you and the dealer agree on the type and extent of repairs included.

Be sure that whoever does your repair work is not only skilled but conscientious. If the skill of the repair person is not readily ascertainable or if the estimate is higher than anticipated, contract to have the work done in stages so that the quality of the work can be reviewed before you commit yourself to further expense. Don't be shy about discussing your expectations: as you will learn later, there are some cost-cutting measures that are acceptable and others that aren't.

At the low end of the functional repair ladder is a type best described as stitch-and-patch, which is acceptable only for rugs that have suffered irreversible harm but are still useful as furnishing pieces. This includes rugs that have been awkwardly reduced in size and rugs with extremely worn pile or with holes in foundations weakened by dry rot. In the last case, a patch cut from a similar rug or a neat darn may be the only practical solution. A collectible rug's original size should never be reduced; however, the appearance of a worn furnishing rug can sometimes be markedly improved by removing severely frazzled edges and ends or by cutting and rejoining—known in the trade as cut-and-shut—in order to eliminate a large hole or disfiguring stain that cannot be painted out.

RESTORATION

The goal of a restorer is to re-create the original condition of a rug through the virtual duplication of the materials, the weaving of the foundation, and the knotting of the pile. An expert restorer will often spend as much time studying the construction of a rug and matching colors and fibers as it takes to do the actual restoration work.

Richard Newman, a Manhattan-based craftsman, says that a close study of rug structure is like deciphering a code. Once he becomes familiar with the subtle interrelationships between the warps, wefts, and knotting that characterize not only the type of rug given him to repair but the style of the weaver of that particular rug, the actual process of restoration is like playing a well-rehearsed song. Every element falls into place in rhythmic progression without strain or hesitation.

Although the performance of this song of restoration is extremely expensive, if you own a carpet of exceptional quality or rugs that represent tribal design and weaving skill at its characteristic best, you could consider it a capital investment. Short of a worldwide collapse, the choicest examples of any of the arts often increase in value at the same time that the merely good ones are declining.

CONSERVATION

Conservation of a rug possessing significant historical or design interest requires that the methods of display and of chemical and mechanical preservation affect its integrity as little as possible. Strictly interpreted, this rules out the removal or addition of materials, which the process of repair or restoration necessitates and in the doing blurs the historic information contained in the rug's original materials and structure. Even a worn and damaged rug with little market value may, if it is old enough and rare enough, be worthy of conservation; so if you have inherited any antique rugs, it would be wise to have them assessed by an expert eye before turning them over for stitch-and-patch repairs.

You may wonder why a rug considered to have little value or interest in the past should now be thought a possible candidate for conservation. Well, it could, for instance, be a type of tribal rug of which only a few are represented in Western collections. Even a battered rug becomes important to conserve for technical analysis and study if it provides an essential link in the design progression of a particular weaving group or contains a unique combination of motifs and colors.

Then, too, tastes and opinions change in rugs as they do in everything else. It is not always easy to predict what future generations will consider important or beautiful. Even as I write, textile curators are acquiring rugs containing early synthetic dyes because they represent a significant chapter in the history of weaving, and a few collectors have already begun speaking of "classic early synthetics" because at the same time the scarcity of fine old rugs drives prices up, it changes the standards of acceptability.

Scientific conservation of an object presupposes treatment, storage, and display under strictly controlled conditions, as prescribed by a specialist. Informal conservation can be undertaken by collectors through the exercise of a prudent policy of limited use in an environment with moderate temperature, humidity, and light-level ranges and of having repairs made with reversible techniques.

The question of whether a rug should be repaired, restored, or conserved is complicated and often controversial. When all is said and done, the final decision rests with the owner, who, unfortunately, is not always as informed as one might hope. Not long ago, on a visit to a carpet and tile shop near my home, I noticed a fine old Baluch rug rolled up in a corner. The proprietor told me it had been brought in for repairs, which he had undertaken reluctantly—

he admittedly knew nothing about oriental rugs—because the insistent owner was a valued customer. These "repairs" entailed cutting off the rug's exceptionally beautiful brocaded skirts and replacing the characteristic goat-hair-wrapped edges—with glued-on cotton twill binding, no less—because both were somewhat frayed and the owner wanted to "tidy the rug up a bit." The sorriest part of it all was that an acceptable, workmanlike repair job would probably have cost very little more than this needless butchery.

If you decide *your* rugs could use a little tidying, I hope the following sections will enable you to make informed decisions based on an intelligent assessment of the problems and of the repair options available to you. For the venturesome, a marvelous book offering step-by-step instruction in rug repairs on an advanced level is included in the Resource Guide in the back of this book. But before you snip a single warp or weft thread or remove a knot of pile, please consider the following:

1. The average rug owner is unlikely to have a sufficient variety of discardable worn rugs or fragments suitable for practicing and perfecting repair skills.

2. The variety and colors of fibers necessary for a first-rate major repair may be difficult to acquire in small quantities.

3. Rug repair is a slow and painstaking craft requiring a high degree of patience, a keen sense of observation, and the kind of temperament that relishes work involving the exact duplication of small details.

4. A carelessly or incorrectly performed *irreversible* repair can do more harm than good.

SIMPLE HOME REPAIRS

Since the primary audience for this guide is beginning collectors, I will not discuss except in passing those problems whose repair requires a familiarity with rug structure beginners are unlikely to possess. A list of tools and materials required for the basic repairs presented here will be found at the end of this section. To readers interested in pursuing the craft beyond this elementary stopgap level, I unhesitatingly recommend Peter Stone's *Oriental Rug Repair*, which may be obtained from booksellers listed in the Resource Guide at the back of this book.

RUG REPILING

Although replacing lost, worn, moth-eaten, or discolored pile is a task more demanding of patience than of skill, there are too many variables among rugs to allow a general approach to the subject. If all rugs were knotted coarsely and all knots were lined up on a single plane and easily accounted for, a beginner's knowledge of rug structure and a few glib paragraphs of mine might suffice; unfortunately, this is not the case.

In addition to familiarity with structure, an acceptable repair requires wools matched to the original in texture as well as color: light reflected from a long, thick glossy pile will not have the same value as light glancing off a short, fine, less lustrous pile dyed exactly the same color. The difference can, in fact, be startling. Unless one is willing to spend the money necessary to amass a wide variety of wools, not to mention the time needed to blend and re-ply them to effect an exact match, a repiled area will betray itself no matter how skillfully copied the knotting technique may have been.

An alternative to knot replacement in very worn rugs is a type of rug darning known as *kashmiring*, which covers the exposed warps and, assuming the color match is good, can approximate the look of the adjoining low pile closely. It is, however, a cosmetic or conservation repair and should not be substituted for pile replacement in an otherwise sound and serviceable rug. This technique is described in greater detail in a later section on conservation methods.

Speaking of conservation, at the risk of offending fellow cat owners I feel obligated to point out that cats that develop a fondness for exercising clawed paws on rugs can literally destroy a low-piled fragile carpet in short order. If you find the thought of declawing too horrible to contemplate, either hang your antique rugs or resign yourself to a battle of wills your cat is almost certain to win.

REPAIRING FLATWEAVES

Since flat-woven rugs have no knots to assist in containing damage, a small hole in a flat-woven rug will usually enlarge more rapidly than it would in a pile rug. Damage to flatweaves used as floor furnishings should therefore be promptly attended to even if the resulting "repair" is less than expert. In the long run, it will be cheaper to have your small repair redone than a large hole rewoven from scratch.

If you are unable to trace out the pattern of the weave—some are quite complex—a neat darn accomplished with a blunt tapestry needle and needlepoint yarns reasonably well color-matched will temporarily suffice. Do try, however, to approximate as closely as possible the tension of the original weave so as to minimize the strain on adjacent areas. The names of craftspeople qualified to do flatweave restoration will be found in the Resource Guide.

EDGE AND END FINISHES

The first areas of a rug to show wear are usually the edges and ends. Even some brand-new rugs have unraveling ends due to careless or hasty finishing. Anchoring these weak points requires more time than skill. If consigned to a professional, the cost will be high; the collector who elects to do them at home will not only stand to gain in self-satisfaction, but in the

Reweaving a slit-tapestry kilim.

Reweaving a soumak flatweave.

doing will learn more about the way rugs are constructed than any book can teach. It is an ideal task to accomplish while television-viewing: tedious but requiring little judgment in the process.

Many people think rug edges and ends serve a function that is primarily cosmetic, like a frame around a picture. But a picture removed from its frame remains intact; a rug so deprived will inexorably disintegrate. A pile knot here and a weft thread there can add up to a very expensive repair job by the end of a year. Because it is so important to attend to the first signs of damage, one should, ideally, possess a work box kept stocked with well-chosen materials and the solemn sense of duty that impels one to do a proper repair in timely fashion.

Perfection being in short supply in this imperfect world, I suggest instead you seize the moment when both your mood and available time are in happy conjunction and use anything you have on hand. Overcasting the edges of an antique Ladik prayer rug with lavender acrylic knitting wool may offend your sensibilities, but arresting further disintegration takes priority. Amends can be made when you acquire satisfactory materials.

Fortunately, it isn't necessary to know much about rugs to do simple edge and end repairs *as long as you allow the rug to guide you*:

1. Don't remove any more of the original material than is necessary: the color, weight, ply, and style of application of the original finish helps establish age and origin.

2. Don't apply a finish of your own devising because it's easier or, in your opinion, more attractive than the original. Rug repair, and especially rug conservation, is an inappropriate field for creative needlework.

Edges

There are four fairly distinct stages of edge disintegration:

1. *Breakage, loosening, and minor loss of the fibers used in overcasting.*

The overcasting material protects the edge warp structure, and although it is often distinctive or decorative, it is not an integral part of the structure. Its replacement, therefore, is the easiest of the edge repairs and can be accomplished successfully by anyone willing to first match the original material in color and density and then copy the tension and angle of the existing, adjacent material.

If the damaged overcasting is itself not original, you may choose to reovercast the entire edge with a more suitable material. If, however, the replacement nearly duplicates the original, you need redo only the damaged portion.

The fuzziness and plumpness of new overcasting can be corrected by applying a flame to the former—a quick pass with a kitchen match or lighter should do the trick—and a wooden mallet to the latter, preferably in that order.

2. *Small sections of the edge warp cords have become separated from the wefts extending from the rug foundation and woven into or around them.*

This repair can also be done at home. First, pull or clip away any broken bits of overcasting and wefts clinging to the side cords. Then, before proceeding further, take the time to closely inspect the weft-weaving technique used originally to secure the edge cords to the foundation warps. The more closely you can duplicate the damaged wefts in both weave and color, the less visible your repair will be.

Thread a large-headed, sharp-pointed needle with a stout linen or button thread color-matched as closely as possible to the broken wefts. Knot the end.

Insert the needle on the back of the rug. Draw it through up to eight sound foundation warps (if the weave is tight, you may need a small pliers to pull the needle through) and, depending on the number of cord-bundles in the original edge finish, loop the thread around a single bundle or over

(a) Securing a single bundle of edge warp cords into the foundation of a rug; (b) overcasting exposed edge warp cords.

and under two or three or more. Then return the needle and new weft thread through sound warps into the body of the rug.

Repeat the process along the length of the damaged section, taking pains to maintain the original tension. A thread drawn too tightly can cause puckering; if left too loose, gaps may occur.

Finish the repair by overcasting as described above in No. 1.

3. *Sections of the warp cords comprising the edge have not only separated from the wefts securing them to the foundation warps but are severely frayed or broken.*

This problem presents several technical challenges: first, the edge cords must be duplicated—which in most cases involves the respinning and plying of wool threads—then joined inconspicuously both vertically

(a–c) Securing and overcasting a damaged double-cord edge.

and horizontally to the remaining warps, a task that should be done on a frame and under carefully adjusted tension so that the new edge will lie smooth and flat, without bulges or puckers. This repair is best undertaken by a professional.

4. *Broken edge warp cords are missing in part or entirely, and the exposed, loosened pile knots have begun to erode.*

When edge damage is this extreme, a proper repair exceeds the ability of all but the most determined amateur, especially if the damage includes a dog-eared corner.

Rug owners are often shocked to learn that reconstruction of edges, eroded guard borders, and dog-eared corners is more difficult, and therefore more expensive, than the reweaving of a hole in the middle of a rug. If professional repairs must be delayed, either take the rug out of service or retard further erosion of the pile knots as follows: (a) Closely overcast the damaged area with wool or stout thread, or (b) fold cotton twill tape around the damaged portions, attaching it as neatly as possible front and back with large, loose zigzag stitches. The tape can be dyed if the color difference is extreme. You may be tempted to apply an adhesive tape: *don't*!

False Edgings

Are there any acceptable alternatives to the above procedures? In regard to the first two relatively simple problems described above, both of which can be easily remedied at home, the answer is no.

Complex edge repairs on a rug in generally good condition should be undertaken by a professional, but if the rug has additional serious problems—unevenly worn pile, for example, or unsightly dye runs—you might consider a handmade false edge, a ready-made edging, or machine overcasting. Personally, I would have no qualms about having a false edging applied to a decorative but otherwise undistinguished worn rug if the alternative was unsightly edges and a continued erosion of pile, but it must be pointed out that the choice of any of these less expensive alternatives can create a new problem in the place of the one it was intended to solve.

This new problem originates with the cutting away of what remains of an original edge to make way for a new one. If the pile knots have already begun to loosen along the edge, this may include a portion of the border guard stripe as well. In either case, the largely invisible but structurally important weft reversals that the edge structure was designed to protect will be irreversibly compromised. A false edging, which is attached *to*, rather than incorporated *into*, the newly trimmed edge, may in time require occasional reinforcement with a few turns of button thread to prevent it and the warps to which it is precariously attached from pulling loose under the normal stress of household use.

Because false edgings of one kind or another are so much less costly than reconstruction, the average journeyman repair person may assume this is what you want done unless instructed otherwise. It is desirable, of course, to match any type of edging as closely as possible to the original, but an expert won't be fooled by a false edge no matter how cunningly devised.

Ends

In general, the ends of all oriental rugs, new as well as old, should be securely overcast, as shown, to prevent the unraveling of wefts and eventual loss of pile knots, unless the warps are firmly braided or knotted across the entire width. However, although the loss of original rug end finishes is always regrettable—especially if distinctive or decorative—as long as there is enough of a stub end left to firmly secure so as to prevent the pile knots from working loose from the warps, the structural integrity of the rug will be preserved. Whether that justifies lopping off worn or partially missing end finishes and overcasting the remainder depends on the rug in question: if it is a fine antique Baluch with long, elaborately brocaded skirts, reconstruction may be warranted; ordinary fringes may be treated more cavalierly, depending on the extent of the loss.

1. *The fringe is unevenly worn and has no distinctive features.*

If the wear does not extend into the wefts or the edge finishes, the warp ends that make up the fringe can be artfully evened by snipping off a few at a time so that the result has the slight imprecision characteristic of a hand-made rug. Remove no more than is necessary to minimize the damage, and try to resist the temptation to remove a perfectly good length of fringe at one end to match what is left of the other.

(a) Right: This is the recommended way to overcast the ends of rugs to prevent the loss of wefts and knots. (b) Wrong: This method will not sufficiently secure wefts and knots against working loose from the foundation.

To soften the bluntness of the newly cut ends, comb out the fibers with a fine-tooth comb or suede brush. Finish by overcasting.

2. *The uneven fringe wear extends into a section of plain weave.*

Some village and tribal rugs have sections of warp and weft plain weaving between the body of the rug and an end fringe, which in this instance is a secondary finish and usually quite short. The plain-weave strip may be purely functional and only ¹/₂ inch to 2 inches long; in others, Baluch and Turkoman rugs in particular, it may be an elaborately decorated 6 inches or more.

If the plain weave is functional, or the decoration consists of no more than plain-woven stripes repeating the colors of the pile, the wefts can be removed one by one, gently prying them out with a blunt needle, until an undamaged row of wefting is reached. Secure this row by overcasting before turning your attention to the fringe. This should be judiciously evened as described above, with special attention to teasing out the crimped look of warps from which damaged wefts have been removed.

3. *A section or sections of fringe have been cut, torn, or chewed off along the edge of the pile, but the remaining fringe is undamaged.*

In this case, new warp threads must be manufactured and anchored into the foundation, then trimmed and the ends teased out as described above.

If the warp fiber is wool, hand-spun knitting or needlepoint wools can be used, depending on the texture of the original warps. If white and brown wools were combined in a single warp, you can achieve a similar barber-pole effect by plying together strands of similarly colored wool. If the fringe to be replaced is cotton, it can probably be matched to cording used in macramé craft work.

The new fringes, whether of wool or cotton, may have to be tinted to blend with the original fringe. The most effective method involves a solution of permanganate crystals. Its preparation and use will be described later in this chapter.

Replacing a section of missing fringe. (a) Anchor new yarns an inch into the foundation; (b) trim new yarns to the length of the existing fringe.

Until a professional repair can be done, a gouged edge should be closely overcast to prevent further erosion of rug fibers.

4. *The damage to the fringe extends into the body of the rug, causing a loss of pile.*

The technical challenges involved in making a stable and inconspicuous repair warrants consigning this problem to a professional, particularly if the damage includes dog-eared corners, which are notoriously difficult to reconstruct. If repairs must be delayed, closely overcast the affected area with wool or stout thread to prevent further loss of pile.

Manufactured Fringes

It is tempting to add a commercially manufactured fringe to an old rug that has little of its own remaining, but a fringe sewed onto the end of a rug can, unless placed in a protected area, soon pull away under the stress of daily foot traffic, taking with it the wefts and pile knots to which it was attached.

However, if you are unable to accustom yourself to the appearance of a rug without fringes, a variety of styles of uniformly good quality are available by mail order from a reliable source listed at the end of this chapter. Remember that these fringes are cotton and therefore are unsuitable for rugs with wool warps.

CURLED CORNERS AND EDGES

Rugs with turned-over edges and corners curling like a breaking wave are not only unsightly but potentially dangerous, especially if the afflicted rug lies in a busy passageway. Tacking a curling edge or corner to the floor will succeed only in eventually separating it from the rest of the rug, and steam-pressing curls into submission is at best a temporary remedy. The most effective approach is to counteract the curling tendency with a strong backing material.

A cotton twill tape may suffice for a lightweight or limply curled rug, but a rug of any substance will in time bend even a stoutly woven fabric to its will. What is needed, I have finally concluded—and have since had confirmed by other sources—is a dimensionally stable material that can be

Attaching a stiffening strip to a curling edge.

attached to the curling portion of the rug without damaging the foundation. Satisfactory choices include dense cardboard, linoleum, thin vinyl tile or masonite, or a sturdy leather like cowhide, all of which can be sewed—never glued!—to the underside of the rug with linen or button thread once holes have been drilled or punched in the backing strip as illustrated.

HOLES, SPLITS, AND TEARS

Holes, splits, and tears often seem more alarming than they are in fact because, unlike damaged edges and ends, they disrupt the overall harmony of the rug design. Actually, hole repairs usually present a skilled, well-equipped craftsperson with fewer technical problems than the reconstruction of a severely dog-eared corner. On the other hand, an eager, inexperienced collector, with only book knowledge of structure and an insufficient variety of wool yarns, can rapidly transform a flaw into a fiasco.

This does not mean one need just stand there helplessly wringing one's hands. There are conservation procedures an amateur can safely undertake, assuming a rug so treated will be used as a wall hanging or placed in a lightly trafficked place. If the condition and quality of a rug are such that the expense of a proper repair cannot be justified, then one or another of these procedures may help extend its life of useful service.

Holes

Everyone knows what a hole is, but the cause of a hole has a direct bearing on the type and extent of the repair required. If a hole has been chewed or burned into a rug that is in otherwise very good condition, it should be professionally rewoven, not only because of the gratifying improvement in appearance but because its restored value will, in most cases, compensate for the cost of the repair.

Sometimes a repair person will suggest stitch-and-glue patching of a hole with a plug cut from a fragment of a similar rug. Although patching is less expensive than reweaving and a very tempting alternative if the match will be nearly exact, resist it. It is a shoddy and devaluing practice not worth considering for a collectible rug.

When a hole results from the wearing away of both the pile and foundation by hard use, it may be difficult to find adjacent warps sound enough to anchor the new foundation materials. In these cases, it is often necessary to enlarge the original hole before reweaving can begin, and the expense of the repair may overtake any value it could add to a rug that was in poor condition to begin with.

If a hole is the first visible sign of an extensive area of dry rot in a cotton foundation, reweaving may not be possible; if it is, the cost may be prohibitive for all but rugs of great historical or sentimental value. In cases of damage this extreme, backing the affected area with an adhesive tape in the hope of consolidating the rotting fibers may be your only alternative. Although this will not solve the problem—nothing can—it can delay the inevitable disintegration. However, since taping is irreversible, do not proceed without confirmation by an experienced dealer or repair person that dry rot is, in fact, the underlying problem. In that unhappy case, *and in that case only*, the use of an adhesive tape can be justified.

Splits and Tears

Tears may be the result of rough or careless handling, but since it isn't easy to rip through the foundation threads of a hand-knotted rug in sound condition, tears or splits may indicate either a hardened spill that has made the fibers stiff or brittle or a dry-rotted cotton warp, weft, or both.

If the tear is clean, affecting only a few foundation threads and pile knots, carefully realign the edges. Insert a needle threaded with button or linen thread an inch above and beyond the tear and work it through the foundation and across the tear, emerging about an inch beyond it on the other side. Continue working your needle back and forth as closely as possible along the tear's entire length. Then tack a *nonadhesive* backing strip to the foundation over the joining. Although reweaving is always the preferred solution, if the rug is not distorted by your mend, it can probably continue in service if placed in a lightly trafficked area.

A split occurring at the site of a hardened spill may resist being joined; indeed, it may be impossible to work a needle through the stiffened fibers without enlarging the split. If this is the case, either try to pick out or, if you know what substance was spilled, dissolve the hardened residue (see the section on stain removal) and proceed as described above. If the substance resists removal, the affected area will have to be removed and rewoven.

Removal and reweaving will also be required when foundation fibers have been weakened by dry rot or mildew, unless the rot proves on examination to be extensive, in which case an adhesive backing tape may be your last, if worst, resort.

CONSERVATION MEASURES

Conservation "repairs" are, without exception, reversible. This rules out such things as adhesive tapes, glued patches, and the cutting of weft reversals at rug edges.

Since they are largely intended for rugs planned to be hung, none of the measures described below are suitable for rugs expected to withstand heavy foot traffic. In all cases, however, they are preferred to turning a blind eye.

Kashmiring

An embroidery technique known as kashmiring is sometimes employed to minimize the insult to a rug's appearance by carrying wool yarns around the warps in a figure-eight stitch. This can be used either as a simple wrapping stitch to strengthen areas along the edges or can be chained around the foundation threads in areas where the pile is either very low or missing. The success of the effect depends largely on how well the colors are matched to the pile.

Because it is reversible, kashmiring has been employed extensively for museum collections so that pile replacements could be easily distinguished from the original on close inspection yet not be so obvious as to distract from the overall harmony of design when seen from a normal viewing distance.

Today purists frown upon even this minor degree of manipulation of original materials. They claim this warp-wrapping technique, which is similar to that used in flat-woven soumaks, creates tensions dissimilar to those set up by the original weaving and may in time weaken the structure. Whether or not one agrees, this is a serious danger in fact as well as in theory. It must be conceded that even the most elegantly accomplished kashmiring provides no more than a cosmetic masking of severe wear and should not be considered a permanent substitute for pile replacement except for rugs you intend to hang on a wall.

Fabric Patches

When a hole is rewoven, the damaged ends of the warps and wefts protruding into the hole are removed, including any loose knots, and the hole is enlarged. This is done to remove irregularities so that the alignment of the new foundation threads and subsequent knotting of new pile wool can be more precisely accomplished. For a temporary conservation repair, the loose knots can be removed, but the damaged warps and wefts should be drawn through to the back and securely tacked all around the perimeter of the opening. If the rug is finely woven or densely packed, a pliers may be needed to pull the needle through the foundation.

Once the broken threads have been secured, the hole may be backed with a heavyweight fabric of a color and texture that will be both harmonious and relatively inconspicuous—for example, a coarsely woven wool home-spun for a tribal rug, a sturdy ribbed cotton or wool for flatweaves, and an upholstery-weight, smooth-surfaced wool or velvet for a fine, low-piled Persian carpet.

Cut the fabric into a patch about 2 inches larger in all dimensions than the hole to be backed. Overcast the edge to prevent fraying, and attach it to the foundation with strong thread.

If used as a floor furnishing, a rug temporarily patched in this fashion should be placed on a dense underlayment in a low-traffic area.

Silk-Screened Patch

An interesting new technique combining photography and silk screening enables visual duplication of damaged or missing areas of historically sig-nificant textiles with a minimum of fiddling with the original materials.

As reported in *Hali*, the international magazine devoted to carpets and textiles, this technique is best suited to flatweaves, but wall-hung low-pile rugs, especially those with finely detailed patterning, would seem candi-dates for this approach, too.

In brief, an area similar to the missing section in pattern and coloration is photographed, and the image is silk-screened onto a backing fabric matched as closely as possible to the thread count and weave structure of the original. The patch is then carefully incorporated into the damaged piece. For the benefit of those who do not themselves possess the necessary skills and equipment, the facility cited in the *Hali* article, the Textile Con-servation Workshop, is listed in the Resource Guide in the back of this guide under Care and Repair.

Although the creation and attachment of a silk-screened patch is undoubtedly expensive—all first-class conservation services are—it would probably cost less than expert restoration of the same area. As always, let your decision be guided by the use expected of the rug in question.

MATERIALS NEEDED FOR REPAIRS MADE AT HOME

The tools required to execute the simple repairs discussed in this chapter are inexpensive and easily assembled. None is traditional, but their use is familiar, and they will allow you to perform the described tasks satisfactorily.

1. Large-eyed, sharp- and blunt-ended tapestry needles (needlepoint, crewel) in a variety of sizes.

2. Thimble.

3. Small pliers for pulling needles through rug foundations.

4. Tweezers for removing pile knots and damaged edge overcastings.

5. A small, stiff brush—a toothbrush will do—and a fine-toothed comb to separate, straighten, or align pile fibers. (If you can find one, a little gadget known as an embroidery fluffer, with fine, hooked, wire teeth, is ideal.)

6. Scissors: (a) a pair of medium-size shears; (b) curved-blade scissors (the type manufactured for shearing pile are expensive; for the procedures described here, a good-quality cuticle scissors will prove quite adequate).

7. A magnifying device of the hands-free type used by needlepointers is useful and sometimes essential when working with finely woven rugs.

8. A wooden mallet for flattening new edge cords and blending other kinds of new work with the original structure.

9. Wooden kitchen matches for singeing the fuzz from new overcastings.

10. An adjustable work light of the extensible-arm, multipositional type. Art supply stores often stock several varieties.

THREADS AND WOOLS

Closely matched fibers, colors, and textures are essential to a satisfactory repair. Although the use of any material is acceptable in an emergency to arrest disintegration, there are a few basic fibers you would be wise to have always on hand:

Threads

A *linen thread* is the best choice for overcasting rug ends, attaching curling corner reinforcements and Velcro strips, anchoring loose edge wrappings, and securing raw edges of holes and tears. Linen thread is very strong and rot-resistant, and being a natural fiber itself, it is compatible with other natural fibers found in rugs. Unfortunately, it is expensive and difficult to find. A reliable mail order source is listed in the Resource Guide. Because of the expense, I settle for a medium-weight thread (#25) in neutral beige, dark red, brown, and blue, which I have found to be the most commonly needed colors. Depending on the type of rug you decide to collect, your needs may be somewhat different.

Button and carpet threads are an acceptable, much less costly alternative to linen. They are usually a cotton-and-synthetic blend and are widely available in a range of colors at sewing and notions counters.

Transparent synthetic threads and small-diameter fishing lines are a tempting choice because of their ability to blend with any color. But their unyielding quality makes for uneasy partnering with natural fibers, and they grow less resistant to breakage over time, especially if exposed to heat or sunlight.

Wools

There is, theoretically, a wool available to match every conceivable repair need; practically speaking, you will find your choice limited to the wool yarns made for needlepoint, crewel, and tapestry work unless you live in or near a large urban area. The goat-hair still used in edge finishes by many tribal weavers is not available, so far as I can determine, from any source here. Sometimes yarns hand-spun from natural brown sheep's wool can be reasonably well matched in color, but none have the wiry texture and gloss of Middle Eastern goat hair.

Purists advocate using only wools colored with natural dyes, but in the vast majority of cases this is not a practical choice. Vegetable colors painstakingly—and expensively—matched may mellow in such a way that the once invisible repair becomes apparent. The best of today's synthetic dyes allows an experienced dye master to reproduce any hue found in antique rugs, and a skilled restorer using this wool can, through re-plying, very closely approximate the subtle variations and spin of the original material.

Old-time rug dealers with repair facilities on the premises often display hanks of wool yarns in an awesome range of muted colors. They were obtained years ago directly from the rug-producing areas, but there are no retail suppliers of these wools in the United States. If you are on very cordial terms with such a dealer, he might spare you a length or two of his precious dusty bounty, but I wouldn't count on it.

For emergency repairs it is useful to have a black wool and two or three shades of ivory, brown, red, and blue in your work basket. These wools and the linen or button threads discussed earlier will allow you to perform relatively inconspicuous temporary repairs on just about any rug.

MATCHING WOOLS FOR COLOR AND DENSITY

Assuming you have access to a well-stocked needlework shop, take your *clean* rug with you and match the colors to the yarns in daylight. If the rug is too large, the shopkeeper may allow you to borrow packets of yarns in promising colors—or even the yarn sample books—over a weekend.

Pile colors are matched to the cut ends of the yarns because fibers seen on end absorb light and thus appear darker than the same yarn lying in a flat, light-reflective strand. It is, therefore, important always to keep in mind the use to which repair wools will be put when matching colors. If you are choosing yarns for the edge and flatweave repairs discussed here, match the original to a flat-lying strand.

When deciding between closely matching colors, bear in mind that a repair requiring, for example, a blue-toned red wool will be more successful if done with yarns of the same tone, even if lighter or darker, than an orange-toned wool with the same intensity of color. If, however, a yarn of the same tonality as the original is not available, choose a lighter-colored yarn of the nearest tonality. A lighter yarn's tone can be drabbed with a solution of potassium permanganate (see below), but nothing much can be done to lighten a darker wool except mixing it with lighter-colored strands.

Matching by Mixing

If you look closely at the wools in an old, naturally dyed rug, you will often be able to distinguish strands of varying values and tones that, at a distance, your eye sees as a single, pleasantly vibrant color. This is especially true of colors achieved by overdyeing, like greens and aubergine. To approximate this effect or to match an unusual color, yarns can be separated into single strands and combined with strands of lighter, darker, or different tones.

Needlepoint, crewel, and tapestry yarns are made up of three, two, and four strands of wool, respectively, which are plied or twisted together. Since the strands tend to curl up on each other like agitated snakes in the process of untwisting, I suggest you hold a length of the yarn tautly between your teeth and one hand while with the other you wind the threads down one by one in the direction opposite to the original ply.

For edge and flatweave repairs the strands can be used without replying, either singly or in combinations up to about six, depending on the color and density required. But since unplied wool is easily pulled apart when subjected to the strain of being repeatedly drawn through a rug foundation, it's advisable to work with short lengths.

Although edge and flatweave repairs can often be accomplished with unplied or home-plied wools, the warp cords used for rug edges are generally denser and more firmly plied than the other fiber threads used in rug construction. If sections of these cords are missing, it may be necessary to have them replaced by a professional.

Matching by Drabbing

Even the brightest colors found in rugs are, more often than not, less bright than the closest match available with commercial wools, despite the enormous range of hues available in the various lines of fine needlework yarns. A concentrated brew of tea or coffee, often recommended to darken or "sadden" colors, will fade in time or with washing, but a permanent drabbing may be effected with a solution of potassium permanganate ($KMnO_4$), an oxidizing agent used as an antiseptic.

This dark purple crystalline salt is available only by medical prescription. It is poisonous if ingested, and the label warns that the chemical renders textiles highly inflammable. Not wishing to advise the use of anything that might cause a cherished rug to burst into flame, I wrote the manufacturer of the brand I purchased and received a reassuring reply from the manager of their science products laboratory.

The compound is so highly colored, he wrote, that if the yarn is rinsed until there is no purple color deposited in the water, it can be safely assumed that there would not be enough left to be of any danger, as appreciable amounts have to be present to cause spontaneous combustion.

After expressing interest in this unusual use of the chemical, he went on to say that what probably occurs is a reaction between the $KMnO_4$ and the oil in the wool itself, producing the dioxide of manganese (MnO_2), which is dark brown and may even be self-mordanting.

Assuming you obtain a prescription from your doctor or dentist, about 4 ounces of the crystalline form of potassium permanagante should be sufficient for a lifetime of anything short of frenzied home repair activity. The solution will impart to wool yarns an ecru to brown coloration, but its use is so inexact that to obtain the degree of drabbing desired you will have to experiment with the strength of the solution and duration of immersion for each type and color of yarn to be treated. In general, however, the following guidelines should be observed.

Equipment

1. Two glass bowls for preparing the solution and for wetting and rinsing the wool.

2. A metal tray or aluminum foil roasting pan.

3. A pair of metal tongs or long fork and a mixing spoon.

4. Rubber gloves and a large apron to protect hands and clothes from stains.

Procedure

1. Place bowls in tray next to sink.

2. Dissolve 1 teaspoon of the crystals in 2 cups of warm water in one of the bowls. Mix well.

3. Fill the other bowl with lukewarm water, immerse the yarn and gently squeeze until the fibers are evenly wetted. (A drop or two of detergent will facilitate absorption.)

4. Transfer the yarn to the permanganate solution. Stir only long enough— seconds, not minutes—to ensure even absorption of the purple color.

5. Immediately remove the yarn with tongs or fork and rinse under running water until the water runs clear. (If the sink is not stain-proof, place a large bowl under the faucet to catch and further dilute the rinsed-out solution.)

Color Matching. If, after the purple color is rinsed away, the resulting brown drabbing is too pale, repeat the process. If it seems too dark, remember that a color dries lighter than it appears when wet.

Even quite a dark shade can result from a surprisingly short immersion time, so I suggest you proceed with caution, drabbing the wool a few strands at a time. If successive batches do not quite match, wools can be blended to minimize the variations.

Store any remaining solution in a screw-top glass jar. *Be sure to place both the leftovers and the unused crystals out of the reach of children.*

Note: If you have a number of rugs requiring extensive edge overcasting, the cost of the yarns can mount up; so if you fancy yourself a kitchen Dr. Frankenstein, you may wish to experiment with bargain bin yarns. Unlike the doctor's poor monster, truly repellent colors can often be tamed and rendered eminently usable through treatment with the permanganate solution.

RUG PAINTING: PROS AND CONS

The easiest but least acceptable treatment for a faded or worn rug is painting the altered colors, eroded pile, or exposed foundation. You might think that this cosmetic subterfuge would be obvious upon even the most casual inspection, but a reasonable amount of care in matching and applying color can achieve magical results, although whether that magic should be considered black or white depends on the circumstances and one's point of view.

The conservative view is that painting is never acceptable, not only because it is employed by unscrupulous dealers to mask major defects but also because little is known about the long-term effect of the pigments and solvents on rug fibers. Rugs painted with the specific intent of deceiving the unwary are quite commonly encountered at auctions, especially the type known in the trade as "short notice," typically held on weekends at motels. For this reason alone, no one should bid on a rug unless it has been inspected carefully beforehand, preferably in daylight.

There are, however, a few cases in which it can be argued that painting is, acceptable both ethically and aesthetically. These include (1) old, expertly executed repairs performed with wools colored with dyes that, although they matched the original colors at the time of the repair, have subsequently faded or altered; (2) spots bleached noticeably paler than surrounding pile; and (3) the bright white tufts that occasionally work up through the pile from the knots of joined weft or warp threads of rugs with cotton foundations. Finally, there are the rugs that for one reason or another—primarily visible wear—possess little or no market value, yet with "freshened" colors or partially repainted designs could continue to serve as decorative furnishings for years to come, albeit in a dark corner or hallway.

Owners of classic antique rugs should, of course, adopt the conservative view and leave well enough alone. Wear may dim a fine old piece, but a faded beauty will always command greater respect than a painted floozy.

MATERIALS

Colored inks and felt marker pens are often used for rug painting, but neither is a good choice. The inks contain dyes that, although transparent and usually waterproof, have limited color-fastness in bright light. The brilliant marker-pen colors share this impermanency and in addition are glaringly incompatible with even poor rug dyes.

The most satisfactory coloring agent for home use is acrylic paint used as watercolor. The acrylics, also known as polymer paints, are made by dispersing colored pigments in an acrylic emulsion. When thinned with water and applied to paper or cloth, the paint spreads out in a thin layer that, when the water evaporates, leaves a continuous, flexible, waterproof and virtually fadeproof film of plastic. I have used acrylics to paint designs on needlepoint canvas, and I know from experience that a modestly priced starter set can be used to mix and match an enormous range of colors and shades. For muting purposes, I suggest adding to your stock a few tubes of gray and brown shades. Avoid using white: it tends to make the colors chalky and clumps the wool fibers into stiff little tufts.

Because acrylics are so versatile and easy to use, they are usually available in stationery and variety stores as well as art supply outlets. One caution: it is not advisable to intermix different brands, as incompatible formulas may cause curdling.

Aside from the acrylic paints, very little equipment is required for achieving a satisfactory result:

1. A couple of stubby brushes—you may have to clip the tips—of the type used for oil painting. Watercolor brushes are too soft to push the paint into wool fibers.

2. A small brush or cotton swabs with which to mix the paint and water until you receive the right shade and consistency.

3. A medicine dropper for dispensing water.

4. A shiny white plate or two on which to mix colors.

PROCEDURE

Unless you are familiar with the mixing of colors, it may take a bit of experimentation before you get a feel for combining colors to achieve just the odd, subtle shade you need. Stick with it, and resist settling for approximate matches. Always mix and match colors in daylight, keep the paint quite thin—thick paint will clog the fibers—and work fast. Once the mixture you are working with dries, it will not redissolve. Depending on the condition of the rug, adequate coverage may require two or three thin applications of paint, each of which should be allowed to dry before adding the next.

When you have completed the touch-up, be sure the paint is entirely dry before walking on the rug or rolling it up. And keep in mind that although a well-worn rug may *look* better after painting, the foundation remains very vulnerable to breakage under normal conditions of daily use. To minimize the effect of stress, provide the rug with a well-cushioned underlayment.

After painting, wash your brushes immediately with soap and water. Never allow acrylic paint to dry on a brush; in fact, never allow it to dry on any textured or absorbent surface you don't want it on because it will be almost impossible to remove. It does, however, wash or peel off smooth, oily, or shiny surfaces like hands and paint-mixing plates.

To sum up, although rug-painting has its legitimate uses, it should never be used as a substitute on rugs for which pile replacement is obviously the preferred solution. By postponing minor repiling, which is a relatively easy and inexpensive repair, the risk of severe foundation damage is increased and the extent and cost of repairs multiplied.

RESOURCE
GUIDE

RUG BOOKS AND PERIODICALS

PERIODICALS

Hali, an international journal of carpets and textiles, with the emphasis on oriental rugs. Many fine color pictures of rugs in both the advertising and editorial sections; news of exhibits, conventions, rug societies; reviews of books and auctions; articles ranging from scholarly research reports to expressions of aesthetic appreciation. Published six times a year, 1996 subscription rates are $114 and $213 for one and two years respectively. Hali Publications Ltd., Circulation Dept., Kingsgate House, Kingsgate Place, London NW6 4TA, U.K. Subscriptions hotline: (44 171) 328–1998; Fax (44 171) 372–5924.

Oriental Rug Review, an American publication long popular with collectors, ceased print publication with the December 1995–January 1996 issue, Volume 16, Number 2. Originally intended to focus on auction reviews and reports, it expanded over the years to reflect primarily the intellectual dealer and collector points of view in well-illustrated articles ranging from scholarly to tongue in cheek. Always fun to read, sometimes ground-breaking, the good news is that all of *ORR*'s back issues and a searchable index will be available on the Internet on their Home Page: http//www.rugreview.com.

ORR's editor, Ron Callahan, plans to mount rug exhibitions; news of these and other ventures will be posted on the *ORR* web site.

BOOKS

Publications about oriental rugs, many of which are issued in limited editions, sometimes offer a better return on one's original investment than the rugs themselves. The first issue of *Hali*, for example, now sells for over one hundred times its original price of $7.50.

Most of the titles listed below are difficult to obtain from conventional booksellers; some included in the first edition of this guide were dropped because of their skyrocketing prices. Since pricing is based on print status and availability, current prices should be obtained from the specialist dealers listed at the end of this section. If the cost gives you pause, you might try your interlibrary loan service.

GENERAL

Bennett, Ian, ed. *Rugs and Carpets of the World.* New York: A & W Publishers, 1977. (OP)

A well-illustrated basic reference covering fine handmade rugs of all kinds, but especially orientals. There is more emphasis on old than new production; color reproduction is mediocre.

Denny, Walter. *Oriental Rugs.* New York: Cooper-Hewett Museum, 1979. (OP)

Dr. Denny, an Islamic Arts scholar, has written and lectured widely on oriental rugs. Gracefully written, this book packs a lot of authoritative information into its relatively few, handsomely produced pages.

Eiland, Murray L. *Oriental Rugs.* Boston: NYGS/Little, Brown and Co., latest edition.

A complete, well-organized, and universally recommended introduction to the subject, including useful information about dyes and structure. A good selection of black-and-white photos illustrates the nononsense prose. The color plates are dreadful.

Ettinghausen, Dimand, Mackie, and Ellis. *Prayer Rugs.* 1974

Illustrated Textile Museum catalog for a major exhibit of examples from Turkey to Turkestan. Scholarly essays and carpet analysis.

Ford, P. R. J. *The Oriental Carpet.* New York: Harry N. Abrams, 1992 reprint.

Lavishly illustrated in color, with good chapters on dyes and structure, the subtitle is *A History and Guide to Traditional Motifs, Patterns and Symbols.* The author is a knowledgeable member of the international rug trade; the rugs, including some Chinese examples, are largely late-19th and 20th century.

Hawley, Walter A. *Oriental Rugs, Antique and Modern.* New York: Dover, 1970. Reprint of 1913 edition.

The chief value of this venerable, inexpensively reprinted handbook is the lucidly presented information about rug structure and the line drawings illustrating the discussion of rug motifs. Hawley was one of the first Westerners to point out the importance of weave analysis in rug identification.

Herrmann, Eberhart. *Seltene Orienteppich.* Munich.

Catalogs issued by a leading European dealer in world-class collector pieces. The text is in German, but the appeal of the rugs is universal. Excellent color plates. Now very expensive, one or two would be an edifying investment for those with limited access to galleries and auction house previews.

Jacobsen, C. W. *Oriental Rugs: A Complete Guide.* Rutland, VT: Tuttle, 1969.

If your library has only one book on oriental rugs, it is likely to be this one by an American dealer, since deceased, with a lively gift for self-promotion. It is an engaging book, spiced with the author's pet peeves and dubious historical information, and although by no means a basic reference, provides useful information about commercial carpets imported into the United States in the first six decades of this century.

Jerrehian, Aram K., Jr. *Oriental Rug Primer, Buying and Understanding New Oriental Rugs*, latest edition. Paperback.

Nicely illustrated and knowledgeable introduction to modern decorative rugs.

O'Bannon, George. *Oriental Rugs: The Collector's Guide to Selecting, Identifying and Enjoying New and Antique Oriental Rugs.* 1995.

Written by a former editor of *Oriental Rug Review* and intended for novice enthusiasts, this elegantly produced slim volume, which "explores the history and craft of carpet-making with advice on buying and assessing," offers a wealth of color plates of fine rugs at a remarkably modest price. Consumer Reports would undoubtedly rate it as a best buy.

Opie, James. *Tribal Rugs.* 1992.

Very informative and beautifully illustrated guide to the weavings and traditions of tribal peoples in Anatolia, Iran, Afghanistan, Central Asia, and the Caucasus. Expensive, but there's nothing else like it.

Thompson, Jon. *Oriental Rugs from the Tents, Cottages and Workshops of Asia.* 1993. (Formerly listed as *Oriental Carpets.*)

One of the two best introductory books (Murray Eiland's *Oriental Rugs* is the other), it is peerless in terms of production and writing style. Its organization, in which rugs are grouped according to purpose and technical skill employed rather than geographical origin, is illuminating, and the color illustrations are gorgeous.

HISTORICAL SURVEYS

Bode, Wilhelm Von, and Kuhnel, Ernst. *Antique Rugs from the Near East*, 4th ed. Ithaca, NY: Cornell University Press, 1984.

A classic scholarly introduction to early oriental carpets with a very useful annotated list of books about rugs made in the classical period. Well-chosen photographs, mostly black and white.

Ellis, Charles Grant. *Oriental Carpets in the Philadelphia Museum of Art.* Philadelphia, PA: Philadelphia Museum of Art, 1988.

A catalog of a distinguished museum collection written by the quirky Grand Old Man of oriental rug studies. Good black-and-white and color photographs accompanied by complete structural analyses.

Gantzhorn, Volkmar, *The Christian Oriental Carpet.* 1991.

This rather odd entry is a lavishly illustrated treatise, originally written as a doctoral thesis, which purports to find Christian symbols lurking in oriental rug motifs. The thesis may be dubious, but the book offers very good plates of many classical carpets at a relatively modest price.

Kirchheim, Heinrich. *Orient Stars: A Carpet Collection*, 1993. Paperbound extract.

A handsome oversize affordable paperbound extract from a truly splendid—and very expensive—scholarly survey of one of the world's great collections of 13–19th century Turkish, Caucasian, and Persian rugs.

SPECIALIZED BOOKS

Baluch Weavings

Adraskand, Inc. *Belouch Prayer Rugs.* 1983.

Long on good color plates, structural analyses, and speculative attributions.

Boucher, Jeff W. *Baluchi Woven Treasures.* 1989.

Baluch tribal rugs are notoriously difficult to photograph, a truism belied by this book displaying the best of the late Col. Boucher's distinguished collection. Conservative attributions, structural analyses, and superb color plates make this a valuable resource for tribal weaving enthusiasts.

Caucasian Rugs

Bennett, Ian. *Oriental Rugs: Volume 1. Caucasian Rugs.* 1993 reprint.

The English text accompanies plates from a German auction house. The color isn't accurate, but the many examples of almost every type of 19th- and early 20th-century Caucasian rugs offers an unequaled wealth of detail.

Burns, J. D. *The Caucasus: Traditions in Weaving.* Seattle, WA: Court Street Press, 1987.

The color could be better, but overall an impressive selection from a well-known collection of 18th- and 19th-century rugs and flatweaves. Few collectors can afford to assemble rugs of this quality, but they provide an ideal to approach as best we can.

Wright, Richard E., and Wertime, John T. *Caucasian Carpets and Covers.* Hali Publications Ltd., 1995.

A long-awaited and highly recommended book on Caucasian carpets and flatweaves with scholarly commentary drawn from original documentary sources and including detailed technical notes.

Chinese Rugs

Eiland, Murray L. *Chinese and Exotic Rugs.* Boston: NYGS/Little, Brown and Co., 1979.

Recommended with certain reservations in the first edition, this book is now out-of-print and when available is priced in the $125–150 range. The only in-print publication on the subject is Lee Allane's *Chinese Rugs: A Buyer's Guide*, 1993.

East Turkestan Rugs

Bidder, Hans. *Carpets from East Turkestan.* Accokeek, MD: Washington International Associates, 1979.

The best single source of information about these handsome rugs, including motifs, dyes, and structure. Illustrated with numerous sketches, black-and-white photos, and good color plates.

Flatweaves

Acar, Belkis Balpinar. *Kilim-Cicim-Zili-Sumak: Turkish Flatweaves.* Istanbul, 1983. English edition available.

Ms. Balpinar, who organized an exemplary exhibit of Turkish flatweaves at the Sultan Ahmet Mosque in Istanbul, knows her subject very well indeed. Good color plates.

Davies, Peter. *The Tribal Eye: Antique Kilims of Anatolia.* 1993.

Based on the author's field work and research, the text of this paperbound book describes the weaving process of kilims and the tribal culture which produced them.

Hull, Alistair, and Luczyc-Wyhowska, Jose. *Kilim, The Complete Guide.* 1993.

And complete it is, including history, pattern, technique, identification, and buying information. Lots of illustrations, many in color.

Justin, Valerie. *Flat-Woven Rugs of the World.* New York: Van Nostrand Reinhold, 1980.

Although many books have been written about kilims, this is one of the very few which discusses and illustrates flat-woven techniques in general. Now out of print, the price may discourage all but budding flatweave collectors.

Indian Rugs

Gans-Ruedin, E. *Indian Carpets.* New York: Rizzoli, 1984.

Although out of print and expensive when available, information about Indian rug weaving is so scarce, this remains a recommended title. The first half of this handsomely produced book deals with Indian carpet production, both past and present, and the materials and dyes used. Next is a section devoted to classical Indian court carpets, followed by examples of 20th-century rugs. Very good color plates.

Kurdish Rugs

Eagleton, William. *An Introduction to Kurdish Rugs and Other Weavings.* New York: Interlink Publishing Group, 1988.

The author, a diplomat and rug collector, researched Kurdish tribal weaving while stationed in the Middle East in the 1980s. The color plates are only so-so, but the information is unobtainable elsewhere.

Stanzer, Wilfried. *Kordi: Lives, Rugs, Flatweaves of the Kurds in Khorassan.* Vienna: Adil Besim OHG, 1988.

An important book based on extensive fieldwork. Handsomely produced; good color plates.

Persian Rugs

Edwards, A. Cecil. *The Persian Carpet.* London: Duckworth, 1953; often reprinted.

The author's 50 years in the London rug trade account for the authoritative tone of this down-to-earth, thorough account of commercial Persian rug production in the first half of this century. Flawed somewhat by grayed black-and-white illustrations, it is nonetheless an often-quoted basic resource.

Opie, James. *Tribal Rugs of Southern Persia.* Portland, OR: James Opie Oriental Rugs, 1988.

The author is a respected dealer-cum-scholar writing from personal knowledge of the areas he specializes in. The informative, appealingly written text is illustrated with beautiful color plates.

Structure and Repair

Emery, Irene. *The Primary Structure of Fabrics.* Washington, D.C.: The Textile Museum, 1980. 1994 reprint.

Published by The Textile Museum, this is the standard reference work on textile structure and a must for collectors of flatweaves. The intelligently organized text is illustrated by clear, consistent, and concisely captioned photo diagrams.

Stone, Peter. *Oriental Rug Repair.* Chicago: Greenleaf Co., 1981.

The only book of its kind, so good there is no need for another. A must for every collector, even those who have no interest in doing repairs, because it sets forth in very clear terms not only what should be done in the way of repair but tips on how to avoid the need for it. Well illustrated, but some of the photo diagrams are a bit hard to decipher due to the fuzziness of the rug fibers.

Turkish Rugs

Brüggeman, Werner, and Böhmer, Harald. *Rugs of the Peasants and Nomads of Anatolia.* Munich, 1983. English translation available.

A prize-winning book containing clear and authoritative information on dyes and design development and wonderful color plates keyed to rug descriptions, accompanied by structural and dye analysis. Recommended as a necessary resource for every collector in the first edition of this guide, the price is now over $300.

Yetkin, Serare. *Historical Turkish Carpets.* Istanbul, 1981. Paperback.

Available through specialist book dealers, this is a valuable, modestly priced resource for Turkish rug enthusiasts. The color illustrations are fair, the black-and-white photos poor, but there are many of them, some of material unavailable elsewhere.

Zipper, Kurt, and Fritzche, Claudia. *Oriental Rugs: Volume 4, Turkish.* 1989. Published in German; English edition available.

Introduction to Turkish rugs with many illustrations of 16–20th century rugs and kilims.

Turkoman Weavings

Hoffmeister, Peter. *Turkoman Carpets in Franconia.* 1980.

This book, which has a text both in German and English, features two superior collections of antique Turkoman rugs and trappings. A structural analysis of each piece is supplied. Good color plates.

Mackie, Louise, and Thompson, Jon, eds. *Turkmen: Tribal Carpets and Traditions.* Washington, D.C.: The Textile Museum, 1980.

A well-illustrated collection of scholarly essays written for a major exhibition at The Textile Museum. Interesting material about tribal life. The color is quite good and the structural analyses notable for their completeness, but the keying of text to illustrations is confusing and the lack of index regrettable.

Parsons, R. D. *Oriental Rugs: Volume 3, Afghanistan.* 1983 (1994 reprint).

The third in the Antique Collectors' Club Series. Most of the many examples pictured are fairly recent, but the information about rug weaving and nomadic life in Afghanistan is detailed and interesting.

Tzareva, Elena. *Rugs and Carpets from Central Asia: The Russian Collections.* New York: Penguin, 1984.

A selection from Russian collections, most never published before, with Uzbek, Kerghiz, Kazakh, and Karakalpak tribal rugs in addition to the more familiar Turkoman examples. The introduction discusses the place of weaving in tribal culture, the kinds of articles woven, and the significance of the motifs. Good color plates are accompanied by detailed structural analyses.

SOURCES FOR BOOKS ABOUT
ORIENTAL RUGS AND RELATED TOPICS

Adraskand, Inc., 15 Ross Avenue, San Anselmo, CA 94960; (415) 459–1711. Principally tribal and village rugs, but books about rugs, too.

The East-West Room, Myrna Bloom, 3139 Alpin Drive, Dresher, PA 19025; (215) 657–0178, Fax (215) 657–6685. Large stock; book lists on request.

George F. Gilmore, 2150 Newport Boulevard, Costa Mesa, CA 92626; (714) 646–7847. *Hali* backlist in addition to rug books.

Renate Halpern Galleries, Inc., 325 East 79th Street, New York, NY 10021; (212) 988–9316. Rugs, tapestries, textiles, and books.

Dennis B. Marquand, P.O. Box 1187, Culver City, CA 90232-1187; (310) 313–0177, Fax (310) 915–9922. Large stock of books on rugs, textiles, and related subjects. Also carries a good selection of auction catalogs. Lists available.

Paragon Book Gallery, 1507 South Michigan Avenue, Chicago, IL 60605; (312) 633–5155, Fax (312) 663–5177. Rare, out-of-print, and scholarly books on Asia.

The Rug Book Shop, 2603 Talbot Road, Baltimore, MD 21216-1621; (410) 367–8194, weekends and evenings. Large stock; book lists on request.

Strand Book Store, 828 Broadway (corner of 12th Street), New York, NY 10003; (212) 473–1452. "Eight miles of books on all subjects" including oriental rugs. Remainders and review copies at 50 percent off. Worth a visit when in New York.

The Textile Museum Shop, 2320 S Street NW, Washington, D.C. 20008; (202) 667–0441, Ext. 29, Fax (202) 483–0994. A good selection of books on rugs and other textile arts. Ten percent discount to members. Book list available.

The Tolstoy Press, P.O. Box 40405, Portland, OR 97240-0405; (503) 226–0126, Fax (503) 227–4069. Books about rugs and the cultures that make them. Book list available.

DEALERS IN COLLECTIBLE ORIENTAL RUGS

GENERALISTS

The following dealers represent only a fraction of the reputable firms to be found nationwide and in Canada. The bulk of their business is in old and antique decorative carpets augmented by the best of the new productions, but most also have a good selection of collectible village and tribal weavings. Retailers who stock only new commercial goods are unlikely to have anything of collectible interest.

If you live far removed from the principal urban centers, I suggest you leave your name and wants with the dealers in your area, as pieces of unusual interest taken in on trade are apt to be shipped to the major auction houses, where, because of the exposure to the international trade, a good price can usually be obtained more quickly than from a local clientele.

In addition to a good selection of fine rugs, well-established dealers can supply rug repair and washing services either in-house or by recommendation. All are qualified to do appraisals, but the basis for determining the fee varies: in some cases it is a percentage of the rug's value; some dealers, like Washington, D.C.'s Elsie Nazarian, who considers appraisals a courtesy service to her clients, charge a nominal flat fee.

Always call first: Some dealers have limited hours; others can be seen only by appointment; still others may have moved or gone out of business. This applies to all dealers on all lists.

Please note: A bullet (•) preceding a dealer's name indicates a new listing.

CALIFORNIA

Ami Negbi Gallery, Inc., 7736 Fay Avenue, Suite 102, La Jolla 92037; by appointment: (619) 456–0131 or 552–9328.

•*Artex Rug Gallery*, 530B Pacific Design Center, 8687 Melrose Avenue, Los Angeles 90069; (310) 659–4530, Fax (310) 659–0632.

Baktiari Gallery, Arky Robbins, 2843 Clay Street, San Francisco 94115; (415) 346–0437. Superior decorative rugs; fine collectibles.

•*The James Blackmon Gallery*, 2140 Bush Street, San Francisco 94115; (415) 922–1859. This exceptionally knowledgeable dealer, restorer, and conservator promotes antique rugs and textiles as art.

Carpets of the Inner Circle, 444 Jackson Street, San Francisco 94111; (415) 654–8661.

Emmett Eiland Gallery, 1326 Ninth Street at Gilman, Berkeley 94710-1503; (510) 526–1087.

Oriental Carpet Gallery, 2150 Newport Boulevard, Costa Mesa 92626; (714) 646–7847.

•*Peter Pap Oriental Rugs of San Francisco, Inc.*, 470 Jackson Street, San Francisco 94111; (415) 956–3300, Fax (415) 956–3320.

•*Keith Rocklin and Victoria Marie Payne*, Los Angeles; by appointment: Tel./Fax (310) 277–4127. Antique oriental rugs and textiles; also pre-Columbian textiles.

COLORADO

•*Franklin Price Oriental Carpets*, 1825 Blake Street, Denver 80202; (303) 295–1824.

Shaver-Ramsey, 2414 East 3rd Avenue, Denver 80206; (303) 320–6363, Fax (303) 320–1541. Large selection of rugs, kilims, textiles, including the best of the new natural-dyed, hand-spun wool productions.

CONNECTICUT

•*Kalamian's Rug Shop*, 963 Bank Street, New London; (860) 442–0615. Mostly new stock, but worth checking for old rugs taken in trade.

Kebabian's, 73 Elm Street, New Haven 06355; (203) 865–0567.

•*Orkney & Yost Antiques and Oriental Rugs*, 148 Water Street, Stonington Village 06378; (860) 535–4402.

Tschebull Antique Carpets, 8 West Avenue, Darien 06820. By appointment: (203) 655–6610. Very knowledgeable scholar/dealer offering rugs of exceptional quality.

DISTRICT OF COLUMBIA

Nazarian Bros., Inc., 5101 Wisconsin Avenue NW, Washington, D.C. 20016-4120; (202) 364–6666.

•*Trocadero, Oriental Rug and Textile Art*, 2313 Calvert Street NW, Washington, D.C. 20008-2644; (202) 328–8440.

David Zahirpour, 4918 Wisconsin Avenue NW, Washington, D.C.; (202) 338–4141, 244–1800.

ILLINOIS

•*Connoisseur Oriental Rugs*: Moe Jamali, 1000 Chicago Avenue, Evanston 60202; (708) 866–6622.

Joseph W. Fell, Ltd., 3221 North Clark Street, Chicago 60657; by appointment: (312) 549–6076.

•*Heart Antiques*: Roy Flachs, 1821 2nd Avenue, Rock Island 61201; by appointment: (309) 788–5454.

INDIANA

•*Sarver's Oriental Rugs*, Indianapolis; by appointment only: (317) 255–3066.

KENTUCKY

Dana Kelly Oriental Rugs, Inc., Chevy Chase Place, 870 East High, Lexington 40502; (606) 266–7802/9274.

MASSACHUSETTS

Thomas Caruso, 76 Beech Street, Belmont 02178; (617) 489–6512, Fax (617) 489–2952. Antique and classical carpets and textiles.

John J. Collins, Jr., 11 Market Square, Newburyport 01950; (508) 462–7276. Gallery with exceptional decorative and collectible rugs.

Lawrence Kearney, P.O. Box 302, Newton 02161; by appointment: (617) 964–0012.

•*Mario Ratzki Oriental Rugs*, Cambridge; by appointment: (617) 354–0238.

Yenian Oriental Rugs, 57 Pearl Street, Springfield 01101; (413) 737–0368.

MICHIGAN

Azar's, 670 South Woodward, Birmingham 48009; (810) 644–7311, Fax (810) 644–7314.

MINNESOTA

Keljik's Oriental Rugs (formerly listed as Shahidi Oriental Rug Co.), 4255 Bryant Avenue South, Minneapolis 55409; (612) 823–6338.

Persia International Carpets, 323 1st Avenue N, Minneapolis 55401; (612) 339–4771.

MISSOURI

Bendas Oriental Rug Co., 7505 Delmar Boulevard, St. Louis 63130; (314) 862–4410.

NEBRASKA

Souq Ltd., Kirk Wynn, 1018 Howard Street, Omaha 68102-2815; (402) 345–1762.

NEW HAMPSHIRE

Peter Pap Oriental Rugs, Inc. (see also: California), Route 101, Dublin

03444; (603) 563–8717, Fax (603) 563–7158. Exceptional decorative and collectible rugs in elegant gallery; very knowledgeable staff.

NEW JERSEY

Ronnie Newman, P.O. Box 14, Ridgewood 07451; by appointment: (201) 563–8717, Fax (603) 563–7158. International dealer in rare and esoteric tribal, village, and decorative weavings.

Sandler & Worth, 760 Georges Road, North Brunswick 08902-3350; (908) 247–1212.

NEW YORK

Berdj Abadjian, 201 East 57th Street, New York 10021; (212) 688–2229.

•*George Anavian*, 942 First Avenue (at 52nd Street), New York 10022; (212) 879–1234, Fax (212) 838–3889.

Bergi Andonian, 102 Madison Avenue (at 29th Street), New York 10016; (212) 532–4688. International dealer in classical, collectible, and decorative rugs.

A. Beshar & Co., Inc., 611 Broadway, New York 10014; (212) 529–7300, Fax (212) 529–7668.

Doris Leslie Blau, 724 Fifth Avenue, New York 10021; (212) 586–5511. More likely than most to have classical carpets.

Dennis Dodds, 19 West 55th Street, Suite 6A, New York 10019; by appointment: (212) 977–3603, Fax (212) 977–5814.

The Ghordian Knot, 136 East 57th Street, New York 10022; (212) 371–6390. More likely than most to have classical carpets.

Renate Halpern, 325 East 79th Street, New York 10021; (212) 988–9316.

Kermani Oriental Rugs, Inc., 3905 State Street, Schenectady 12304; (518) 393–6884.

•*Krikor Markarian, Inc.*, 151 West 30th Street, Room 1102, New York 10001; (212) 629–8683, Fax (212) 564–3747. More likely than most to have classical carpets.

•*Symourgh International*: David Zadeh, 34 East 34th Street, New York 10016-4302; (212) 686–3756/5599, Fax (212) 683–3032. Large stock of fine decorative rugs, some collectibles.

NORTH CAROLINA

Boone's Antiques, Inc., Highway 301 South, P.O. Box 3796, Wilson 27895-3796; (919) 237–1508, Fax (919) 237–8609.

Fargo-Hanna Ltd., 4422 Chapel Hill Boulevard, Durham 27707; (919) 419–0963.

•*The Persian Carpet*, 5634 Chapel Hill Boulevard, Durham 27707; (919) 489–8362, (800) 333–1801, Fax (919) 493–3529.

OHIO

House of Davidian, Inc., 7 North Franklin Street, Chagrin Falls 44022; (216) 247–3868.

Markarian Oriental Rugs, 3420 Edwards Road, Cincinnati 45208; (513) 321–5877.

OREGON

James Opie Oriental Rugs, Inc., 1025 SW Washington Street, Portland 97205; 1–800–252–8878, Fax (503) 227–4069. Superior selection of old rugs and the best of the new natural-dyed, hand-spun wool productions.

PENNSYLVANIA

Dennis R. Dodds, P.O. Box 4312, Philadelphia 19118; by appointment: (215) 247–4774, Fax (215) 247–4777.

O'Bannon Oriental Carpets, 5666 Northumberland, Pittsburgh 15217; (412) 422–0300. Reliable source for the best of the new rug productions as well as fine antiques.

Peter Scholten, Oriental Rugs, 117 West Main Street, Boalsburg 16287; (814) 466–7576, Fax (814) 466–2264. Also by appointment in New York City.

•*Woven Treasures*, 2211 South Street, Philadelphia 19146; (215) 546–8448, Fax (215) 735–1208. (For information on an exemplary new production of village-woven carpets see section on contemporary collectibles.)

TENNESSEE

Ro's Oriental Rugs, 6602 Highway 100, Nashville 37205; (615) 352–9055, 665–0094, Fax (615) 665–1743. Antique rugs and tapestries.

TEXAS

Goravanchi Co. Persian Rugs: Nader Goravanchi, 1800 Post Oak Boulevard, Suite 110, Houston 77056; (713) 626–4200, Fax (713) 622–1023.

•*Texas Oriental Rugs, Inc.*, 2809 Fondren Road, Houston 77063; (713) 965–0922, Fax (965) 784–2264.

VERMONT

Vincent J. Fernandez, a new shop on Route 7 across from the Shelburne Museum, Shelburne 05482; (802) 985–2275. Old and antique rugs and the best of the new contemporary productions.

VIRGINIA

Edgeworth-Trent Oriental Rugs, 1111 North Thompson Street, Richmond 23230; (804) 278–9699.

Salem M. Eways, Inc., 1895 Seminole Trail, Charlottesville 22901; (804) 975–3136, Fax (804) 975–1570.

•*John R. Hall*, 131 Church Street NW, Vienna 22180; (703) 242–8805, Fax (703) 281–4366.

•*Alan Marschke's Oriental Rug Gallery*, 687 South Washington Street, Alexandria 22314; (703) 548–0909.

John Murray, 10 Horseshoe Drive, Williamsburg 23185; by appointment: (804) 220–2114.

WASHINGTON

•*Doug Curtis Rugs*, 6104 Roosevelt Way, Seattle 98115; (206) 524–5475.

•*Honeychurch Antiques*: Fine Asian art and antiques, 1008 James Street, Seattle 98104; (206) 622–1225, Fax (206) 622–1204. Primarily old and antique Chinese rugs.

•*Rugs and Kilims International*, 129 Lake Street SE, Kirkland 98033-6419; (206) 889–2129.

WEST VIRGINIA

•*Gerald W. Thompson*, P.O. Box 193, Shepardstown 25443; by appointment: (304) 876–2218.

WISCONSIN

Edward S. Gulesserian, Inc., 8 South Breese Terrace, Madison 53711; (608) 256–8000.

CANADA

Ararat Rug Company, Ltd., 3457 Park Avenue, Montreal, Quebec H2X 2H6; (514) 288–1218, Fax (514) 288–1210.

SPECIALISTS IN VILLAGE AND TRIBAL RUGS AND TRAPPINGS

CALIFORNIA

Adraskand, Inc., 15 Ross Avenue, San Anselmo 94960; (415) 459–1711. Nirvana for the tribal rug collector.

Alex Chis Oriental Rugs, P.O. Box 2944, Niles Station, Fremont 94536; by appointment: (510) 489–8554.

Anahita Gallery, Santa Monica; by appointment: (310) 455–2310, Fax (310) 455–2490.

Michael Andrews, Mill Valley; by appointment: (415) 381–8048, Fax (415) 381–8021.

•*Thomas Cole*, San Rafael; by appointment: Tel.Fax (415) 485–1652.

Rudolf Geissman, 143 Cedros Avenue, Suite B 103, Solana Beach 92075; (619) 481–3488.

Hazara Oriental Rug Gallery, 6042 College Avenue, Oakland 94618; (510) 655–3511; Fax (510) 655–5223.

•*John Webb Hill*, San Francisco; by appointment: (415) 647–4068.

•*Tony Kitz Oriental Carpets*, 2843 Clay Street, San Francisco 94115; (415) 346–2100, Fax (415) 346–3548.

James D. Waterbury Oriental Rugs, Camarillo 93010; by appointment: (805) 987–5761.

COLORADO

Shaver-Ramsey, 2414 East 3rd Avenue, Denver 80206; (303) 320–6363, Fax (303) 320–1541. Rugs, kilims, textiles. Antique, old, and best of the new natural-dyed hand-spun wool productions. Rug maven Paul Ramsey travels frequently to the Middle East in search of stock.

FLORIDA

•*Don Edwards, Yunus Gallery*, P.O. Box 692323, Orlando 32869; by appointment: (407) 876–0869, Fax (407) 352–5535.

GEORGIA

Afghanistan's Nomadic Rugs, 3219 Cains Hill Place, W. Buckhead 30625; (404) 261–7259.

ILLINOIS

•*Connoisseur Oriental Rugs*: Moe Jamali, 1000 Chicago Avenue, Evanston 60202; (708) 866–6622.

•*Heart Antiques*: Roy Flachs, 1821 2nd Avenue, Rock Island 61201; by appointment: (309) 788–5454. Specializing in Baluch weavings.

•*The Nomad's Loom*, 3227 North Clark Street, Chicago 60657; (312) 248–5544, Fax (312) 248–0171.

KANSAS

•*Richard Golder, Jr.*, Overland Park; by appointment: (913) 381–4834.

MAINE

A. E. Runge, Jr., 139 Main Street, Yarmouth 04096; (207) 846–9000. Usually open daily, but phone ahead to make sure.

MASSACHUSETTS

Yayla Tribal Rugs, 283 Broadway, Cambridge 02139; (617) 576–3249, Fax (617) 492–3459.

MINNESOTA

•*Zabol*, 911 West 50th Street, Minneapolis 55419; (612) 824–0467, Fax (612) 827–7342.

NEVADA

•*Khyber Pass Rug Co.*, 230 Evans Avenue, Reno 89501; (702) 786–1050, Fax (702) 786–1050.

NEW YORK

•*Brooke Pickering*, 16 East 23rd Street, New York 10010; Moroccan rug specialist, by appointment: (212) 780–9125.

•*Shiv Sikri*, 254 East 95th Street, New York 10128; by appointment: (212) 996–9196.

OREGON

James Opie Oriental Rugs, Inc., 1025 SW Washington Street, Portland 97205; 1–800–252–8878, Fax (503) 227–4069. Specializes in fine old Southwest Persian rugs and trappings.

PENNSYLVANIA

O'Bannon Oriental Carpets, 5666 Northumberland Street, Pittsburgh 15217; (412) 422–0300.

Peter Scholten Oriental Rugs, 117 West Main Street, Boalsburg 16827; (814) 466–7576, Fax (814) 466–2264. Also by appointment in New York.

TEXAS

Caravanserai Ltd.: Casey Waller, Oriental Rug and Textile Gallery, 1435 Dragon Street, Dallas 75207; (214) 741–2131, Fax (214) 741–2137.

•*Donna Endres' Istanbul to Samarkand*, Antique Marketplace, 5350 Burnet Road, Austin 78756; (512) 452–1000. Tribal rugs and Anatolian kilims. Appointment recommended to view antique weavings: (512) 451–8533.

VIRGINIA

Sun Bow Trading Co., 108 Fourth Street NE, Charlottesville 22902; (804) 293–8821. Antique, old and new stock hand-picked at the source by knowledgeable, well-traveled proprietor Saul Bardofsky. Also has early antique fragments.

•*John and Suzan Wertime*, Oriental Rug and Tribal Art, P.O. Box 16296, Alexandria 22302; by appointment: (703) 379–8528.

WASHINGTON

•*J. H. Terry, Antique Tribal Rugs*, 313A 1st Avenue S, Seattle 98104; (206) 233–9766, Fax (206) 621–0831.

FLATWEAVES

Most of the dealers listed in this resource guide stock at least a few old kilims; those listed alphabetically below either deal in flatweaves exclusively or to an extent that qualify them as better-than-average mentors for beginning collectors:

•*Donna Endres' Istanbul to Samarkand Antique Marketplace*, 5350 Burnet Road, Austin, TX 78756; (512) 452–1000. Specializes in old and antique Anatolian kilims.

George Fine, Kilims, 1615 East Fort Lowell Road, Tucson, AZ 85719; (520) 795–9377, Fax (520) 795–9923.

•*Marla Mallett*, 1690 Johnson Road NE, Atlanta, GA 30306; by appointment: (404) 872–3356. Kilims, tapestries, and antique textiles. Expert knowledge of structure.

•*Kilim: Linda Miller*, 150 Thompson Street, New York, NY 10012; by appointment: (212) 533–1677.

Mark Shilen Gallery, 109 Greene Street, New York, NY 10012; (212) 925–3394.

Sun Bow Trading Co., 108 Fourth Street NE, Charlottesville, VA 22902; (804) 293–8821. Very large stock of old and antique kilims.

•*Turkana Gallery*: Peter Davies, 125 Cedar Street, Penthouse, New York, NY 10006; by appointment: (212) 732–0273, Fax (212) 349–6484. Mr. Davies, the author of a well-respected book on kilims (see Flatweaves in annotated book list), specializes in early Anatolian examples.

John and Suzan Wertime, P.O. Box 16296, Alexandria, VA 22302; by appointment: (703) 379–8528. Scholarly knowledge of flatweaves.

Yayla Tribal Rugs, 283 Broadway, Cambridge, MA 02139; (617) 576–3249.

AUCTION HOUSES

The following five houses hold sales devoted to oriental rugs as well as sales in which rugs are offered together with fine furnishings. The number of rug-only sales varies from house to house and year to year, but all hold previews of from two days to a week in length immediately prior to the sale, and all offer a variety of services.

Buyer's premium: Successful bidders now pay an additional premium of 15 percent of the final bid price up to and including $50,000, plus 10 percent of any amount over $50,000.

Catalog subscriptions: All of the houses offer subscriptions to catalogs pertaining to specific interests. The price includes postsale results and the illustrated bulletins published several times a year.

The detail provided in catalog descriptions of condition not only varies from house to house but from rug to rug and should always be double-checked either in person or by phone with the rug experts.

Estimates of values: As a courtesy to potential consignors, the auction house experts will supply free verbal estimates of what your property may bring at auction. Call the rug department to inquire how this may best be done. Clear photographs of the front and back, the ends and edges, and close-ups of details may suffice; sometimes it may be necessary for a rug to be shipped to the auction house for a hands-on inspection.

Appraisals: The cost of a formal written appraisal varies from house to house, but in all cases it is more than the fee most dealers charge.

Packing and shipping: All of the houses can arrange for the packing and shipping of items bought at auction. This charge, which can be considerable, should be figured into the total price you are willing to pay. It would be wise to ask for an estimate before deciding to bid.

Absentee and phone bids: As a courtesy to buyers who are unable to attend, verbal or written bids may be left prior to a sale. For important rugs, it may be possible to arrange to bid during the sale over the telephone through an auction house representative. There are no fees for these services.

Butterfield & Butterfield, 220 San Bruno Avenue, San Francisco, CA 94103. For catalogs and information about buying and selling at auction and related fees, call (415) 861–7500; call the same number, ext. 292, for the rug department.

Seventy to eighty percent of the buyers at Butterfield's rug auctions are dealers, and the majority of rugs offered fall into the decorative commercial carpet category. The catalogs have fewer photographs than others do, and the descriptions are bare bones: no dating is provided, and only major repairs and significant reductions in size are reported. However, the Butterfield rug department is knowledgeable and happy to provide detailed information at previews—held in Los Angeles as well as San Francisco—and over the phone.

Christie's, 502 Park Avenue, New York, NY 10022; (212) 546–1000, Fax (212) 980–8136, and *Christie's East*, 219 East 67th Street, New York, NY 10021; (212) 606–0400, Fax (212) 737–6076. For catalogs, contact Christie's Publications, 21–24 44th Avenue, Long Island City, NY 11101; (718) 784–1480. For a brochure about buying and selling at auction call the Customer Service Department, (212) 546–1128.

The regrettable period of Islamic Arts doldrums reported in the first edition of this guide has been succeeded by a revitalization of Christie's oriental rug sales department (212–546–1187) with the expert assistance of James Ffrench. Rug-only sales are once again being held three times a year, and rugs are also offered throughout the year in conjunction with furniture sales. Well-illustrated catalogs are available either singly or by subscription at the number given above, but the formerly informative condition reports now leave a lot to be desired.

Grogan & Company, 268 Newbury Street, Boston, MA 02116. Call (617) 437–9550, Fax (617) 437–0513 for catalog sales and buying and selling information. For information about rugs, ask for Michael Grogan.

Michael Grogan, founder and president of this up-and-coming auction house, cut his teeth in Sotheby's rug department in New York. Grogan & Company cannot yet compete in numbers with the established houses, but the quality of the rugs being offered, usually together with silver or other fine furnishings, is attracting more and more collector attention, and the house is small enough to be both friendly and flexible. The catalog descriptions are basic; the photographs, although few in number, are good.

Skinner, Inc., 357 Main Street, Bolton, MA 01740; (508) 779–6241, Fax (508) 779–5144, and 63 Park Plaza, Boston, MA 02116; (617) 350–5400, Fax (617) 350–5429. Call the Bolton office for catalog sales, buying and selling information, and to speak with Skinner's personable rug expert, Jo Kris.

Skinner holds rug-only sales three times a year (spring and early and late fall) and offers a good selection throughout the year in conjunction with other sales. Major rug sales are now held in the Boston gallery. Unlike the New York houses, preview hours extend to the hour preceding the sale, and the informal atmosphere and relaxed selling style assure attendees a pleasant as well as educational day's outing. A subscription to the well-illustrated catalogs (color and black-and-white; condition reports provided) is a worthwhile investment.

Please note: If unfamiliar with Boston, I strongly advise you to call or fax for directions and parking information for both the Grogan and Skinner sales.

Sotheby's, 1334 York Avenue, New York, NY 10021. Call Client Services (212) 606–7116 for information about buying and selling and catalogs; rug specialists Mary Jo Otsea and Daisy Edelson may be reached at (212) 606–7886, Fax (212) 606–7886.

Sotheby's offers rugs at three to four major rug-only sales each year and at arcade sales when warranted. Collectors should consider as essential a subscription to the well-illustrated catalogs: the major sales provide structural analyses for the important collector pieces and condition reports for all rugs; the arcade sale catalogs, which offer only basic information, are generously illustrated in black and white. The rug experts here are knowledgeable and willing to be helpful to all comers, but beginning collectors unable to enter the competition at a fairly high level should not expect much in the way of TLC from this powerhouse organization as a whole.

Oriental rugs are offered from time to time by other auctions houses as well, but reliable information about origin, age, and dyes is usually lacking except for those able to afford expert consultant advice. However, collectors wishing to pursue these opportunities may profit from a subscription to *Antiques and Arts Weekly*, which despite its New England origin and emphasis, provides current information about nationwide offerings:

Antiques and Arts Weekly, The Bee Publishing Co., Inc., P.O. Box 5503, Newtown, CT 06470-5503; for current subscription information call (203) 426–3141 or Fax (203) 426–1394.

Previews and reviews antique shows and auctions of major importance or unusual interest, publishes feature pieces on notable collections, and carries detailed advertisements of upcoming auctions and antique shows.

ORIENTAL RUG SOCIETIES AND CONFERENCES IN NORTH AMERICA

The following list of rug societies was compiled in the fall of 1995 by the Board of Directors of the American Conference on Oriental Rugs (see end of list for more information about this and other rug conference opportunities). It was the most complete list available at the time of writing, but since meeting dates and places are subject to change, current information and membership particulars should be obtained from the contacts given below:

ORIENTAL RUG SOCIETIES

UNITED STATES

Hajji Baba Club, founded 1932
Elena Goff, Weston, CT
Evenings: (203) 227–2783
International Hajji Baba Society, founded 1965
Wendel Swan, Alexandria, VA
Evenings: (703) 960–0343
Fax (703) 683–7545

Arizona
Arizona Oriental Rug/Textile Association, founded 1994
Sally Komerska, Tucson
Days: (602) 323–0320
Fax (602) 299–7802 (c/o O'Bannon)

California
Rug Society of San Diego, founded 1991
Alan Campbell, San Diego
(619) 281–3084

San Francisco Bay Area Rug Society, founded 1981
John Sommer, Fremont
(510) 793–5828
Fax (510) 791–0271
The Textile Group of Los Angeles, founded 1979
Stephanie K. Morehouse, Los Angeles
(Tel.Fax) (213) 931–4987
Textile Museum Associates of Southern California, founded 1985
Cheri Hunter, Pacific Palisades
Days: (310) 454–8221
Fax (310) 454–8604

Colorado
Colorado Textile Group, founded 1984
Franklin Price, Denver
Days: (303) 295–1824

Florida

Central Florida Rug Society,
founded 1989
    Doug Connor, Tampa
    Evenings: (813) 935–8827
South Florida Oriental Rug Club,
founded 1990
    Sharon Kerwick, Fort
    Lauderdale
    Days: (305) 565–9031
    Evenings: (305) 564–4325
    Fax (305) 564–0648

Georgia

Georgia Rug and Textile Society,
founded 1992
    Cheryl Rodgers, Atlanta
    Evenings: (404) 351–2437
    Fax (404) 351–7117
    E-Mail crrodgers@aol.com

Illinois

Chicago Rug Society, founded
1973
    Suzanne Kaufman, Rockford
    Evenings: (815) 963–6543
    Fax (815) 963–6543*51

Kansas

*Oriental Rug Society of Kansas
City,* founded 1987
    Jessie Fisher, Kansas City
    Days: (816) 221–0422
    Fax (816) 472–1820
*Textile Museum Associates of
Kansas City,* founded 1993
    Bill Griffith, Kansas City
    Days: (913) 362–2006

Massachusetts

New England Rug Society, founded
1985
    Mark Hopkins, Lincoln

    (617) 259–9444
    Fax (617) 259–1529
    E-Mail mopkins@aol.com

Michigan

Detroit Oriental Rug Society, 1994
    David Morrison, Huntington
    Days: (810) 542–7200
    Evenings: (810) 542–1491
    Fax (810) 542–8936
    E-Mail davdhmorr@aol.com

Minnesota

Minnesota Rug Society (now
organizing)
    Glenn Miller, Rochester
    Days: (507) 289–4565
    Fax: (507) 289–2516

New Jersey

Princeton Rug Society, founded
1972
    Jeffrey K. McVey, Lambertville
    (609) 397–1326

New York

Moroccan Rug and Textile Society,
founded 1991
    Brooke Pickering, New York
    City
    (212) 780–9125
    Fax (212) 475–7370
New York Rug Society, founded
1970
    Sally Sherrill, New York City
    Evenings: (212) 249–2497

North Carolina

Triangle Rug Society, founded
1985
    Lucille Kimble, Durham
    Days: (919) 489–2702

Ohio

Cleveland Rug Society, founded
1984
    Joan Long, Akron
    Evenings: (216) 666–4876
    Fax (216) 972–5574
    E-Mail jclong@uakron.edu

Oregon

Portland Area Rug Society
    Leslie Atiyeh, Newbergh
    (503) 538–7560
    Fax (503) 538–8239

Pennsylvania

*Textile Arts Society of
Philadelphia*, founded 1983
    Anne Sims, Wayne
    Days: (610) 293–9542
    Evenings: (215) 684–7585
    Fax (215) 236–4063

Texas

Houston Oriental Rug Society,
founded 1989
    Lee Ann Kozak, Houston
    Evenings: (713) 661–3978
    Fax (713) 661–4326

Washington, D.C.

Washington Textile Group, founded
1988
    Richard Wright, Bethesda, MD
    Evenings: (301) 320–4456

CANADA

Armenian Rug Society, founded 1980
    Eileen Bedoukian-Hampshire,
    Hudson, Quebec
    Days: (514) 458–4050 (Tel./Fax)
    Evenings: (514) 694–1996
Calgary Rug and Textile Club,
founded 1991
    Peter Haley, Calgary
    Days: (403) 244–7568
    Fax (403) 229–3817
*Montreal Carpet Appreciation
Society*, founded 1975
    Eileen Bedoukian-Hampshire,
    Hudson, Quebec
    (514) 458–4050 (Tel./Fax)
*Quebec Oriental Rug and Textile
Society*, founded 1993
    Janice Summers, Montreal
    Days: (514) 288–1218
    Fax (514) 288–1210
Toronto Oriental Rug Society,
founded 1975
    Katherine Green, Markham,
    Ontario
    Evenings: (905) 471–7381

ORIENTAL RUG CONFERENCES

THE AMERICAN CONFERENCE ON ORIENTAL RUGS

The first ACOR conference, a weekend-long combination of workshops and panel discussions, eye-boggling dealer displays, and ruggie schmoozing was held in Boston in 1992. A second took place in 1994 in Chicago, and a third in Santa Monica in 1996. This enormously popular biennial event, largely the result of the efforts of members of North American rug societies, owes at least part of its success to its policy of limiting the number of participants. Held in February, details are provided well in advance by *Hali*, and may also be requested from the rug groups listed previously, but be warned: he or she who hesitates to sign up will lose out on the hands-down best opportunity to advance one's rug-collecting knowledge.

INTERNATIONAL CONFERENCE ON ORIENTAL RUGS

The name tells it all. Held every two or three years in late fall, the conferences are held in locations offering the best rug-viewing and researching opportunities for rug collectors and scholars from around the world. Hamburg/Berlin hosted the 1993 conference; Philadelphia, whose Museum of Art houses a splendid collection of classical carpets, was selected as the site for the seventh ICOC in 1996. Site, program, and registration information are provided by *Hali*.

TEXTILE MUSEUM CONVENTION

These annual October events focus on particular topics. In 1995, for example, the area of concentration was tribal rugs. A popular and entertaining feature of the TM conventions is the informal show-and-tell session held Sunday mornings to which participants bring their "mystery" rugs, trappings, and textiles for a panel of experts to discuss and, it is hoped, identify. Details are published in *Hali* and can be obtained from the Textile Museum, 2320 South Street NW, Washington, D.C. 20008; (202) 667–0441.

NOTABLE RUG COLLECTIONS

MUSEUMS

Although the following museums have collections worth seeing, usually only a few rugs—if any—are on view at any one time, so phone first to avoid disappointment. *Hali* provides subscribers with news of special exhibitions at these and other institutions, and the catalogs prepared for these events are usually a relatively inexpensive source of authoritative, up-to-date information. Since they are subject to change, days and hours are not given.

UNITED STATES

California
Berkeley Lowie Museum of Anthropology
Los Angeles County Museum of Art
San Francisco M. H. de Young Memorial Museum
The H. McCoy and Caroline Jones collection of tribal rugs and kilims was donated to this museum in 1980; additional items have been added since. An endowed center for the study of rugs and textiles is planned.

Delaware
Wilmington Winterthur Museum (rug tours by appointment)

Illinois
Chicago Chicago Art Institute

Kansas
Kansas City Nelson-Atkins Museum

Massachusetts
Boston–Cambridge Boston Museum of Fine Arts
Fogg Art Museum, Harvard University
Springfield George Walter Vincent Smith Art Museum (exceptional Turkoman examples)

Missouri
St. Louis The St. Louis Art Museum

Ohio
Cincinnati The Cincinnati Art Museum
Oberlin The Allen Art Museum

Pennsylvania
Philadelphia Museum of Art (stellar collection of classical carpets)

New Jersey
Morristown Macculloch Hall Historical Museum

New York
New York The Brooklyn Museum
            The Frick Collection
            Hispanic Society of New York
            The Metropolitan Museum of Art (renowned and comprehen-
            sive collection)

Virginia
Richmond Virginia Museum of Fine Arts

Washington, D.C.
The Textile Museum. Membership, which is tax-deductible, should be
considered a priority for all collectors. The only institution of its kind in the
United States, it supports a conservation laboratory and research library,
issues scholarly publications, hosts an annual convention devoted to oriental
rug topics, and mounts frequent and superior rug and textile exhibitions.

West Virginia
Huntington Huntington Museum of Art

CANADA

Toronto Royal Ontario Museum
           Museum for Textiles

OTHER COLLECTIONS

UNITED STATES

California
Yosemite National Park: The Ahwahnee Hotel, a National Historic Land-
mark completed in 1927. Decorated with oriental flatweaves by noted
Persian art scholars Phyllis Ackerman and Arthur Upham Pope.

North Carolina
Asheville Biltmore Estate
New Bern Tryon Palace restoration

Pennsylvania
Bryn Athyn Glencairn Museum

South Carolina
Greenville Liberty Textile Collection, the Liberty Corporation

Virginia
Williamsburg The Williamsburg Restoration

EUROPE AND THE MIDDLE EAST

Berlin, Islamic Museum in the Museum Island
Berlin, Islamic Galleries in Dahlem
Budapest Museum of Applied Arts (strong on early Turkish examples)
Cairo Museum of Islamic Art
Istanbul Museum of Turkish and Islamic Art
       Vakiflar Carpet Museum (may be closed)
Lisbon Calouste Gulbenkian Museum
London Victoria and Albert Museum (extensive, renowned collection)
Lyons Museum of Historical Textiles
Milan Poldi Pezzoli Museum
Paris Museum of Decorative Arts
Vienna Museum of Applied Arts (superb classical carpets)

CARE AND REPAIR SERVICES AND SUPPLIES

Most dealers in old rugs employ workers able to make serviceable repairs but who may or may not be sufficiently skilled to provide restoration services. The restoration specialists listed below may not wish to do basic repairs and may have work backed up for as much as a year. However, since good craftspeople invariably know who the other good ones are, additional names can probably be provided on request. To help you decide what level of skill will best serve your particular needs, please first read or review the sections dealing with rug care and repair.

Please note: A bullet (•) preceding a name indicates a new listing.

RESTORATION

FLATWEAVES

•Aziz Antique Rug Repairs: Aziz Arwandeli, 1104 Sutter Street, San Francisco, CA 94109; (415) 474–4102.

Barnett, Ronee, 580 Broadway, New York, NY 10012; (212) 966–3520.

•Hayko Restoration and Conservation: Hayk Oltaci, Chelsea Antiques Building, 110 West 25th Street, Suite 705, New York, NY 10001; (212) 633–0700.

Kane, Tina, 8 Big Island Road, Warwick, NY 10990; (914) 986–8522.

•Oriental Rug Hospital, 50 Rose Place, Garden City Park, NY 11040; (516) 746–0000, 1–800–RUG–HELP, Fax (516) 746–0157.

•Pittenger, Robert, 158 West 23rd Street, New York, NY 10011; (212) 691–6948.

Sanford Restoration Works: Emily Sanford, 2102 Speyer Lane, Redondo Beach, CA 90278; (310) 374–7412, Fax (310) 798–2292.

•Sany, Ahmad, 29 West 30th Street, Room 901, New York, NY 10001; (212) 868–3240. Walk-in clients welcome, but scheduled appointments appreciated.

•Senatro, Mary Ann, Bedford, NH 03110; (603) 627–6276.

•Talisman, David Walker, 719 Swift Street, #10, Santa Cruz, CA 95060; (408) 425–7847.

•Textile Conservators: Maury Bynum, 215 West Ohio Street, Suite 600, Chicago, IL 60610; (312) 329–0097, Fax (312) 329–7847.

•Textilian: Kathryn T. Van Sciver, P.O. Box 1386, Jamaica Plain, MA 02130; (617) 524–2830.

Zahirpour, David, 4918 Wisconsin Avenue NW, Washington, D.C. 20016; (202) 338–4141.

PILE

Altay Tribal Rugs, 213A Highland Avenue, Somerville, MA 02143; (518) 623–5526.

Atenian, Vartanoush, 34 East 34th Street, New York, NY 10016; (212) 686–3756, (718) 263–0049 (home).

•Aziz Antique Rug Repairs: Aziz Arwandeli, 1104 Sutter Street, San Francisco, CA 94109; (415) 474–4102.

Buckland-Rasmussen: Mary Rasmussen, 1451 Sherbrooke Street W, Montreal, Canada H3G 2S8; (514) 937–6273.

Costikyan Cleaning and Restoration, 32–16 37th Avenue, Long Island City, NY 11101; (212) 786–9684.

Thomas J. Dwyer Ltd., 304 East Genesee Street, Fayetteville, NY 13066; (315) 637–4988.

•Fenlon, Sharon, Appleton, WI 54911; (414) 734–0864.

•Hayko Restoration and Conservation: Hayk Oltaci, Chelsea Antiques Building, 110 West 25th Street, Suite 705, New York, NY 10001; (212) 633–0700.

Newman, Richard E., 337 East 81st Street, New York, NY 10028; (212) 249–9797. Expert, highly selective specialist in tribal weavings.

•Oriental Rug Hospital, 50 Rose Place, Garden City Park, NY 11040; (516) 746–0000, 1–800–RUG–HELP, Fax (516) 746–0157.

•Pittenger, Robert, 158 West 23rd Street, New York, NY 10011; (212) 691–6948.

Sanford Restoration Works: Emily Sanford, 2102 Speyer Lane, Redondo Beach, CA 90278; (310) 374–7412, Fax (310) 798–2292.

•Sany, Ahmad, 29 West 30th Street, Room 901, New York, NY 10001; (212) 868–3240. Walk-in clients welcome, but scheduled appointments appreciated.

•Senatro, Mary Ann, Bedford, NH 03110; (603) 627–6276.

Shallcross and Lorraine, 60 Pinckney Street, Boston, MA 02114; (617) 720–2133.

•Talisman: David Walker, Santa Cruz, CA; (408) 425–7847.

•Textile Conservators: Maury Bynum, 215 West Ohio Street, Suite 600, Chicago, IL 60610; (312) 329–0097, Fax (312) 329–7847.

•Textilian: Kathryn T. Van Sciver, P.O. Box 1386, Jamaica Plain, MA 02130; (617) 524–2830.

•In addition to the craftspeople listed above, a repair and restoration facility in the Aegean Free Zone in Izmir, Turkey, opened and supervised by Woven Legends of Philadelphia, offers a comprehensive range of services at very competitive prices. Inquiries should be directed to Robert Mann at Woven Legends Restoration's estimating and service center at 2540 Walnut Street, Denver, CO 80205; (303) 292–9865, Fax (303) 292–9801.

TEXTILE CONSERVATION

Buckland-Rasmussen, 1451 Sherbrooke Street W, Montreal, Canada H3G 2S8; (514) 937–6273.

•Fenlon, Sharon, Appleton, WI 54911; (414) 734–0864.

•Hayko Restoration and Conservation: Hayk Oltaci, Chelsea Antiques Building, 110 West 25th Street, Suite 705, New York, NY 10001; (212) 633–0700.

Sanford Restoration Works: Emily Sanford, 2102 Speyer Lane, Redondo Beach, CA 90278; (310) 374–7412, Fax (310) 798–2292.

•Sany, Ahmad, 29 West 30th Street, Room 901, New York, NY 10001; (212) 868–3240. Walk-in clients welcome, but scheduled appointments appreciated.

•Senatro, Mary Ann, Bedford, NH 03110; (603) 627–6276.

•Talisman: David Walker, Santa Cruz, CA; (408) 425–7847.

•Textile Conservators: Maury Bynum, 215 West Ohio Street, Suite 600, Chicago, IL 60610 (312) 329–0097, Fax (312) 329–7847.

The Textile Conservation Workshop, 3 Main Street, South Salem, NY 10590; (914) 763–5805.

CLEANING SERVICES

•George Anavian, 942 First Avenue, New York, NY 10022; (212) 879–1234, Fax (212) 838–3889.

A. Beshar & Co., 5 Canal Place, Bronx, NY 10451; (212) 292–3301.

•Bobcat Carpet Care: Al Casas, 2705 Pico Boulevard, Santa Monica, CA 90405; (310) 478–4438.

•Leonard Contardo, 409 North Lee Street, Alexandria, VA 22314; (703) 548–4140. Hand-washing specialist.

K. Costikyan, 38–10 29th Street, Long Island City, NY 11101; (718) 786–9684.

Danbury Rug Works, 13 Summit Street, Danbury, CT 06810; (203) 743–1691.

Fred Remmers Rug Cleaners, 2186 Central Avenue, Memphis, TN 38104; (901) 278–3704.

Kouri's, 95 North Clinton Street, Poughkeepsie, NY 12601; (914) 471–4909.

Nazarian Bros., Inc., 5101 Wisconsin Avenue NW, Washington, D.C. 20016-4120; (202) 364–6666.

Newman, Richard E., 337 East 81st Street, New York, NY 10028; (212) 249–9797. Hand-washing specialist.

Oriental Cleaning Services, 3907 Ross Avenue, Dallas, TX 75204; (214) 821–9135.

Rug Renovating Co., 532 North Grove Street, East Orange, NJ 07017; (201) 675–8313 or (718) 361–7900.

Shishadeh, 116 Cricket Avenue, Ardmore, PA 19003; (610) 649–2000, Fax (610) 649–6463.

•Talisman: David Walker, Santa Cruz, CA; (408) 425–7847.

Zahirpour, David, 4918 Wisconsin Avenue NW, Washington, D.C. 20016; (202) 338–4141.

CLEANING AND REPAIR SUPPLIES

Chatalbash Rug Co., Inc., 20 East 30th Street, New York, NY 10016; (212) 532–5260, Fax (212) 696–1764. Write or phone for catalog. Source for Paternayan and Appleton yarns suitable for rug repair, linen carpet thread, replacement edgings, stair rods and clips, rug hanging clips, cotton fringing, rug underlayments, and Chemtreat, the powder used to mix a mothproofing solution as discussed in the section on storage problems in the chapter on oriental rug care.

Talas Conservation Supplies (catalog $5), 568 Broadway, New York, NY 10012; (212) 219–0770, Fax (212) 219–0735. Talas stocks Orvus Paste, the low pH anionic detergent mentioned on page 217.

BIBLIOGRAPHY

AUCTION CATALOGS

Christie's: Sale #8080, 12/16/94; Sale #8120, 4/10/95; Sale #7751, 9/12/95; Sale #8292, 12/15/95

Skinner, Inc.: Sale #1619, 12/10/94; Sale #1640, 4/8/95; Sale #1657, 7/7/95; Sale #1667, 9/16/95; Sale #1685, 12/9/95

Sotheby's: Sale #6643, 12/15/94; Sale #6687, 4/13/95; Sale #6735, 9/13/95; Sale #6793, 12/14/95

PERIODICALS, JOURNALS, BULLETINS, AND EXHIBITION CATALOGS

"All About Oriental Rugs." *Rug News*, Vol. 8, No. 10, January 1987.

Badische Co. Catalog of dye materials, 128 Duane Street, New York, NY, no date, c. 1900.

Baker, George P. OCM Catalog, 1886.

Bogle, Michael M. "The Mounting of Textiles for Storage and Display." *Textile Conservation Center Notes, No. 15*. North Andover, MA: Merrimack Valley Textile Museum, 1979.

———. "The Storage of Textile." *Textile Conservation Center Notes, No. 14*. North Andover, MA: Merrimack Valley Textile Museum, 1979.

———. "Technical Data on Moth-Proofing." *Textile Conservation Notes, No. 10*. North Andover, MA: Merrimack Valley Textile Museum, 1979.

———. "Technical Data on Silk Textiles." *Textile Conservation Center Notes, No. 1*. North Andover, MA: Merrimack Valley Textile Museum, 1979.

———. "Technical Data on Wool Textiles." *Textile Conservation Center Notes, No. 2*. North Andover, MA: Merrimack Valley Textile Museum, 1979.

Böhmer, Harald. Notes titled "Dyeing of Wool with Natural Dyes," 1984.

———. "The Revival of Natural Dyeing in Two Traditional Weaving Areas of Anatolia." *Oriental Rug Review*, Vol. 3, No. 9, December 1983.

Bulbach, Stanley. "The Weaving Arts: An Ancient Technology." Reprinted in *Rug News*, Vol. 10, No. 8, January 1989.

Columbus, Joseph V., ed. "Principles of Practical Cleaning for Old and Fragile Textiles." *Museum News Technical Supplement*, Conservation

Department, Textile Museum. Washington, D.C.: American Association of Museums, 1956.

"The Decorative Rug." Rug Basics Series, updated reprint. *Oriental Rug Review*, Vol. 10, No. 3, 1990.

Diyarbekirli, Nejat. "New Light on Pazyryk Carpet." Translated by Alan Mellaart. *Hali*, Vol. 1, No. 3, 1978.

Eiland, Murray. "A Look at the Word Tribal." *Oriental Rug Review*, Vol. 9, No. 5, 1989.

Engerisser, Franz. "Ornamentale Kufi-Schrift und Flechtbandmotive in Borduren von Orientteppichen." *Hali*, Vol. 3, No. 1, 1980.

Ford, P. R. J. "Kelardasht Weaving." *Rug News*, Vol. 7, No. 8, pp. 16–17, October 1985.

Gardiner, Roger F. *Oriental Rugs in Canadian Collections*. Catalog of 1975 exhibition. Toronto, Canada: The Oriental Rug Society, 1975.

Gross, Laurance. "Reducing the Perils of Textile Display," *Museum News*, Vol. 38, No. 1, September 1979.

Gupta, Dr. D. K. "Carpet Trade in India," *Rug News*, Vol. 19, No. 8, 1987.

"Hand-Laundry Detergents." *Consumer Reports*, February 1982.

Hazeldine, Tony, "On the Road to Zakatala," *Hali* #78, 1995.

Hopkins, Mark, "Rug Collecting in New England: The View Through the Collector's Eye," *Oriental Rug Review*, Vol. X11, No. 3, February/March 1992.

Lindquist, David P., "Using This Guide," *The Official Price Guide to Antiques and Collectibles*, 13th edition, 1993, Random House.

Mailand, Harold F. *Considerations for the Care of Textiles and Costumes*. Indianapolis, IN: Indianapolis Museum of Art, 1980.

Mallett, Marla, "Tracking the Archetype," *Oriental Rug Review*, Vol. 14, No. 2, 1994.

Mast, Ted. *Oriental Rug Review*, Vol. 10, No. 4, pp. 25–26, 1990.

———. "Rethinking Caucasian Soumak Production," *Oriental Rug Review*, Vol. 10, No. 4, 1990.

Merritt, Jane. "A Considered Choice: Selecting a Textile Conservator." *Hali*, #40, 1988.

Moore, William G. "Collecting Rugs: The Great Middle Class Thing," *Oriental Rug Review*, Vol. 9, No. 3, 1990.

Mushak, Paul. "Dye Use in Caucasian Rugs," *Oriental Rug Review*, Vol. 10, No. 4, 1990.

———. "Use of Certain Rug Dyes as Markers of Age in Oriental Rugs," *Oriental Rug Review*, Vol. 15, No. 5, 1995.

Myers, George Hewitt. "Rugs: Preservation, Display and Storage." *Textile Museum Workshop Notes*, Paper No. 5. Washington, D.C.: Textile Museum, June 1952.

O'Bannon, George. "Caucasian Rug Nomenclature and Structure," *Oriental Rug Review*, Vol. 10, No. 4, 1990.

———. "Interview of Collectors Ralph and Linda Kaffel," *Oriental Rug Review*, Vol. 10, No. 4, 1990.

———, ed. Auction reports and previews. *Oriental Rug Review*, issues dated 1989 through February/March 1991.

———, ed. "Price Guide to Five Caucasian Rug Types from 1983 to 1990," *Oriental Rug Review*, Vol. 10, No. 4, 1990.

O'Callaghan, Ron, Editorial, *Oriental Rug Review*, Vol. 15, No. 5, 1995.

Palmai, Clarissa. "Caring for Your Rugs." *Rug News Digest*, Vol. 2, No. 1, 1980.

———. "Textile Mounting." *Textile Museum Journal.* Washington, D.C.: The Textile Museum, 1979.

Pinner, Robert, and Stanger, Jackie. "Kufic Borders on Small Pattern Holbein Carpets." *Hali*, Vol. 1, No. 4, 1978.

Price, Steven, "A Very Old Shahsevan Mafrash: How Old Is 'Very Old'?" *Oriental Rug Review*, Vol. 14, No. 1, 1993.

Rice, James W. "The Conservation of Historic Textile Colorants." *Principles of Textile Conservation Science*, No. 4. Washington D.C.: Textile Museum, n.d.

Ruters, Nils, et al. "Cleaning and Restoring Oriental Carpets." *Hali*, Vol. 1, No. 4, 1978.

Sakisian, Armenag. "Dragon Rugs and Their Armenian Origin." *Rug News Digest*, Vol. 33, March 1980.

Schetky, Ethel Jane McD., ed. "Dye Plants and Dyeing." *Plants and Gardens*, Vol. 20, No. 3. Brooklyn, NY: Brooklyn Botanic Garden, 1964.

Shelley, Louise, and Wright, Richard E. "Caucasian Rugs in the Late Nineteenth Century." *Hali*, Vol. 3, No. 1, 1980.

Sherrill, Sarah B. "The Islamic Tradition in Spanish Rug Weaving: Twelfth through Seventeenth Centuries." *The Magazine Antiques*, March 1974.

Steinert, Stefan. "Coloring Antique Woollen Fabrics with Water and Lightfast Colors." *Hali*, Vol. 1, No. 4, 1978.

Stroh, Leslie. "Traditional Sizes and Shapes in Oriental Rugs." *Rug News*, Vol. 8, No. 12, March 1987.

The Textile Museum, *Pest Busters*, 1989.

Tschebull, Raoul. "The Development of Four Kazak Designs." *Hali*, Vol. 1, No. 3, 1978.

Weigle, Palmy, ed. "Natural Plant Dyeing." *Plants and Gardens*, Vol. 29, No. 2. Brooklyn, NY: Brooklyn Botanic Garden, 1973.

Wertime, John T. "Flat-Woven Structures Found in Nomadic and Village Weavings from the Near East and Central Asia." *Textile Museum Journal*, Vol. 18. Washington, D.C.: Textile Museum, 1979.

Whiting, Mark. "The Dyes of Turkoman Rugs." *Hali*, Vol. 1, No. 3, 1978.
———. "Dye Analysis in Carpet Studies." *Hali*, Vol. 1, No. 1, 1978.
Wilber, Donald N. "Heriz Rugs." *Hali*, Vol. 6, No. 1, 1983.
Wright, Richard E. *Rugs and Flatweaves of the Transcaucasus.* A catalog for the Pittsburgh Rug Society exhibition, 1980.
U. S. Department of Agriculture. "Controlling Household Pests." *Home and Garden Bulletin*, No. 96, 1976 revision.
———. "How to Prevent and Remove Mildew." *Home and Garden Bulletin*, No. 68, 1971 revision.
———. "Protecting Woolen Clothes against Clothes Moths and Carpet Beetles." *Home and Garden Bulletin*, No. 113, 1980 revision.
———. "Removing Stains from Fabrics." *Home and Garden Bulletin*, No. 62, 1978 revision.

BOOKS

Acar, Belkis Balpinar. *Kilim-Cicim-Zili-Sumak: Turkish Flatweaves.* Istanbul: Eren Yayinlari, 1983.
Allane, Lee. *Oriental Rugs: A Buyer's Guide.* New York: Thames and Hudson, 1988.
Alsop, Joseph. *The Rare Art Traditions.* New York: Harper and Row, 1982.
Alth, Max, and Alth, Simon. *The Stain Removal Handbook.* New York: Hawthorn Books, 1977.
Azadi, Siawosch. *Turkoman Carpets.* Fishguard, Wales: The Crosby Press, 1975.
Bacharach, Jere L., and Bierman, Irene A. *The Warp and Weft of Islam.* Seattle: Henry Art Gallery, University of Washington, 1978.
Bayer, Friedr. and Co., dye catalog, 1898.
Beattie, May H. *Carpets of Central Persia.* Kent, England: World of Islam Festival Publishing Co., 1976.
Bennett, Ian. *Complete Illustrated Rugs and Carpets of the World.* New York: A&W Publishers, 1977.
Beresneva, L. *The Decorative and Applied Art of Turkmenia.* Leningrad: Aurora Art Publishers, 1976.
Bidder, Hans. *Carpets from Eastern Turkestan.* New York: Zwemmer, 1964.
Birrell, Verla. *The Textile Arts.* New York: Harper Brothers, 1959.
Blake, Wendon. *Acrylic Watercolor Painting.* New York: Watson-Guptill, 1970.
Bosly, Caroline. *Rugs to Riches.* New York: Pantheon, 1980.
Boucher, Jeff W. *Baluchi Woven Treasures.* Alexandria, VA: Jeff W. Boucher, 1989.
Brüggemann, Werner, and Böhmer, Harald. *Rugs of the Peasants and Nomads of Anatolia.* Munich: Kunst & Antiquitäten, 1983.

Bukhardt, Willy. *Alte Teppiche aus dem Orient.* Basel: Gewerbe-museum, 1980.

Calvert, Dr. F. Crace. *Coal Tar Colors and Recent Improvements in Dyeing and Calico Printing.* Philadelphia: Henry Carey Baird, 18—.

Clarke, Leslie J. *The Craftsman in Textiles.* London: G. Bell and Sons, 1968.

Collingwood, Peter. *The Techniques of Rug Weaving.* New York: Watson-Guptill, 1969.

Croot, Ann. *A Step-by-Step Guide to Woven Carpets and Rugs.* London: Hamlyn Publishing Group, 1974.

Davis, Don R. "Clothes Moth," *Encyclopedia Britannica*, Vol. 7, p. 99, 1973.

Denny, Walter B. *Oriental Rugs.* New York: Cooper-Hewitt Museum, The Smithsonian Illustrated Library of Antiques, 1979.

"Detergents and Detergency." *Encyclopedia Britannica*, Vol. 7, pp. 311–13, 1973.

Dimand, M. S. *A Handbook of Muhammadan Art.* 3rd ed. New York: Metropolitan Museum of Art, 1944, revised and enlarged 1958.

Dimand, M. S., and Mailey, Jean. *Oriental Rugs in the Metropolitan Museum of Art.* New York: The Metropolitan Museum of Art, 1973.

"Dyes and Dyeing." *Encyclopedia Britannica*, Vol. 7, pp. 814–21, 1973.

Eagleton, William. *An Introduction to Kurdish Rugs.* New York: Interlink Publishing Group, 1988.

Edwards, A. Cecil. *The Persian Carpet.* London: Duckworth, 1953.

Eiland, Murray L. *Chinese and Exotic Rugs.* Boston: New York Graphic Society/Little, Brown and Co., 1979.

———. *Oriental Rugs*, 3rd edition. Boston: New York Graphic Society/ Little, Brown and Co., 1981.

Ellis, Charles Grant. *Early Caucasian Rugs.* Washington, D.C.: The Textile Museum, 1976.

———. *Oriental Carpets in the Philadelphia Museum of Art.* Philadelphia: Philadelphia Museum of Art, 1988.

Emery, Irene. *The Primary Structure of Fabrics.* Washington, D.C.: The Textile Museum, 1966.

Erdmann, Kurt. *The History of the Early Turkish Carpet.* London: Oguz Press, 1977.

———. *Seven Hundred Years of Oriental Carpets.* London: Faber and Faber, 1970.

Fichter, George S. *Insect Pests.* New York: Golden Press, 1966.

Finch, Karen, and Putnam, Greta. *Caring for Textiles.* New York: Watson-Guptill, 1977.

Ford, P. R. J. *The Oriental Carpet: A History and Guide to Traditional Motifs, Patterns and Symbols.* New York: Harry N. Abrams, 1981.

Franses, Jack. *European and Oriental Rugs for Pleasure and Investment.* New York: Arco Publishing Co., 1970.

Gans-Ruedin, E. *Indian Carpets.* New York: Rizzoli, 1984.

―――. *The Splendor of Persian Carpets.* New York: Rizzoli, 1978.

Hall, A. J. *A Handbook of Textile Dyeing and Printing.* London: Woodbridge Press, 1955.

Hardingham, Martin. *The Fabric Catalog.* New York: Pocket Books, Simon and Schuster, 1978.

Hawley, Walter A. *Oriental Rugs, Antique and Modern.* 1913. Reprint. New York: Dover Press, 1970.

Herbert, Janice Summers. *Affordable Oriental Rugs.* New York: Praeger, 1970.

Hoffmeister, Peter. *Turkoman Carpets in Franconia.* Edinburgh: The Crosby Press, 1980.

Hubel, Reinhard C. *The Book of Carpets.* New York: Praeger, 1970.

Jacobsen, Charles W. *Oriental Rugs: A Complete Guide.* Rutland, VT: Charles E. Tuttle Company, 1962.

Jerrehian, Aram K., Jr. *Oriental Rug Primer.* Philadelphia: Running Press, 1980.

Joseph, Marjory L. *The Essentials of Textiles.* New York: Holt, Rinehart and Winston, 1976.

Justin, Valerie S. *Flat-Woven Rugs of the World.* New York: Van Nostrand Reinhold, 1980.

Kendrick, A. F., and Tattersall, C. E. C. *Handwoven Carpets, Oriental and European.* 1922. Reprint. New York: Dover Press, 1970.

Knecht, Edmund; Rawson, Christopher; and Loewenthal, Richard. *A Manual of Dyeing.* London: Charles Griffin and Co., 1893.

Konieczny, M. G. *Textiles of Baluchistan.* London: British Museum Publications, 1979.

Kuløy Hallvard Kåre. *Tibetan Rugs.* Bangkok: White Orchid Press, 1982.

Landreau, Anthony N., and Yohe, Ralph S. *Flowers of the Yayla: Yorük Weaving of the Toros Mountains.* Washington, D.C.: The Textile Museum, 1983.

LeFevre, Jean. *The Persian Carpet.* Catalog. London: LeFevre and Partners, 1977.

―――. *Turkish Carpets from the 16th to the 17th Century*, Catalog. London: LeFevre and Partners, 1977.

Linton, George C. *Applied Basic Textiles.* New York: Duell, Sloan and Pearce, 1966.

Loges, Werner. *Turkoman Tribal Rugs.* Atlantic Highlands, NJ: Humanities Press, 1980.

Loughlin, James E. "Dyeing." *McGraw-Hill Encyclopedia of Science and Technology*, Vol. 4, pp. 348–51, 1971.

Lucius and Bruning. *Coal Tar Colours of Farbwerke Vorm. Meister.* Germany, 1908.

Lutz, Frank E. *Field Book of Insects.* New York: G. P. Putnam's Sons, 1918.

Macauley, David. *The Way Things Work.* New York: Houghton Mifflin, 1988.

Mackie, Louise, and Thompson, Jon, eds. *Turkmen Tribal Carpets and Traditions.* Washington, D.C.: The Textile Museum, 1980.

Maerz, A., and Paul, M. Rea. *A Dictionary of Color.* New York: McGraw-Hill Book Co., 1930.

Maritz-Iten, J. *Turkish Carpets.* New York: Harper and Row, 1977.

Mayer, Ralph. *The Artist's Handbook of Materials and Techniques.* New York: Viking Press, 1970.

Mills, John. *Carpets in Pictures.* London: National Gallery, 1975.

Minnis, Wesley. "Dye." *McGraw-Hill Encyclopedia of Science and Technology,* Vol. 4, pp. 336–47, 1970.

Moore, Alma Chestnut. *How to Clean Everything.* New York: Simon and Schuster, 1968.

Neff, I. C., and Maggs, C. V. *Dictionary of Oriental Rugs.* London: A. D. Donker, 1977.

Opie, James. *Tribal Rugs of Southern Persia.* Portland, OR. James Opie Oriental Rugs, 1981.

Petsopolous, Y. *Kilims.* New York: Rizzoli, 1979.

Pluckrose, Henry. *Introducing Acrylic Painting.* New York: Watson-Guptill, 1968.

Proud, Nora. *Textile Printing and Dyeing.* New York: Reinhold Publishing, 1965.

Quick, John. *Artist's and Illustrator's Encyclopedia.* New York: McGraw-Hill, 1977.

Rattee, Ian D. "Dye." *Encyclopedia Americana,* Vol. 9, pp. 508–12, 1973.

Russ, Stephen. *Fabric Printing by Hand.* New York: Watson-Guptill, 1965.

Schorsch, Anita, ed. *The Art of the Weaver.* New York: Universe Books, 1978.

Schurmann, Ulrich. *Caucasian Rugs.* 1974 reprint; distributed by Washington International Associates, Accokeek, MD.

———. *Central-Asian Rugs.* Frankfort: Verlag Osterrieth, 1969.

Schwartz, Anthony. "Detergent." *Encyclopedia Americana,* Vol. 9, p. 21, 1973.

Singer, Max. *La Teinture Moderne.* Paris: Adolphe Delmee, 1875.

Swan, Lester A., and Papp, Charles S. *Common Insects of North America.* New York: Harper and Row, 1972.

Swezey, Kenneth. *Formulas, Methods, Tips and Data for Home and Workshop.* New York: Popular Science Publishing Co./Harper and Row, 1969.

Tanavoli, Parviz. *Shahsavan: Iranian Rugs and Textiles.* New York: Rizzoli, 1985.

Tattersall, C. E. C. *Notes on Carpet Weaving and Knotting.* London: Victoria and Albert Museum, 1969.

Thompson, Jon. *Oriental Carpets: From the Tents, Cottages and Workshops of Asia.* Rev. ed. New York: E. P. Dutton, 1988.

Tschebull, Raoul. *Kazak.* New York: The Near Eastern Art Research Center, Inc., and the New York Rug Society, 1971.

Turkish Ministry of Culture and Tourism. *Turkish Handwoven Carpets.* Catalogs 1 and 2. Ankara: Turkish Republic Ministry of Culture and Tourism, 1987.

Weigle, Palmy. *Ancient Dyes for Modern Weavers.* New York: Watson-Guptill, 1974.

"Wool, Worsted and Woollen Manufactures." *Encyclopaedia Britannica,* Vol. 28, pp. 805–17, 1911.

Wright, Vera Penick. *Pamper Your Possessions.* Barre, VT: Barre Publishers, 1972.

Yetkin, Şerare. *Early Caucasian Carpets in Turkey.* Atlantic Highlands, NJ: Humanities Press, 1978.

———. *Historical Turkish Carpets.* Istanbul: Türkiye iş Bankasi Cultural Publications, 1981.

INDEX

About the Author

JOYCE WARE is a member of the New York and Connecticut rug societies and over the years has assembled an extensive personal library of books about oriental rugs and related subjects. She has written for *Rug News, Oriental Rug Review,* and *Fiberarts* magazine and has lectured about oriental rugs and collecting in general to historical societies in her home state of Connecticut.